D1570765

Madrid

Big City Food Biographies Series

Series Editor
Ken Albala, University of the Pacific, kalbala@pacific.edu

Food helps define the cultural identity of cities in much the same way as the distinctive architecture and famous personalities. Great cities have one-of-a-kind food cultures, offering the essence of the multitudes who have immigrated there and shaped foodways through time. The **Big City Food Biographies** series focuses on those metropolises celebrated as culinary destinations, with their iconic dishes, ethnic neighborhoods, markets, restaurants, and chefs. Guidebooks to cities abound, but these are real biographies that will satisfy readers' desire to know the full food culture of a city. Each narrative volume, devoted to a different city, explains the history, the natural resources, and the people that make that city's food culture unique. Each biography also looks at the markets, historic restaurants, signature dishes, and great cookbooks that are part of the city's gastronomic make-up.

Books in the Series

New Orleans: A Food Biography, by Elizabeth M. Williams
San Francisco: A Food Biography, by Erica J. Peters
New York City: A Food Biography, by Andrew F. Smith
Madrid: A Culinary History, by Maria Paz Moreno

Madrid

A Culinary History

Maria Paz Moreno

ROWMAN & LITTLEFIELD
Lanham • Boulder • New York • London

Published by Rowman & Littlefield
A wholly owned subsidiary of The Rowman & Littlefield Publishing Group, Inc.
4501 Forbes Boulevard, Suite 200, Lanham, Maryland 20706
www.rowman.com

Unit A, Whitacre Mews, 26-34 Stannary Street, London SE11 4AB

British Library Cataloguing in Publication Information Available

Library of Congress Cataloging-in-Publication Data
Names: Moreno, María Paz, 1970– author.
Title: Madrid : a culinary history / by Maria Paz Moreno.
Description: Lanham : Rowman & Littlefield, [2018] | Series: Big city food
  biographies series | Includes bibliographical references and index.
Identifiers: LCCN 2017021863 (print) | LCCN 2017022606 (ebook) |
  ISBN 9781442266414 (electronic) | ISBN 9781442266407 (cloth)
Subjects: LCSH: Cooking—Spain—Madrid—History. | Food industry and
  trade—Spain—Madrid—History. | Cooking, Spanish—History.
Classification: LCC TX723.5.S7 (ebook) | LCC TX723.5.S7 M6743 2018 (print) |
  DDC 641.5946 /41—dc23
LC record available at https://lccn.loc.gov/2017021863

Printed in the United States of America

To the memory of my father, Fernando Moreno Rubio, who loved books, great food, and traveling the world.

Contents

Big City Food Biographies—
Series Foreword

Cities are rather like living organisms. There are nerve centers, circulatory systems, structures that hold them together, and, of course, conduits through which food enters and waste leaves the city. Each city also has its own unique personality, based mostly on the people who live there but also on the physical layout, the habits of interaction, and the places where people meet to eat and drink. More than any other factor, it seems that food is used to define the identity of so many cities. Simply say any of the following words, and a particular place immediately leaps to mind: bagel, cheesesteak, muffuletta, "chowda," and cioppino. Natives, of course, have many more associations—their favorite restaurants and markets, bakeries and doughnut shops, pizza parlors, and hot dog stands. Even the restaurants seem to have their own unique vibe wherever you go. Some cities boast great steakhouses or barbecue pits; others, their ethnic enclaves and more elusive specialties like Frito pie in Santa Fe, Cincinnati chili, and the Chicago deep-dish pizza. Tourists might find snippets of information about such hidden gems in guidebooks; the inveterate flaneur naturally seeks them out personally. For the rest of us, this is practically uncharted territory.

These urban food biographies are meant to be not guidebooks but real biographies, explaining the urban infrastructure, the natural resources that make each city unique, and, most important, the history, people, and neighborhoods. Each volume is meant to introduce you to the city or reacquaint you with an old friend in ways you may never have considered. Each biography also looks at the historic restaurants, signature dishes, and great cookbooks that reflect each city's unique gastronomic makeup.

These food biographies also come at a crucial juncture in our culinary history as a people. Not only do chain restaurants and fast food threaten the existence of our gastronomic heritage, but we are also increasingly mobile as a people, losing our deep connections to place and the cooking that happens in cities over the generations with a rooted population. Moreover, signature dishes associated with individual cities become popularized and bastardized and are often in danger of becoming caricatures of themselves. Ersatz versions of so many classics, catering to the lowest common denominator of taste, are now available throughout the country. Our gastronomic sensibilities are in danger of becoming entirely homogenized. The intent here is not, however, to simply stop the clock or make museum pieces of regional cuisines. Cooking must and will evolve, but understanding the history of each city's food will help us make better choices, make us more discerning customers, and perhaps make us more respectful of the wonderful variety that exists across our great nation.

Ken Albala
University of the Pacific

Acknowledgments

This book could not have been written without the help and generous support of the people and institutions that have assisted me along the way. I am grateful to the University of Cincinnati for granting me a sabbatical semester to work on this project and to the Taft Research Center, also at the University of Cincinnati, for the Taft Faculty Release Fellowship that allowed me to carry out my research in Madrid and devote several more months in Cincinnati to completing it. Thank you as well to the University of Cincinnati Libraries and their staff for processing my never-ending OhioLink and interlibrary loan requests efficiently and smoothly. I am grateful, too, to the staff at Madrid's Biblioteca Nacional de España and to Ester García Guillén at Madrid's Real Jardín Botánico for her generosity and kindness in opening the Jardín's archives for my research.

I am especially indebted to Professor Ken Albala from the University of the Pacific, series editor for the Big City Food Biographies at Rowman & Littlefield, for his support of the project and the excellent feedback that greatly improved this manuscript. To Professors Salvador García Castañeda from the Ohio State University and Marina Bettaglio from the University of Victoria, British Columbia, thank you for supporting the idea for this book when it was just a project in its early stages. My sincere thanks also to my Madrid friends, Almudena Tomás, Julián de Unamuno, CSIC professor Maria del Carmen Simón Palmer, and researchers Pilar Bueno and Raimundo Ortega, for all their advice and hospitality. Heartfelt thanks, too, to Professor Connie Scarborough from Texas Tech

University and Charles Tepe, who showed me some of the most interesting places to eat and drink in Madrid.

I am forever indebted to my dear friends Ned Heeger-Brehm of the Cincinnati Public Library for his superb editing and Angie Dresie for her insightful comments and suggestions. They both provided honest and invaluable feedback that vastly improved this work. *Gracias* also to my mother, Maria Vega, whose delicious cooking both feeds and inspires me and who never stops encouraging me to keep up the good work. Additional *gracias* to all my incredibly supportive Spanish friends; my siblings; my brother-in-law-turned-Madrid-guide, Sergio Esteve; and my big and loving family back in Spain. I must also thank my colleagues at the Department of Romance Languages and Literatures at the University of Cincinnati, especially its chair, Professor Carlos Gutiérrez, for their support and friendship, and thanks to the many friends on both sides of the Atlantic who believed in this project and were eager to see the finished product. Finally, my deepest thanks to my husband, Eric, who enjoyed discovering Madrid's gastronomic wonders as much as I did and whose care, love, and unwavering encouragement have accompanied me at every step of this adventure. *¡Muchas gracias!*

Introduction

"*De Madrid, al cielo*" ("From Madrid, to the heavens"). These words, often spoken by those singing the praises of Spain's capital, capture perfectly the devotion that Madrileños have for their beloved city. The saying implies is that there is no higher pleasure, except ascending to heaven, than enjoying the wonders the city has to offer, especially food and drink, which hold a privileged place in every Spaniard's heart. It is no exaggeration to say that Spaniards in general—and the people of Madrid are no exception—are obsessed with their food and drink. Spaniards derive tremendous pleasure from culinary delights, and they are at the center of social and family life. Time spent with friends and relatives always involves a meal, be it a few tapas (small plates meant to be shared) or a full three-course meal, as well as a glass of wine, beer, vermouth, or the like. Eating is truly a social activity in Spain, and cooking is still considered an important skill, with those who master it enjoying everyone's respect and admiration.

Madrileños like to cook at home, but they also love to eat out, and their city offers them a million options—enough to satisfy every taste, craving, and palate. From the humble and affordable to the chic and highly refined cooking of Michelin-starred restaurants, from the domestic and traditional to the cosmopolitan and exotic, from the classic to the avant-garde, for carnivores as well as vegetarians and even vegans, Madrid has something to offer everyone and is a great place to be hungry. Food is also intertwined with history in Madrid in truly extraordinary ways. I invite you to read this book as a way of learning about this history, and

1

perhaps it will pique your interest and tempt you to visit or, at the very least, travel there vicariously with me.

Before venturing any further, however, I must make a confession: I was not born in Madrid, and for a long time I did not even like Madrid all that much. I was born in a much smaller town called Murcia in southeast Spain, and my family then moved to Alicante, a city on the Mediterranean coast that was, during the 1970s and 1980s, a nice, quiet, and slow-paced town with a pleasantly provincial feel. (It has since experienced a serious touristic boom, and this has changed things some-what, although it still retains some of its laid-back air.) Alicante is blessed with a very mild year-round climate and about 350 sunny days per year. Every time I visited Madrid, I felt overwhelmed and stressed by its fast pace, its size, the enormity of its buildings and avenues, and the time it took to get anywhere in such a large city. To me, the weather felt too cold in the winter and too hot in the summer, and even though I enjoyed visiting the city occasionally for its world-class museums and theaters, it never felt like home.

On one of those visits, my brother-in-law Sergio, whose family has deep roots in Madrid and who knows the city like the back of his hand, became determined to make me change my mind about Madrid. After years of knowing each other, he knew my weaknesses, so he and my sister deployed an unfailing strategy—taking me and my husband on a memorable tapas and wine tour of old Madrid. For those not familiar with the concept of tapas, I'll explain: They are small plates of incredibly tasty food served with a drink at every bar in Spain, often eaten standing up by the counter and shared with friends or family. These heavenly bites range from the simple to the sophisticated but are always intensely flavorful. They may consist of a slice of tomato-soaked bread with ham or chorizo; or a portion of potato omelet, garlic shrimp, cheese, fritters stuffed with ham or cod, or *patatas bravas* (potatoes with a spicy sauce); or a long list of other delicious options. *Tapeo*, bar-hopping for tapas, is a casual affair but a wonderfully bonding one since you're with your friends, sharing one after another of these delicious bites and usually no less delicious glasses of Rioja or Ribera del Duero wine.

On this particular occasion, we roamed the streets of the Cava Baja—a street known for its eating and drinking establishments since the sixteenth century and where some of the most traditional bars, *gastrobars*, and *tabernas* can still be found today—making frequent stops in the places my brother-in-law wanted to show us, trying the specialty at each one. They were all busy and filled with hungry crowds that left no doubt about these being the places to be on a Saturday afternoon. Seeing how these bars competed to offer the best tapas, the friendliest atmosphere, or the smoothest vermouth, it was easy to understand their fame and the reasons for such large crowds. After a few stops, I was hooked. They say the shortest way to a person's heart is through the stomach, and in my case that's exactly what happened.

I fell in love with Madrid's food, tapas bars, *tabernas*, and restaurants but also with the lively, narrow streets of the old city. And I fell hard, realizing that I needed to learn more, see more places, and try their mouthwatering specialties. I also wanted to learn about the history of Madrid to fully understand how this beautiful and insanely dynamic city came to be what it is today.

Welcoming people is in the very nature of Madrid, and it is this combination of humanity and cultural traditions that has shaped its identity over centuries. As a Madrileño friend recently put it, "Once you arrive to Madrid, you *are* from Madrid." It truly does not matter how long you've lived there or where you come from—Madrid will take you in and let you become one of its prodigal children. This welcoming quality of Spain's capital is also what has made it such a food mecca. New York may be called "the city that never sleeps," but Madrid is its equally insomniac sister. The heart of Madrid pumps day and night with an extraordinary and infectious energy, making it not only a vibrant and enormously exciting food town but also a cultural center with a never-ending and maddening array of activities and events taking place. There is always something happening in its bustling streets, from outdoor markets to concerts to first-rate art exhibitions at its many museums, such as the Prado, the Thyssen-Bornemisza, or the Reina Sofia. The people of Madrid seem to be in a perpetual state of hunger—both physical and metaphysical—filling the bars and restaurants during the day and late into the night. In fact, restaurants keep their kitchens open until midnight on weekdays and even later on weekends, and the streets are always crowded with people walking, shopping, eating, talking exuberantly—in sum, enjoying the vibrant city and all that it has to offer.

You are sure to find whatever you crave in cosmopolitan Madrid, which is home to a dazzling number of eateries offering fare ranging from traditional Madrileño dishes to those from every region of the country and the world. Spain's capital city admirably balances the old and the new, with the "old" Madrid represented by respected and revered traditional restaurants that are the keepers of tradition and the "new" Madrid spearheaded by a wave of young and highly creative chefs who have chosen to make the city their home. This new wave cooks not just for the rich and elite but also for a gastronomically curious middle class and for young professionals who may not be affluent but who are nevertheless well traveled and sophisticated. As one young food blogger put it, "We like to eat well, take a little escapade now and then, and in sum, be as happy as we can without spending too many euros."[1] The city, having reinvented itself many times over centuries of existence, continues to change and grow, mixing the old with the new, with energy and an openness to embracing new ideas. It is a most exciting process to watch.

This book aims to be a passionate account of Madrid's fascinating food history across its many centuries of existence to today. The first chapter, "Before Madrid:

The Flavors of the Iberian Peninsula," examines food and foodways from antiquity through the Middle Ages, focusing on the contributions of each of the region's successive inhabitants. It looks at the city's origins and its foundation in the ninth century AD as an Arab military outpost, as well as the intriguing archeological evidence of a history that is both rich and amazing. This chapter also shows how the rich gastronomic legacy of Madrid was built slowly over millennia, starting with the survival eating of the prehistoric peoples and evolving with the numerous and complex influences of the Iberian, Greek, Roman, Visigothic, Arabic, Jewish, and Christian inhabitants of Madrid.

The second chapter, "Too Many Kings Spoil the Broth," examines food and cooking in Madrid since 1561, when the city was declared the Spanish capital by Felipe II, through the eighteenth century, showing the role played by the successive monarchies that ruled Castile during this period as vehicles for gastronomic innovation. Differences in diets related to class and social status are presented in this chapter, as is as the major shift in Spanish cuisine that took place with the discovery and colonization of America and the introduction in Europe of products like potatoes, tomatoes, peppers, and chocolate. These New World foods would slowly make their way into Spanish cuisine and become essential ingredients in many of Madrid's traditional dishes.

Chapter 3, "A New Era of Creative Cuisine," charts the transformation that occurred in the nineteenth century when Spanish cuisine, which until then had been heavily indebted to French cuisine, started to develop its own sense of identity and a desire to break free from French influences. Several important cookbooks and food writers of the time made food a relevant social topic with political and ideological implications. Some of the most legendary of Madrid's establishments date from this time, as do many of its best-known dishes. The turbulent start of the twentieth century in Spain is also presented in this chapter. During the Spanish Civil War (1936–1939), the city suffered a siege and frequent bombings, and its population had to endure extreme food shortages. An examination of food availability in Madrid during the civil war and the years after highlights the resourceful strategies adopted by Madrileños in order to survive, from the rise of the *estraperlo* (black market) to the use of ingenious recipes like potato omelets without eggs or potatoes, and the recipes included in this chapter are a testament to the strength and resilience of Madrid's citizens. The last section of chapter 3 focuses on the birth and rise of star-chef Ferrán Adriá and the molecular gastronomy movement, as well as the stature of Spain in today's culinary world, with nine restaurants in the country currently holding a Michelin three-star rating.

Chapter 4, "Madrid, a Gastronome's Playground: Markets and Food Retailing through History," looks at Madrid's numerous markets, specialty shops, bakeries, and other types of establishments, which have helped Madrileños stock their pantries for centuries. The chapter traces the evolution of markets from open-air street markets into covered structures during the nineteenth century and the eventual crisis and rebirth of these historic markets into contemporary gourmet spaces catering to modern tastes in the twenty-first century. Centenary shops still in operation in Madrid are described in this chapter, along with the impact that the increasing presence of modern supermarkets is having on the city's food-retailing landscape.

The fifth chapter, "Historic Cookbooks," looks at the canonical works that have both shaped and reflected the evolution of Madrid's cuisine across the centuries. From the medieval books written by royal cooks for their use at court or by monks needing to feed their congregations to more recent cookbooks aimed at busy housewives and hungry postwar citizens, the history of Madrid is embedded in these recipes and deserves to be told.

In chapter 6, "Historic Restaurants, *Tabernas*, and Cafés," these Madrid culinary establishments are presented, digging into their past, the stories around them, and their specialty dishes. More than a dozen restaurants over one hundred years old are still in operation in Madrid, including the oldest restaurant in the world, Sobrino de Botín, amazingly open since 1725. These fascinating places are full of charm and culinary wisdom and keep the spirit of the old city alive by continuing to prepare traditional dishes that are as historic as they are delicious.

Finally, in the last chapter, "Madrid's Traditional Dishes," the city's typical and signature dishes are presented, and historical background on each is provided, along with recipes for their preparation. From tapas to main courses and desserts, these are some of the most popular specialties that can be enjoyed while visiting Spain's capital.

Madrid: A Culinary History provides a glimpse of what, how, and where people have eaten in Madrid throughout the ages. Tracing the role of food in the life of the city over its long and convoluted history has been a fascinating journey for me. I hope that reading these pages will give you an understanding and appreciation of the remarkable, complex, sometimes woeful, sometimes joyful culinary history of Madrid, and perhaps you will even find yourself transported to Madrid's boisterous streets while enjoying something delicious. *¡Buen provecho!*

Madrid, Spain, June 2016–Cincinnati, Ohio, January 2017

1

❖ ❖

Before Madrid

The Flavors of the Iberian Peninsula

Matrice, Mayrit, Magerit, Madrid. The city's many names over the centuries bear witness to its long history and rich cultural heritage. Madrid has seen a fascinating succession of peoples come and go, from prehistoric inhabitants to Iberians, Celts, Greeks, Romans, Visigoths, Moors, and Christians. Madrid's rich history is explained by the welcoming landscape, with numerous rivers, small peaks, and fertile valleys, and the hospitable climate, which provided its inhabitants with an abundance of resources for millennia. Evidence of hominid occupation of the Iberian Peninsula has been found dating back more than one million years at the Atapuerca Mountains archeological site, located in present-day Burgos, in the Castile and León region of northern Spain, making Atapuerca the oldest documented human occupation in Europe. There is evidence of at least three hominid species that preceded *Homo sapiens* among the first settlers of the Iberian Peninsula, and recent DNA evidence suggests that several of these species interbred over time, with most modern Europeans having some small percentage of Neanderthal (*Homo neandertalensis*) genes. Conflict between Neanderthals and bigger-brained *Homo sapiens* about twenty-six thousand to twenty-eight thousand years ago in the Iberian Peninsula resulted in the displacement and eventual extinction of the former.[1] Archeological evidence also suggests that the Atapuerca Mountains served as a favored site of several pre–*Homo sapiens* hominid species, with the earliest specimen reliably dated to somewhere between 1.2 million and 600,000 years before the present. Prehistoric art has been uncovered at different locations on the

Iberian Peninsula, including in modern-day Soria, near Madrid, and most famously
in the Caves of Altamira in today's Asturias. The remarkable Altamira caves, for
example, feature charcoal drawings and color paintings of hunting scenes, local
fauna, and human hands created between 18,500 and 14,000 years ago, with ar-
cheologists estimating the oldest paintings in these caves to be 35,600 years old.
The first records of agricultural activity, animal husbandry, and food storage in the
Iberian Peninsula date from 7000 to 5000 BC, with remains of beer dating back to
5000 BC found in caves in Cova Sant Sadurní, near present-day Barcelona.[2]

Archeological findings show that people began to settle in the fertile region of
Madrid's Manzanares Valley as far back as 350,000 years ago, likely attracted by
the abundance of water and other natural resources.[3] Human presence, however,
dates back quite a bit further. In fact, the Museo de los Orígenes, focusing on the
history of Madrid and housed in a sixteenth-century palace presiding over the
charming Plaza de San Andrés (San Andrés's Square), includes in its fascinating
collection a number of hunting tools and other artifacts from a much earlier age—
about four hundred thousand years ago—including ceramic pots and vases, gold
jewelry, and even the prehistoric molar of a young boy. As this collection shows,
the banks of the Manzanares, as well as of the Jarama and Henares Rivers—all
feeding the region of Madrid—are a rich source of archeological clues, with the
remains of ancient elephants, hippopotamuses, mammoths, deer, wolves, and bulls,
among other animals, all being found there. The groups of hominids who lived in
the Manzanares Valley during the Paleolithic period based their lifestyle on the
opportunistic exploitation of this environment, leading them to seek out the best
sites that would provide resources for their survival. The steady supply of water,
abundant riparian vegetation, and variety of wildlife offered by the Manzanares's
and Jarama's riversides must have been a decisive factor for the settling of the first
peoples in the region. This early group of hominids sustained themselves by hunting horses, red and fallow deer, aurochs, and even larger animals like elephants.
They also ate fruits, nuts, and seeds, as well as honey and insects. Prehistoric paintings have been found in the area depicting anthropomorphic figures and animals,
such as bison and deer. The rich flora and fauna that thrived in this area was gradually affected by climatic changes, as well as by hunting, fishing, and the use of land
for cultivation by the first inhabitants, starting around 3500 BC. This appropriation
of the natural space for human occupation caused the progressive disappearance of
streams and the decimation of forests around the area, a process that would acceler-
ate after the sixteenth century, when King Felipe II established his court in Madrid,
marking the beginning of its remarkable growth. In spite of this, today's fauna is
still fairly rich, albeit drastically different from what it used to be. About fifty species of birds can be found in Madrid's urban parks alone, among them magpies,
sparrows, blackbirds, nightingales, pigeons, and finches. Storks are common, and

there are several types of vultures, such as the rare griffin vulture; imperial eagles; kestrels; and great bustards, as well as woodpeckers and even seagulls. The forests around Madrid are home to otters, deer, foxes, wild boars, wild cats, hares, squirrels, and weasels. Today's Madrid region includes about sixty different species of trees, from black poplars to cottonwoods, willows, *madroños* (the strawberry tree, depicted in the city's coat of arms), ash trees, and magnolia trees.[4]

The city of Madrid is situated near the very center of the Iberian Peninsula, the actual geographic center being a little more than eight miles from the city on a hill called Cerro de los Ángeles. The surrounding region occupies a widely varied topographic space, with changes in altitude of up to 6,561 feet. Highest in elevation are the Somosierra and Guadarrama mountain ranges, and in the Guadarrama Mountains, for example, the Peñalara peak rises to 7,969 feet, making it the highest peak in the region. The lowest elevation point, by contrast, is marked by the Alberche River as it passes through the town of Villa del Prado, about thirty-three miles from the capital, at an altitude of merely 1,410 feet above sea level. The city of Madrid itself is at an altitude of 2,132 feet above sea level and has relatively mild winters but hot summers. As a result, most Madrileños flee the city during the summer—especially August, the hottest month of the year—to vacation on the Mediterranean beaches of Alicante and Valencia or on the much cooler northern coasts of Galicia, the mountainous regions of Asturias, or the Basque Country. Madrid is noticeably empty during the summer and traffic is a breeze, a welcome change from the hectic mass of vehicles usually choking the city's main arteries, though this does nothing to improve the reputation of Madrid's famously grumpy cab drivers.

FIRST CIVILIZATIONS: PHOENICIANS, CARTHAGINIANS, GREEKS, IBERIANS, AND CELTS

The many different peoples who have made the Iberian Peninsula their home over the centuries have all left their mark on Spain's culture and its cuisine. Phoenicians, Greeks, and Carthaginians arrived on the peninsula in successive waves starting around 1100 BC, with Phoenician merchants founding the trading colony of Gadir or Gades (modern-day Cádiz) near the mythical city of Tartessos. They settled along the Mediterranean coast and founded trading colonies that flourished for several centuries. The Phoenicians also started the cultivation of olive trees in the Iberian Peninsula and established fish-salting plants in the south. Beef husbandry appears to have been common as well. Fish caught off the coast, such as tuna, mackerel, and sturgeon, were sold and highly prized in the markets of the eastern Mediterranean. The discovery of numerous Phoenician amphorae suggests that olive oil and wine were commonly traded goods.[5] Attracted to the Phoenician trading posts established along the southern and southeastern coasts, Greeks from Turkey's Gulf of Izmir arrived in the eighth century BC and established their first colonies, such as Emporion (modern-day Catalan Empúries), founding several others along the Mediterranean coast on the east and leaving the southern coast to the Phoenicians. The Greeks increased the cultivation of olive trees, as well as almonds and grapes, introducing wine production. Also about this time, the Celts crossed the Pyrenees and began to settle in the north and west of the peninsula, and by the seventh century BC, the Iberian Peninsula consisted of several agrarian and urban civilizations that had been inhabiting the land for centuries, such as the Lusitanians, Celtiberians, Gallaeci, Astures, and Celtici; the Iberians in the eastern and southern zones; and the Aquitanian cultures, which include the Basque, in the western portion of the Pyrenees. In the sixth century BC, while struggling with the Greeks for control of the western Mediterranean, the Carthaginians arrived, founding what became their most important city on the Iberian Peninsula, Carthago Nova (modern-day Cartagena). The Carthaginians established colonies along the south coast of Spain, the north coast of Africa, as well as in Sicily, Corsica, Sardinia, and the Balearic island of Ibiza. For about three centuries, the Carthaginians focused mainly on maintaining a flourishing trading activity of goods such as silver, salt, fish, olive oil, and wine, basically continuing the commercial activities of the Phoenicians. However, after Carthage's defeat at the hands of Rome in the first of the Punic Wars (265–241 BC), with Carthage losing Sicily, Corsica, and Sardinia and also having to pay Rome financial compensation, a more belligerent situation developed. Battles between Carthaginians and Romans for control of the peninsula increased in frequency, with several successive Carthaginian leaders unsuccessfully attempting to defeat Rome. Finally, young and fearless Hannibal attempted to bring as much of the peninsula under Carthaginian control as possible, advancing inland as far as Salamanca. But it was his decision to conquer the town of Sagunto, which was under Roman protection, in 219–218 BC that would lead to the Second Punic War and result in the end of Carthaginian presence on the peninsula. Hannibal's decision to attack Sagunto was a provocation to Rome, and a costly one. The city fell after an eight-month siege, resulting in Rome formally declaring war on Carthage and eventually defeating Hannibal's army. The struggle for Iberia lasted for the following twelve years (218–206 BC),[6] ending with the expulsion of the Carthaginians and the Romans moving to gradually conquer the entire Iberian Peninsula and incorporate it into the Roman Empire, naming it Hispania.

The Iberians, so named by the Greeks because of their connection to the Iber River (today's Ebro River), had arrived on the Iberian Peninsula sometime during the third or fourth millennium BC. Where they came from remains unclear. While some historians contend that they came from the eastern Mediterranean region of Asia Minor, others hypothesize that they originated in western or eastern Europe; another theory is that they were North African tribes who migrated during the Neolithic period. Just as their origin remains a mystery, so does their culture, of which little is known. It is believed, however, that after the Celts arrived on the Iberian Peninsula, they eventually mixed with the Iberians, giving rise to the Celtiberians. This name, given to them by the Romans, has since been used as a convenient way of describing the somewhat confusing medley of tribal groups that inhabited the hinterland. What is clear, however, is that resistance to unification was a constant problem faced by the Romans and throughout Spain's history, as exemplified by the case of the Basques, a people of uncertain origin that some believe are descended from autochthonous peoples, while others speculate that they are perhaps related to the Berbers of North Africa. Isolated from the rest of the peninsula by the barrier of the Pyrenees, the Basques were never fully conquered, successfully resisting even Roman invasion, and to this day they still preserve a strong sense of identity and their mysterious language, unrelated to Latin and unlike any other languages spoken in Europe today.

Some Celtiberian tribes known as Carpetanos settled in the Ebro Valley, spreading progressively toward the southeastern coast of the Iberian Peninsula. Even though we know the name of their capital, Mantua Carpetana, its precise location is not known. Nevertheless, evidence of Celtiberian settlements have been found near modern-day Madrid and along the Jarama and the Manzanares Rivers, and it is clear that the Carpetania region extended beyond the area of Madrid proper, encompassing the areas occupied today by the towns of Alcalá de Henares, Toledo, Cuenca, Ciudad Real, and Guadalajara. Considered by many historians as the most influential ethnic group in pre-Roman Iberia, the Celtiberians were skilled at metalwork and developed a powerful and successful army, leaving behind sophisticated bronze figures of symbolic or religious significance and a number of bronze plaques and inscriptions commemorating notable military events.

The Celtiberians' influence and power would start to decline following a number of disastrous wars against the Roman Empire between the years of 195 BC and 72 BC, and eventually they would submit to Roman domination. As a result, their language was lost, replaced by Latin, and their culture was obliterated by that of the powerful new empire. Very likely, their cuisine suffered a similar fate, influenced by the Roman diet and substituting Celtiberian traditional main staples with wheat bread, olive oil, and wine. This, however, is mostly speculation, since our knowledge of Celtiberian cuisine and its evolution under Roman rule is quite limited.[7]

What is known of this past culture? There is evidence that the Celtiberians raised livestock for meat, milk, and wool, and the presence of sheep, goats, cows, pigs, and chickens is well documented. Other sources of meat, which in general was only a small part of their diet, were the animals they hunted, as the bones uncovered in archaeological excavations show deer, wild boar, hare, and rabbit, as well as partridge, quail, and duck. However, their diet seems to have been based more on grains and vegetables, growing vegetables and fruits such as pears and plums, grains like barley and wheat, pulses such as bitter vetches and fava beans, and nuts such as walnuts and acorns, which were often dried and ground for flour.[8] Also well documented is the production of alcoholic drinks, among them a high-proof wheat beer (*caelia*), mead, and wine made from grapes.[9]

ROMAN *MATRICE*, "MOTHER OF WATERS"

The Romans began their expansion through the Iberian Peninsula, which they named Hispania, in 206 BC. Realizing the strategic importance of the Madrid region, they seized the Carpetano settlement situated by the Manzanares River and called the new settlement Matrice, "mother of waters," in reference to the river flowing nearby.[10] Matrice was not, strictly speaking, a city, but rather a sort of crossroads where several roads connecting the Vía Augusta met. The Vía Augusta, an impressive 932-mile-long road that was the principal commercial road crossing Hispania, was of enormous economic importance to the Roman Empire. It connected major Roman cities such as Toledo (Tolutum) and Alcalá de Henares (Complutum), while Matrice lacked an urban core and instead was composed of a number of villas, surrounded by vast extensions of cultivated land. Some of these villas were quite large and luxurious and served as rest stops for travelers along the way. These villas would eventually be abandoned after the arrival of the Visigoths on the peninsula in the fifth century AD, but some of their splendor survives today as archaeological treasures. Excavations under Madrid have uncovered fascinating ruins, gorgeous mosaics, stunning jewelry, ceramics, and coins, as well as a wide variety of utensils dating from this time. Today these areas are hopping with city life, such as Casa de Campo; Villaverde Bajo;[11] Carabanchel; Jarama-Henares; Barajas, the town where the Adolfo Suárez Madrid–Barajas Airport is located; and Cuatro Caminos.

The Romans remained on the Iberian Peninsula for a period of six hundred years and introduced many of the changes and innovations that were decisive in the making of today's Spain. Especially important was the institution of a well-structured legal and administrative system, as well as the Christian religion and the Latin language. Castilian Spanish—along with other Romance languages still spoken in Spain, such as Galician or Catalan—is derived from Latin. Also, the first Jewish populations arrived on the peninsula with the Romans, who, given their polytheistic tradition, were fairly tolerant of other religions as long as they didn't pose a political problem. Since their arrival to Hispania and for at least a thousand years—until 1492, when they were forced to choose exile or conversion to Christianity—the Jews figured prominently in the history of Spain, greatly influencing its gastronomic culture.

The Romans carried out an impressive number of public works projects, building aqueducts, amphitheaters, roads, and bridges for commercial, military, and civil purposes, many of which are, remarkably, still standing today. One of the most impressive examples of Roman urban architecture can still be seen in the town of Segovia, about fifty-six miles north of Madrid. The stunning aqueduct that rises in the center of this friendly and charming town was built during the second century AD for the purpose of transporting water from the mountains in the Acebeda region, running for about twenty miles before it reaches the town. This wonder of engineering is composed of 167 arches and 20,400 unmortared granite blocks, held together by nothing more than gravity. It is still in remarkably great shape for having been in use until the middle of the twentieth century. This imposing and beautiful architectural wonder is well worth an excursion from the capital. Segovia is also famous for its legendary *cochinillo asado*, an extremely tender roast suckling pig that is an absolute must-try of melt-in-your-mouth deliciousness. The most famous place to try this delicacy is a restaurant called Mesón de Cándido, which has been wowing customers with this dish since 1905. Cándido has been visited by a long list of celebrities, from Hollywood actors, writers, and painters to stars from the world of sports and even royals and heads of state, their photographs proudly decorating the walls of the restaurant.

The Romans made a number of important contributions to the cuisine of Hispania: the introduction of sophisticated ovens and methods to bake bread, the production of large quantities of wine and olive oil, and the use of the pungent and popular fish sauce known as *garum*, produced in the Mediterranean region of the Iberian Peninsula and exported throughout the entire Roman Empire. As Rafael Chabrán points out, "There is evidence of bread in Spanish archaeological sites from the Mesolithic Age, but most certainly it was the Romans who revolutionized bread production in Spain by introducing their way of making bread and by constructing their Roman ovens." The importance of this Roman culinary heritage to Spanish cuisine cannot be overstated, since "much of what we think of today as being typically Spanish were, in fact, the staples of the Roman diet. Bread, cheese, olives, and olive oil, wine, and roasted meat, when it was to be had, were the standard fare of the Roman soldiers in Hispania."[12] The Roman pantry was well stocked—and, by extension, Madrid's was as well—with a variety of meats, poultry, fish, and abundant fruits and vegetables. The Roman and, presumably, Madrileño diet included bread, olives, honey, cheese, lamb, pork, beef, duck, goose, chicken, eggs, fruits (pears, figs, apples, grapes, and the like), and vegetables like wild asparagus and carrots. *Lucanica*, a short and rustic sausage made from pork that originated in the southern Italian region of Lucania, made its way to Hispania, possibly brought over by Roman soldiers. Mentioned by Apicius in his treatise on Roman cooking, *De re coquinaria*, *lucanica* is the clear predecessor of contemporary Spanish *longaniza*, the Catalan *llonganissa*, and also the Portuguese *linguiça*, all of them sausages made with pork and different spices and still widely enjoyed today.

Just as in contemporary Madrid, the Romans considered snails a delicacy. Noted in the writings of Pliny and backed by archaeological research, evidence of snail farms has been found throughout the area occupied by the Roman Empire; in the case of the Iberian Peninsula, they were mostly located in the northern region of Asturias.[13] The breeding of snails was a big business in ancient Rome, according to Felipe Fernández-Armesto: "The ancestors of our escargots de Bourgogne were packed into breeding cages in ancient Rome and stuffed with milk until they were too big for their shells."[14] The result was a gourmet and nutritious delicacy enjoyed by the wealthy as well as invalids. Today, Madrileños *love* their snails, prepared with a tasty tomato sauce and served in the numerous taverns, bars, and restaurants around the city. Madrid's oldest tavern, La Taberna de Antonio Sánchez, a beautifully preserved establishment, has been serving this gourmet dish for almost two centuries since first opening its doors in 1830.

The Romans were very skilled at agriculture, and they took advantage of the fertile soil of the Iberian Peninsula, realizing early on that land and climate conditions in Hispania were ideal for the cultivation of a number of foodstuffs such as wheat, olive oil, and wine and, in the coastal areas, the production of salted fish.[15] Xavier Medina notes that the Roman villas and their surrounding land were agriculture centers of production devoted to crops, especially grains. Madrid was also used as farmland, and it is likely that it was used to grow some of these staples, such as wheat and grapes, and to procure meat from livestock and poultry and eggs from chickens. A detailed description of Roman cuisine and its many dishes, some of them rather exotic and sophisticated even by today's standards, can be found in Apicius's previously mentioned *De re coquinaria*, a fascinating cookbook dating back to the late fourth or early fifth centuries AD. Apicius's book contains recipes for lamb, kid, and chicken stews, dishes made with pulses and vegetables, and the preparation of different types of fish and birds, such as peacocks and flamingos. Despite the documented existence of these exuberant dishes, however, historians like Medina believe that the cuisine practiced in Roman Hispania was not as lavish as the one that could be found in the capital of the empire.[16] Rather, the diet of farmers around Matrice was more likely a simple diet composed of a few staples (bread, wine, olive oil, pulses, vegetables, and fruit) and the occasional meat, often salted or in sausage form.

THE VISIGOTHS

In the year AD 456, the Visigoths, a Germanic tribe that had separated from the Ostrogoths in the fourth century, entered the Iberian Peninsula through the Pyrenees. Led by the Visigoth king Theodoric II, they would eventually defeat the Romans and rule Hispania until being themselves defeated by the Moors, who would invade the peninsula in 711 and remain there for eight centuries. By AD 476, the Visigoth conquest of Hispania was completed, and in the year 507 Visigoth king Leovigild established the kingdom's capital in the city of Toledo, located about forty-six miles from present-day Madrid. Newly discovered archaeological evidence suggests that Madrid then became an area of Visigoth settlement, albeit consisting only of a small and sparsely distributed population that occupied some of the abandoned Roman villas and established a few small villages throughout the region.

Even though the Visigoths introduced new laws and created a centralized government, they also maintained many Roman traditions. Latin was maintained as the language used for all official communications and was the language of choice for writers and historians. The Roman name for Madrid, "Matrice," was kept, and Christianity was adopted as the official religion. The works of Saint Isidore of Seville are the most important surviving texts from this period, providing detailed documentation on many aspects of Visigothic society and culture. In his *Etymologies* and *Regula Monachorum*, Saint Isidore speaks of the changes that Roman culture and society underwent under Visigoth rule. Saint Isidore's books are rich with information about food and eating during this time. He thoroughly describes Spanish cooking under the Visigoths, including cooking utensils and equipment, and he even details food rituals and traditions regarding the preparation of popular dishes. The influence of the Roman legacy is apparent in his account. He mentions stews made using legumes popular among the more humble segments of the population, as well as the common Visigothic dish *pulte*, a sort of porridge inherited in its essence from Roman cuisine and made from coarsely ground wheat or millet, to which mashed legumes were added. Wine, apple cider, and barley beer were also very popular and were consumed in large quantities. The Visigoths did not introduce many cuisine changes, however, judging from Saint Isidore's observations about what and how people ate. Mostly, the Visigoths continued to eat the staples introduced by the Romans, cultivating lentils, beans, chickpeas, peas, lettuces, chards, and leeks, as well as figs, pears, plums, grapes, pomegranates, and peaches. The Visigoths were, as Claudia Roden notes, stock-raising herders who kept pigs, sheep, and goats; cooked with lard instead of using olive oil, thus deviating slightly from the Roman custom; and raised geese and hunted from the lush forests around the area, which provided them with rabbits, game, and various types of birds.[17]

THE FOUNDATION OF MEDINA MAYRIT
AND SPAIN'S ARABIC FOOD HERITAGE

The Visigoth rule ended with the arrival of Muslim armies in 711, whose expansion through the Iberian Peninsula was rapid. The Visigoth kingdom was crumbling and was easily defeated; their army was no match for the Islamic hordes, and the Iberian Peninsula soon came under Moorish rule and was named Al-Andalus. By the eighth century, most of the peninsula was under Muslim control, with the exception of the mountainous and rugged Basque region, Asturias, and part of Catalonia. Thus started the subsequent campaign to gain back the land for Christianity, known as the *Reconquista*, which would last until 1492. Despite its power and splendor, Al-Andalus was, for most of its existence, in permanent conflict with the northern Christian Visigoth kingdoms.

The establishment of Madrid as a significant urban nucleus took place in the mid-ninth century, possibly in the year AD 865, according to most historians. The Arabs saw the Manzanares River region as an important strategic spot, and Muhammad I, Córdoba's emir at the time, was deeply aware of its value and established a military outpost there with an imposing fortress and an agricultural settlement to feed its population. Muhammed called this military outpost Magerit—a name that would eventually evolve into Mayrit. Even though no consensus exists about the meaning and etymology of the name, the most widely accepted interpretations translate it as "place of many *mayrits* [subterranean waters]," or "place with abundant water."[18] There is no question that the river was an important point of reference: the *alcázar* (castle) was built on a hill on the left bank of the Manzanares River, on the grounds of what is now the Palacio Real, or Royal Palace—a must-see for any Madrid visitor today—and to the south of the hill, the *al-mudayna*, or citadel where the civil population lived, was erected, surrounded by a protective wall. Eventually, these two areas would be united and surrounded by a single, expanded wall. Over time, small neighborhoods of peasants, artisans, and merchants began to appear outside the citadel's gates, and the city spread steadily. The numerous springs, rivers, and streams that had been flowing since ancient times created a very fertile land that was ideal for agriculture and teaming with wildlife. The abundant produce that was grown in the land outside the city was brought to be sold in the early city's street markets, such as the one found in the Plaza de la Paja (Straw Square, named as such for being the spot where the straw was weighed each season and its price set). This square continued to be used as marketplace well after Madrid was reconquered under Christian rule, and it remained the most important marketplace in the city during the thirteenth and fourteenth centuries. Peasants, shepherds, and artisans would gather there to sell the fruits of their labor, providing the city's population with meat, milk, eggs, fruits and vegetables, grains, olives and olive oil, wine, cheese, and honey, among other products. No longer a marketplace, today the Plaza de la Paja is a delightful square surrounded by several buildings dating back to the sixteenth century, such as the Casa del Obispo (Bishop's House) and the Vargas family palace. It is dotted with pleasant cafés where visitors can take a break from exploring the city's old streets.

Mayrit became known for its green landscape and rich orchards, which the Moors exploited fully with their mastery of agricultural techniques. As Ana Ruiz points out, those who did not belong to the military turned to farming and agriculture for income, while others became artisans and makers of handicrafts, pottery, and other commodities. "Farming and agriculture became the fundamental drivers of the economy, and excellent hunting, crop-growing, and cattle-raising conditions eventually added an agricultural element to the existing military character of Mayrit."[19] These orchards produced famously delicious figs, cherries, apples, quinces, plums, pomegranates, pears, apricots, walnuts, and many other fruits. Vines and wheat were also prevalent, as were olive trees.

References to the *medina* (city) of Mayrit abound in the literature about Al-Andalus. Abd al-Mun'im al-Himyari, a Muslim geographer and historian from the fourteenth century, mentions it in his work *The Book of the Fragrant Garden*, a notable source of information about Muslim Spain: "Mayrit, constructed by the Emir of Córdoba, Muhammad I, was a small town containing an impenetrable fortress and a major mosque." He says that Mayrit "had the strongest and best defensive architecture that existed at this time."[20] These references are significant as they reveal the true purpose of the first Madrid and its foundation. Mayrit was a defense outpost, a fortress built to maintain control over the territories of Al-Andalus. The vantage point upon which Mayrit sat was the perfect strategic enclave from which to fend off the advances of the Christian armies coming from the north and also served as headquarters for Muhammad I's army. In Muslim Spain, *marcas* (marches) were established by the Caliphate of Córdoba as defensive regions separating Al-Andalus's territories from those under Christian control. Mayrit belonged to the Marca Media, or Middle March, the central frontier territory whose capital city was Toledo and which quickly became one of the most important centers of Al-Andalus's power. The fragmentation of the Caliphate of Córdoba into small kingdoms, or *taifas*, beginning in the year 1031 weakened their power, however, and facilitated the efforts of the Christian kings to regain their lost territories. Ultimately, after a series of bloody battles, the Christian kingdoms from the north overpowered the Muslim armies, and in 1085 Christian king Alfonso VI captured Toledo. The Christian reconquest of what is now Spain continued, concluding in 1492 when Isabel and Fernando, known as the *Reyes Católicos* ("Catholic Kings"), took control of the city of Granada—the last remaining Muslim stronghold in all the Iberian Peninsula—and forced all Muslims to either convert to the Catholic faith or leave.

It must be noted, however, that a period of *convivencia*, or coexistence, characterized the southern territories of Al-Andalus for several centuries before the Catholic Kings dictated the expulsion of non-Christians from the Iberian Peninsula in 1492. Under Muslim rule, the different ethnic groups lived alongside and influenced each other's culture, language, and, more notably, each other's cuisine. Generally speaking, "daily contact between Christian, Jewish and Muslim communities led to a substantial degree of tolerance and coexistence, that marked the difference between Spain and the rest of Europe for much of the Medieval period."[21] For example, the Mozárabes or Mozarabs (Christians who lived under Moorish rule in Al-Andalus) dressed as Muslims, adapted the Arabic diet, and even spoke Arabic but kept their Christian faith and religious practices. Both Mozarabs and Jews enjoyed a special status in Al-Andalus that allowed them to maintain their faith and traditions, although they were subject to certain restrictions and payment of several taxes. As Claudia Roden notes, during the eight centuries of Muslim occupation, there were constant and ongoing wars, but there were also treaties and long periods of peace that allowed for continuous trade exchanges.

> During and after the Reconquista, there were many towns where Muslims lived among Christians and Jews. . . . The communities fraternized despite condemnation by the Church. . . . They did business together, they ate and drank together, sang and played games together, and invited each other to festivals and weddings. The style of cooking that had at first been rejected as part of the enemy Muslim culture by Christians was eventually assimilated by them.[22]

Food in Arabic Mayrit was plentiful and varied. The Moors brought a new sophistication to the cuisine of the Iberian Peninsula, along with new cooking and food preservation techniques such as *escabeche* (cooking in vinegar) and the distillation of alcohol. Grains were an important part of the diet, with wheat, millet, barley, oats, sorghum, and semolina, among others, used for porridge but also ground to form flour to create pastries and cakes. Many kinds of beans were eaten as well, such as broad beans, chickpeas, and lentils, along with a stunning variety of vegetables, such as eggplants, cucumbers, onions, artichokes, lettuces, celery, and squash. Many of these vegetables, along with olive oil cultivated in Andalusia, would eventually make their way to other parts of the caliphate via commercial trade. Rice was an important crop, and milk and cheese were also important elements of the cuisine, as were fruits and sweet desserts. Meat was scarce in Al-Andalus and seems to have been reserved for special occasions, not being within the reach of the lower classes. Poultry was an exception, while other types of meat, such as lamb, were mostly reserved for religious celebrations. Once sacrificed, every part of the lamb was used through roasting, drying, and baking the different parts of the animal and preserving them as sausages or jerky.[23]

Many traditional dishes were enjoyed in Al-Andalus, such as *altamandria*, a finely chopped mix of chicken, hen, pigeon, and other small birds cooked with rice and flavored with spices; *harees* or *harissa*, made with coarsely ground flour from wheat or another type of grain, which was then boiled and mixed with deboned chicken meat; *sajina*, a flour porridge topped with vegetables; and *alcuzcuz*, a mix composed of flour and made into small pellets, steamed, and eaten with vegetables and lamb meat (known today by the name couscous). Added to this was, of course, a wide array of honey-dripping sweets made with honey, sugar, wheat flour, dates, raisins, and dried nuts, including dishes such as *alajú*, a baked paste made of almonds, walnuts, pine nuts, toasted bread, spices, and honey; *albardilla*, a seasoning for meat made with beaten eggs, flour, and sugar; *alelijo*, prepared by boiling milk, flour, abundant sugar, and sesame seeds; and *almorí*, flour dough with salt, honey, raisins, pine nuts, hazelnuts, and almonds.[24] The legacy of some of these medieval recipes is still evident in many of Spain's sweets, as it is in the Spanish language itself: numerous words referring to foods derive from Arabic, signaling the origin of the foods themselves, such as *azúcar* (sugar), *alcachofa* (artichoke), *berenjena* (eggplant), *almendra* (almond), *espinaca* (spinach), *azafrán* (saffron), *limón* (lemon), *arroz* (rice), and *alcohol*, among many others; the word *alfeñique*, a term used today to refer to someone who is weak and with little strength or resolve, comes from the name of one of these desserts, made by boiling sugar and twisting it to create thin, fragile strings that were then enjoyed with custard cream. Curiously, this dessert survives in modified form in modern Mexico, having been introduced by the Spanish in the seventeenth century as part of the Catholic tradition, and

Window of a traditional Madrid pastry shop, showing the typical *rosquillas* and *huesos de San Expedito. Photo by the author.*

today *alfeñiques* are present in Mexican celebrations of the Día de los Muertos (Day of the Dead). Traditional desserts of Arab origin still popular in Madrid include the tasty *buñuelos*, the many versions of *rosquillas*, and the peculiarly named but nevertheless delicious *huesos de San Expedito* (Saint Expedite's bones).

By the eleventh century, Madrid had reached a population of three thousand, which was devoted mostly to two kinds of activities: the military and those who worked indirectly for the army, such as blacksmiths, carpenters, tanners, stablemen, and the peasant population, whose job was to produce food to sustain the military. As a result, a strong agricultural economy developed, and Madrid became known for the quality of its fruits, vegetables, and grains. Other economic activities flourished as well, including pottery, which became highly prized for its quality and durability: "In Madrid a certain type of clay is found with which they make pots that can be used for twenty years without breaking, and the foods prepared in them do not spoil during very hot seasons."[25]

The influence that almost eight hundred years of Muslim rule left on Spanish culture and cuisine cannot be overemphasized. The recent discovery in modern Madrid of dozens of silos built for food storage by the Arabs during this time illustrates the many layers of history, peoples, and flavors that intermingled over the centuries to form the complexity of modern-day Madrid. The medieval cuisine of Spain's capital city should no doubt be considered a mix of Arabic, Jewish, and Christian influences. As many scholars note, these ethnic groups would eat each other's dishes and influence each other's cuisine. Christian king Alfonso VI, for example, ate and dressed "*a lo morisco*"—that is, in the style of the Muslims from Al-Andalus—showing just how much the customs of Christians and Moriscos were intertwined.[26]

MEDIEVAL MADRID AND THE JEWISH GASTRONOMIC LEGACY

In the year 1162, the Christian king Fernando II conquered Madrid and established a new political and social system very different from the one of Al-Andalus, though it retained some structures from its Islamic past. The first coat of arms of Madrid bore an inscription that made reference to this past and the origins of the city, built in a fertile space with abundant water and as a military fortress surrounded by a wall:

> *Fui sobre agua edificada.*
> *Mis muros de fuego son.*

"On water I was built. My walls are made of fire." These verses make metaphorical reference to the fact that the city was built near several rivers and streams and that its walls were made of flint, a stone used to start fire and which would create sparks when struck by arrows and other weapons. This poetic inscription can be seen today written on the walls of the Plaza Puerta Cerrada (Closed Gate Square), named as such because it was located by one of the gates of the medieval wall.

Mayrit had become part of the kingdom of Castile in 1085, and the subsequent arrival of new Christian urban settlers changed the landscape of the city, with the city becoming organized in parish districts around the different churches, while Muslims and Jewish minorities occupied specific, segregated spaces designated for them. In this way, Madrid followed a similar pattern to that of other towns during the Christian *Reconquista*, or reoccupation of the Iberian Peninsula. A small Mudéjar community (Muslims who continued to live in Christian territory after the *Reconquista*) remained, but both Muslims and Jews were forced to relocate to communities called *aljamas*. Madrid had two *aljamas*, located in what today is the center of the lively La Latina district and commemorated with signs in both the Plaza de Puerta de Moros (Moor's Gate Square) and Calle de la Morería (Moorish Quarter Street).[27]

Things worsened progressively for Muslim and Jewish communities. In 1502, King Fernando and Queen Isabel offered the Mudéjares the choice between conversion and expulsion, and a century later King Felipe III effectively banished all Moriscos (converted Muslims) from Christian Spain. The Jewish population had already been forced to convert or leave, with large numbers of Jews becoming *conversos* starting in 1391 and many others abandoning their homes and belongings after the fall of Granada in 1492. The infamous Inquisition, a tribunal created by Queen Isabel and King Fernando in 1480, investigated accusations of false conversions. A number of *limpieza de sangre* (cleanliness of blood) laws were enacted, distinguishing between Old Christians and New Christians—people of Jewish descent who were always subject to suspicions of apostasy. These laws discriminated against New Christian minorities regardless of their sincerity as converts, giving more privileges to Old Christians. Individuals accused of falsely converting were subject to trial and, if found guilty, received punishments that could range from the relatively mild, such as fines, mandatory fasting and prayer, or a pilgrimage to a local shrine, to the severe, such as lashes in public, prison, rowing in the galleys of ships, and, in the worst cases, burning at the stake. In Madrid, the Inquisition conducted its *autos de fe*, or public penances, at the Plaza Mayor (Main Square), in the very heart of the city. One such *auto de fe* took place there on July 4, 1632, when seven people were executed. According to historical sources, this gruesome spectacle did nothing to ruin the appetite of King Felipe IV, who was in attendance at the executions and who, along with his party, consumed the amount of twenty *panes de boca* ("small breads," possibly empanadas, small pastries stuffed with meat, vegetables, or fish popular in medieval Spain), which they washed down with some wine, finishing their meal with a dessert of flavored shaved ice.[28]

There are no Jewish cookbooks from this period, since it could mean death to be found writing or disseminating Jewish recipes. Instead, as David M. Gitlitz and Linda Kay Davidson have observed, "hints about Jewish cuisine and an occasional recipe are scattered through a variety of medieval documents, including the most unlikely of sources: Inquisition trial testimonies." As these documents detail, anyone found keeping the Sabbath or avoiding the consumption of "pork, hare, rabbit, strangled birds, conger-eel, cuttle-fish, nor [eating] eels or other scaleless fish, as laid down in the Jewish law" could be accused of being a false *converso*. Other clues to false conversion included breaking the prohibition on consuming meat during Lent, eating "boiled eggs, olives or other viands" upon the death of a parent, or celebrating "the Festival of unleavened bread, beginning by eating lettuce, celery or other bitter herbs on those days."[29] As Claudia Roden notes,

> Inquisitors could enter their [new Christians—that is, newly converted Muslims and Jews, accused of being false *conversos* and still secretly practicing their original religion] homes at any time to check that they were cooking with pork fat and pork products—perhaps that is the time when the Spanish custom of putting little bits of ham in every possible dish, including vegetable and fish dishes, took root, as converted Muslims and Jews, as well as Old Christians, were forced to show proof of their allegiance to Christianity by eating pork.[30]

Before their expulsion from Christian Spain, however, both Muslims and Jews accounted for a large portion of the population, and their imprint on Spanish cuisine should not be underestimated. Many Jews who remained in Spain but converted to the Christian faith kept many of their culinary tastes and practices and adapted them to the rules of their new religion, leading to many of today's traditional Spanish dishes having Jewish or Arabic origins. For example, the use of mint and spices such as saffron—an essential ingredient to paella, the iconic Spanish dish—cinnamon, cumin, coriander, and caraway is common in many Spanish recipes and reflects a distinctly Arab touch.[31] Culinary historians have noted the Jewish origin of Madrid's most famous dish, *cocido madrileño*, a rich and satisfying stew of chickpeas, potatoes, cabbage, root vegetables such as carrots or turnips, chicken, and an impressive amount of pork in the form of *morcilla* (blood sausage), bacon, chorizo, marrow bones, and other parts of the pig. Its origins can be traced to a Sephardic dish called *adafina*, a filling stew of chickpeas, root vegetables, and lamb meat traditionally cooked in a large clay pot overnight on Friday and eaten on the Sabbath the next day. Historians believe that the name of this dish originates from the classical Arabic word *dafīnah*, meaning "hidden" or "covered," since it was cooked on the hearth and covered by embers or set under an iron pot filled with coals. The existence of this dish is documented as far back as the fifteenth century.[32] Claudia Roden notes that the traditional *cocido* from Madrid "is said

A plate of *cocido* served at Taberna la Bola, a century-old restaurant renowned for this dish. *Photo by the author.*

to be a legacy of the wealthy Conversos (converted Jews) who married into the Castilian aristocracy—an old Sabbath dish into which the Jewish converts piled all kinds of pork to show that their conversion was real."[33] As time went by, this dish evolved and endured, and by the seventeenth century, a typical Madrid meal consisted of an appetizer, usually fruit; one or several main courses, most often a one-pot chickpea and vegetable stew; and a final course, which could be a salad, olives, or a fried sweet.[34]

It is a discomforting truth that most Spaniards today often downplay the role of the Jewish and Arabic influences in their culture, distancing themselves from a heritage that survives stubbornly in Spanish last names and facial features. As Alicia Ríos conjectures, these influences have remained unacknowledged partly because the spices and dishes became so integrated in the country's culinary tradition that Spaniards quickly saw them as purely Spanish but also because of the general hostility toward Arabs and Arab culture, which is still present in the Spanish subconscious, posing a conflict with the Spaniards' sense of identity.[35]

This same heritage has similarly been overlooked in many studies of Madrid's gastronomic traditions, perhaps as a way of erasing a part of Spain's history that involves a time of religious intolerance, prejudice, and xenophobia. Ultimately, however, it must be acknowledged that contemporary Spanish cuisine is greatly indebted to the culinary heritage of the Spanish Jews and the Arabs, both rich and complex cuisines that combine a mesmerizing array of ingredients and techniques to create dishes of delicate flavors and textures. It is commonly noted that Spanish cuisine differs enormously from that of other European countries, and this difference is precisely rooted in the Arabic and Jewish traditions, which give Spanish cuisine a distinct personality, separating it from the less exotic food of other European cuisines. Both Arabs and Jews were culinary innovators, introducing exotic ingredients and spices, a sophisticated palate leading to new flavors not found anywhere else in medieval Europe. As Ken Albala reminds us, "Muslim and Jewish customs and foodways continued to influence Spanish cooking down to the present. . . . the influence of Arab cultures, and especially the use of fruits and vegetables native to the Middle East was stronger here than elsewhere."[36] This rich culinary legacy should be embraced and celebrated in all its variety. Nowhere is this clearer than in Madrid, which, as detailed in the following chapters, continues to be a crossroads of cultures in the twenty-first century.

2

Too Many Kings Spoil the Broth

GROWING PAINS: THE MAKING OF A CAPITAL

Food and cooking in Madrid evolved dramatically when the once sleepy town was declared Spain's capital in the sixteenth century.[1] The amazing variety of dishes, cuisines, eateries, and products that now make Madrid a gourmet's paradise was a long time in the making. In fact, at the end of the fifteenth century, the city census showed only "two fishmongers, seven butchers, one butter maker, one confectioner, one pastry cook and one tavern owner."[2] However, when Felipe II relocated the court from the nearby city of Toledo in 1561, what had been a modest town with a population of around twenty-eight thousand suddenly turned into the capital of the kingdom.[3] The settlement of the royal court in Madrid marked the beginning of extraordinary growth and development, with a rapid rise in population and infrastructure, resulting in a series of both positive and negative consequences.

For several centuries, the capital of Spain had been itinerant, alternating between Madrid and other cities, Toledo being perhaps the most relevant. However, due to its easy access in the middle of the Iberian Peninsula, many state meetings started to take place in Madrid, and the city became a favorite for the royal family, who would visit frequently and stay at the Royal Alcázar (fortress) for relatively long periods. This, along with the urgent need for an administrative center where records could be permanently kept, led to the Habsburgs' establishment of Madrid as the capital of the kingdom, turning it into an administrative and commercial center that grew quickly, spreading to the north, east, and south. Nearby areas around Madrid were swiftly deforested to build housing for the rapidly expanding population, and the wood was used in cooking and heating. The numerous orchards and prolific vegetable gardens outside the city dwindled and eventually disappeared under urbanistic pressure. Court officials and nobles needed lodging, and Madrid's rapidly growing population and numerous visitors needed to be fed. To remedy the lack of accommodations in the city, King Felipe II imposed a room tax called the *Regalía de aposento*, requiring owners of houses with two floors to give up half of the house for use by members of the court. Unsurprisingly, Madrileños were not happy with this mandate and protested, stating that they needed the first floors for their horses and chickens and for grain storage. Other owners resorted to the ingenious trick of building a facade for their houses, giving them the appearance of having only one story and hiding the other stories from view from the street. These buildings were referred to as *casas a la malicia*, or "houses built maliciously," since their purpose was to deceive the authorities in order to dodge the king's mandate.

When the king's attempt to provide free room and board to his court was unsuccessful, the number of establishments offering lodging and food for a price increased dramatically. By the seventeenth century, 843 such establishments were in operation in the city, offering varying types of services at considerably different quality levels depending on their price. At the top of the scale were the many *posadas* (inns) that could be found in the areas near the Palacio Real (Royal Palace) and the city center, most of them on the streets around the Plaza Mayor. One of the most famous during the seventeenth century was the Posada del Peine (Haircomb's Inn), which opened its doors in 1610 and was one of the most elegant establishments at the time, the preferred accommodations for many members of the nobility. Amazingly, it remained in operation until the mid-twentieth century, only closing its doors in the 1960s. Fortunately, it reopened in 2006 after being acquired and thoroughly renovated by a high-end chain and today is a beautiful boutique hotel housed in a charming historic building, and its four hundred years of history makes it, according to some, Spain's oldest hotel. This significant part of Madrid's history can be admired at Calle de Postas, a street adjacent to the Plaza Mayor; the street's name refers to the carriages that entered the city through it, carrying the mail.

Other lodging options included *mesones*, *paradores*, and *fondas*, halfway between inns and boarding houses, which also offered food and had a varying range of prices. These establishments were mostly located around the streets where the carriage lines coming from other cities made their final stops and thus catered mostly to visitors. Of these, *mesones* offered the most affordable prices and provided hay, barley, and stables for the horses of equestrian travelers. *Fondas* and

Posada del Peine Hotel. *Photo by E. J. Tepe.*

paradores offered simple shared rooms in which to spend the night and, for a higher price, cleaner and more comfortable individual rooms. Finally, for the most budget-conscious traveler, the so-called *posadas secretas* (secret inns), which were rooms for rent in a private house, were the equivalent of today's Airbnb.

TELL ME WHAT YOU EAT: FOOD, DRINK, AND CLASS

What kind of gastronomic scene did a city like Madrid offer its visitors in the sixteenth and seventeenth centuries? It was a bit limited, actually. There were no "restaurants," strictly speaking, since neither the word nor the concept existed in Spain at the time; the word *restaurant* was French and would arrive in Madrid, along with other French trends, only in the nineteenth century. Hungry customers would head to one of the numerous *tabernas*, *mesones*, and *fondas* that operated in the city and offered inexpensive meals and drinks—wine being by far the most popular. Food served at these tables was basic but filling, with a bean and meat stew called *olla podrida*—a predecessor of today's *cocido*—being one of the most common dishes. A recipe for this dish given by Francisco Martínez Montiño in his 1611 *Arte de cocina* includes sausage, lamb, beef, pig's feet, hare, tongue, chickpeas, turnips, and onions, among other ingredients. This dish, with some variations, seems to have been quite popular at the time and can be found in numerous European cookbooks of the seventeenth and eighteen centuries. Stuffed meat pies, or empanadas, were also common, as were cheese and dried meats, olives, and several types of offal dishes, of which perhaps the most popular was beef tripe. Known as *callos*, this dish is still wildly popular in Madrid and is served either as a tapa accompanying a drink or as a main dish. Despite how unappealing it sounds, this dish is prepared wonderfully in Madrid, resulting in an extraordinarily tender bite full of flavor, perfectly enjoyed with a glass of red wine, a pleasant surprise to any adventurous soul deciding to give it a try. Lhardy, an elegant 175-year-old restaurant located at the historic Carrera de San Jerónimo, is a classic place to try it; for a less formal experience, casual eateries like Casa Ciríaco or Bar Alonso have equally well-deserved reputations for their outstanding *callos*.

During the seventeenth century, many products arriving from other cities were sold and bought at the *mesones*, which soon became trading posts for agricultural products grown outside of Madrid, such as wheat, wine, fruits, and vegetables, that would then be sold in the city's markets. Aside from *mesones*, the other popular place to get a drink and perhaps some food was the *taberna*, the taverns that sprouted around the city by the hundreds. In 1625, the city boasted no less than 390 taverns, which as some historians point out, exceeded the number of convents by 130, making the city and church officials uneasy and prompting a series of regulations aimed at avoiding the proximity of taverns to churches and convents. In addition, both *mesones* and *tabernas* developed a terrible reputation for uncleanliness and the poor quality of their fare. Heavy regulations were then put in place by the Crown to reduce the occurrence of cases of food poisoning and to curtail the adulteration of wine, both of which were quite common. To this end, the king prohibited the sale of wine that had been watered down and also forbade *mesones* and *tabernas* from serving fish, game meat, or bread to avoid risks of food poisoning due to from the poor hygiene of some of these establishments. Gambling was also banned on the premises after the combination of betting and alcohol proved problematic, causing frequent quarrels and other unpleasant incidents.

Apparently, Madrileños had developed an unquenchable thirst for wine, which attracted winemakers from all over the country; by 1665, a total of sixty-three winemakers from places like Alcalá de Henares, Fuencarral, or Carabanchel but also from Toledo and even Andalusia had set up shop in the city to sell their wines to the masses. And they did, with great success. For the nobility, who had a more discerning taste and were eager to show their status and wealth, it was possible to obtain expensive wines imported from Italy, the Rhine Valley, and other "exotic" lands.

Besides wine, other drinks became popular among the city's population during the seventeenth century; *hipocrás* (a mix of wine, ambergris, sugar, cinnamon, and musk), *carraspada* (wine from Muscat grapes boiled with honey and spices), and *garnacha* (a wine made from the juice of three different types of grapes, plus sugar, cinnamon, and pepper) were served as alternatives to plain wine. On cold winter days, the traditional breakfast was a glass of brandy (*aguardiente*) accompanied by a sweet treat, usually a cookie or a fritter (*buñuelo*) coated with orange jam.[4] The upper classes were by then falling deeply in love with a truly exotic drink: chocolate, which was consumed only in liquid form well until the end of the nineteenth century and soon became the preferred beverage of the nobility and the clergy, quickly turning into a powerful sign of wealth and social status. Chocolate reached Europe for the first time in 1544, though as a commodity the first shipments began to reach Spain in 1585. As Andrew Dalby notes, "In the seventeenth century the Spanish court was well known throughout Europe for its prowess in preparing chocolate drinks."[5] *Chocolatadas* (chocolate parties) came to be part of the protocol at Madrid's Palacio Real. The ladies of the court would regal their female visitors with a cup of chocolate along with a wide variety of sweet treats. The popularity of this drink is responsible for the fact that coffee did not become widely consumed in Spain as early as in other European countries. From Spain, the chocolate craze spread to other European countries, and by 1644 chocolate was known in Italy as a medicine, with Cosimo III's court physician experimenting with it by mixing it with ambergris, musk, jasmine, and lemon peel. In France, chocolate was used it to enhance the flavor of biscuits and sweetmeats, becoming very much in vogue at the court of Versailles. And in England, milk began to be added to the drinking chocolate, which was avidly consumed in the numerous chocolate houses that opened in London during the mid-seventeenth century.

Aside from chocolate, *aloja* was another favorite drink in the Spanish capital, especially during the hot Madrid summers. Popular across all social classes, it was

made with honey, water, and spices like ground ginger, cinnamon, and white pepper and was commonly sold at the entrance to the *corrales de comedias* (open-air
popular theaters). Originally a nonalcoholic drink, some vendors started to add
wine to it, which, despite being illegal, helped boost sales even more.

Plain water was rarely drunk. In fact, the Habsburgs and their court preferred to
quench their thirst with refreshments made with a number of spices and herbs, fla-
voring their water with cinnamon, anise, clove, dill, rosemary, jasmine, or orange
blossom. These flavored waters were highly consumed in Madrid during the hottest
months of the year, and the nobility could enjoy them very cold thanks to snow
brought daily to the Alcázar from the nearby Guadarrama Mountains. Over time,
the juice of some fruits eventually was used. Lemonade and orange waters became
very popular, as did *agua de cebada* (barley water) and *horchata* (tigernut milk).

When available, the Madrileños' preferred meat was lamb, though this gradually became replaced by beef during the nineteenth century.[6] Fish was considered
a luxury given the difficulty of transporting it from the coastal areas and was
thus enjoyed only by the upper classes—with the exception perhaps of dried cod,
which was relatively affordable and could be preserved for a long time. Fruits,
vegetables, and pulses were, by contrast, abundant and readily available and
formed the base of the diet for the popular classes. The nobility's diet included a
much greater quantity and variety of meats, and on special occasions seafood was
transported in boxes buried in snow and straw to maintain its freshness. Bream, for
example, was a favorite delicacy eaten at Christmas for those who could afford it.
The king's diet was predominantly meat and sweets; fish was mostly eaten during
Lent, and fruits, milk, and vegetables were present only in small amounts since
they were considered "unhealthy" by the monarch's doctors and their consumption was hence discouraged.

The culinary disparity between the haves and the have-nots in the quickly developing city of Madrid were, in fact, acute, with a number of wealthy families enjoying a wide variety of foodstuffs out of reach for the majority of the population. This
was not new: since the Middle Ages, the table had become a powerful indicator
of social rank. As Teófilo Ruiz points out, "Besides clothing, there was no greater
marker of social difference in the late Middle Ages and in the early modern period
than eating."[7] This was definitely true for Madrid, whose gastronomy has historically been characterized by the dichotomy between two vastly different cuisines:
on the one hand, there was the cuisine of the royalty, the aristocracy, and the upper
classes (formed by court officials, wealthy landowners, and the high clergy); on
the other hand, there was the cuisine of the middle and lower classes. The latter,
a simple diet consumed for survival, was in fact served at the many convents and
monasteries that ran soup kitchens for the poor, feeding as many as fifteen hundred
people every day.[8]

Bread illustrates well the differences between the two diets. The rich ate white bread made from refined *candeal* flour, while the poor ate *moreno*, a dark bread made from a coarse mix of rye and barley. The two classes did have one thing in common, though: nearly everyone's everyday fare at the time—including even that of the king and queen—was the *olla podrida*, or stew, containing more or less meat depending on each family's economic resources.

A TRAVELER'S VIEW OF THE ROYAL TABLE

The many gastronomic wonders available to those of ample means are recounted in the writings of Lady Anne Fanshawe, who arrived in Madrid in 1664 as the wife of the ambassador of Great Britain for King Charles II. Her memoirs describe the many wonderful delicacies that she enjoyed while living in Madrid. She compares the foodstuffs of Spain to those of her native England, declaring emphatically the superiority of Madrid's wine, water, bread, meats, and produce, both in quality and in flavor:

> I find it a received opinion that Spain affords not food either good or plentiful: true it is that strangers that neither have skill to choose, nor money to buy, will find themselves at a loss; but there is not in the Christian world better wines than their midland wines are especially, besides sherry and canary. Their water tastes like milk; their corn white to a miracle, and their wheat makes the sweetest and best bread in the world; bacon beyond belief good; the Segovia veal much larger and fatter than ours; mutton most excellent; capons much better than ours. They have a small bird that lives and fattens on grapes and corn, so fat that it exceeds the quantity of flesh. They have the best partridges I ever eat [*sic*], and the best sausages; and salmon, pikes, and sea-breams, which they send up in pickle, called *escabeche* to Madrid, and dolphins, which are excellent meat, besides carps, and many other sorts of fish. The cream, called *nata*, is much sweeter and thicker than any I ever saw in England; their eggs much exceed ours; and so all sorts of salads, and roots, and fruits. What I most admired are, melons, peaches, bergamot pears, grapes, oranges, lemons, citrons, figs, and pomegranates; besides that I have eaten many sorts of biscuits, cakes, cheese, and excellent sweetmeats I have not here mentioned, especially manger-blanc; and they have olives, which are nowhere so good; and their perfumes of amber excel all the world in their kind, both for household stuff and fumes; and there is no such water made as in Seville.[9]

Her memoirs serve as a vivid illustration of the social and culinary habits of the Spanish royal family itself. About King Felipe IV and his family, she writes:

> The King and Queen eat together twice a week in public with their children, the rest privately, and asunder. They eat often, with flesh to their breakfast, which is generally,

to persons of quality, a partridge and bacon, or capon, or some such thing, ever roasted, much chocolate, and sweetmeats, and new-laid eggs, drinking water either cold with snow, or lemonade, or some such thing. Their women seldom drink wine, their maids never; they all love the feasts of bulls, and strive to appear gloriously fine when they see them.[10]

Both the king and the queen of Spain also enjoyed a daily bowl of *cocido*, made by one of the few women cooks allowed to work in the court, Ana de Santillana, whose recipe included chickpeas, garlic, onion, parsley, cilantro, mint, lettuce or escarole, five pounds of mutton, two and a half hens, one pound of bacon, pepper, cloves, and saffron.[11]

Clearly, the royal family did not go hungry. However, even the Spanish royal court sometimes strained to feed the large number of people who were living at the king's expense. As María del Carmen Simón Palmer explains, finding employment at Madrid's Palacio Real was the main goal of any Madrid resident since it guaranteed the indefinite livelihood of an individual and his or her family. Since palace jobs were often passed on to descendants, they were highly desired. Hundreds of people worked as butlers, maids, cooks, or servants to the king and queen in some manner, and they all depended on the monarch for their daily sustenance. Under King Felipe V, the number of maids who assisted the queen alone exceeded two hundred. Given the enormous expense that this implied, the Crown began to pay most servants with a daily ration of food rather than in currency. This procedure was economically advantageous for the Crown and ensured that only those who showed up for work were "paid." This explains the large amounts of food that were prepared at the palace every day, with as many as fifty dishes presented to the king, from which he would choose what he wanted to eat. Nothing was discarded, however; the uneaten food was passed on to the queen, and then to the members of the court, and then to several convents that were under the monarchs' protection, always following a strict hierarchical order. Eventually, the remainders would find their way to the *posadas* of Madrid, ensuring that none of the delicious royal food went to waste.[12]

THE ROYAL TABLE

Two fascinating items were never absent from the royal table: a silver tray called a *salva*, where food was placed for a servant to try before the king did, and a bezoar stone. The bezoar was a stony concretion extracted from the stomach of a goat, and since the Middle Ages, the bezoar was believed to act as an antidote to several kinds of poisons. These two items, the *salva* and the bezoar, were intended to prevent the poisoning of the monarch, a not uncommon occurrence in a climate of political intrigue and betrayals.[13] The *salva* was obviously useful as a protective measure, though the effectiveness of the bezoar stone has long been debunked. There were other elements of the royalty's eating rituals—both during the Habsburgs' rule and later on with the Bourbon dynasty—meant to differentiate the court from the commoners of Madrid. Food and the manner in which it was served and enjoyed was a status symbol designed to impress foreign dignitaries and visitors to the Spanish court and to remind them of Spain's place as the most powerful empire of the time. To that end, a convoluted etiquette and protocol surrounded meals and banquets at the palace. Music and entertainment were incorporated; luxurious tablecloths and napkins made from imported fabrics were used, as were delicate porcelain and gold-rimmed plates and gold or silver flatware (the fork would not arrive to the Spanish court until the late sixteenth century). Domestic and imported wines were served in abundance; costly spices brought from faraway lands and heavily guarded under lock and key seasoned the many dishes at a single banquet; sweets, including candied fruit, were plentiful and served with every meal. Everything was designed to be ostentatious and impressive and to give the appearance of abundance and wealth. Banquets multiplied in times of crisis—when the Crown was suffering economic hardships from the cost of wars, conflicts in the colonies, and competition with other European nations—to conceal any sign of weakness from Spain's enemies and to project the image of a prosperous and mighty Spanish empire. Except on Fridays, when fish was eaten according to the Catholic Church's mandate, these feasts always had meat at their center, usually capon, duck, chicken, quail, peacock, deer, boar, lamb, or veal.

One of the most popular dishes of the time, found in nearly every Spanish cookbook from the Middle Ages into the eighteenth century, was the *manjar blanco* or *blancmange* (literally, "white delicacy"). A favorite of the nobility and Habsburg royalty, it was made with chicken breast meat, milk, rice flour, and sugar to create a dish that was rich, creamy, sweet, and savory. There were many variations of this enormously popular dish, changing the type of meat—or using fish instead—and using different spices. Alas, this delicacy did not withstand the test of time and is no longer prepared.

A CHRISTMAS BANQUET FOR FELIPE III

Both rooted in tradition and with a flair for ostentation, the cuisine of the Habsburgs' court was characterized by its magnificence and was meant as an eloquent expression of the power and wealth of the Spanish Crown. Nowhere is this idea better reflected than in the work of Francisco Martínez Montiño, cook of Felipe III and author of one of the most influential cookbooks of this era, *Arte de cocina, pastelería, vizcochería y conservería.* Published in 1560 and reedited profusely during the following centuries, Martínez Montiño's book became a best-seller in its time. It contained more than five hundred recipes, along with instructions to keep a kitchen clean and in good working order. It also provides several examples of menus for a variety of occasions, including a menu for a Christmas dinner that was, truly, "fit for a king":

Christmas Banquet

First Courses: legs of ham, *olla podrida* (meat, bean and vegetable stew), roasted turkey in its own juice, puff pastry veal pies, roasted pigeons with fried bacon, tarts with bird meat over cream soup, stuffed marzipans, roasted quails with lemon sauce, bread pudding with pork loin, sausages and quails, roasted suckling pigs with cheese, sugar and cinnamon soup, puff pastries with pork stuffing, roasted moorhens.

Second Courses: Roasted capons, roasted ducks with quince sauce, chicken with stuffed escaroles, English meat pies, roasted veal with arugula sauce, *costradas* (meat pie with a thick crust) stuffed with veal sweetbreads and liver, roasted thrush over golden soup, pies stuffed with quince, bone marrow and sweetened eggs, hare meat pies, birds *à la tudesca*, fried trouts with bacon, *ginebradas* (puff pastry tartlets filled with curd).

Third Courses: chickens stuffed with roasted cow's udder croutons, bird's meat hash, smothered pigeons, roast larded kid, green citron pies, turkey pies in white sauce, fresh baked seabreams, rabbits with capers, pig's feet turnovers, ringdoves in black sauce, *blancmange*, sweet fritters.

Fruits [and other accompaniments] to be served with these dishes: grapes, melons, oranges, raisins, almonds, dried apricots, fresh butter, pears, olives, cheese, preserves and rolled wafers.[14]

THE HABSBURGS AND THE BOURBONS:
GLUTTONY VERSUS SOPHISTICATION

The Habsburgs were the ruling dynasty in Spain for almost two hundred years, from 1516 until 1700. Their food choices were deeply rooted in medieval tastes and beliefs, and their diets relied heavily on meat and spices, with a strong presence of meat stews, as was the custom in Castile. *Blancmange*, mentioned earlier, was served at least once a week. Lard was the cooking fat of choice; olive oil would not be used much in Madrid until the eighteenth century, when its importation to the city in large quantities and its widespread use are documented.

The diet of King Felipe II provides a good example of the Habsburgs' tastes. A surviving menu from 1536 details a long list of dishes featuring chicken, capon, lamb, quails, pigeon, veal, and beef, among other meats, prepared in various forms and eaten for both breakfast and dinner. It is no surprise that several of Habsburgs kings suffered from acute gout, made worse by their doctors' recommendations to maintain a meat-based diet and avoid fish, vegetables, and fruits.

The nobility, not to be outdone, threw lavish banquets of their own, such as the one given in Madrid in 1612 by a wealthy duke who wowed his guests with a gargantuan feast over the course of several days: "On each meat day the royal pantry supplied him and his entourage with the following items: 8 ducks, 26 capons, 70 hens, 100 pairs of pigeons, 50 partridges, 100 hares, 25 sheep, 40 pounds of lard, 12 hams, 3 pigs, 8 bushels of assorted fruits, and six different kinds of wine." On days when meat was not to be had, the abundance of seafood was equally impressive: "100 pounds of trout, 15 pounds of eels, 100 of mullet, 50 pounds each of four different kinds of preserved fish, 1,000 eggs, 100 pounds of butter, 100 pounds of codfish, and 100 pounds of anchovies."[15]

The almost two-hundred-year-long era of Habsburg rule in Spain, which began in 1516 with Carlos I and continued with his son Felipe II, would come to an end in 1700. The death that year of the last Habsburg king of Spain, the infirm and childless Carlos II, marked the arrival of the Bourbon dynasty on the Spanish throne. This did not happen without conflict, however, as it triggered the war known as the War of the Spanish Succession (1702–1715) between Spain and other European powers.

Under the Habsburgs, Spain ruled over a vast empire that spanned the globe and included numerous territories in both Europe and the Americas. The question of who would succeed Carlos II and inherit such a large empire had long troubled ministers in capitals throughout Europe, with some favoring a division of the empire between the eligible candidates from the royal houses of France (Bourbon), Austria (Habsburg), and Bavaria (Wittelsbach). Carlos II, however, appointed as his sole successor his grandnephew Felipe, a Bourbon who was Duke of Anjou and grandson of King Louis XIV of France. With Felipe ruling in Spain, Louis XIV sought to secure advantages for his dynasty, but the other European countries regarded a dominant House of Bourbon as a threat to Europe's stability and the balance of power.

The struggle for power within Europe resulted in open confrontation between the Habsburg archduke Charles of Austria, who also claimed rights to the Spanish throne, and Felipe, Duke of Anjou. England, the Dutch Republic, and Austria all supported Archduke Charles's claim to the Spanish Crown, formally declaring war with Spain in May 1702. By backing the Habsburg candidate in the War of Spanish Succession, the European powers sought to reduce France's power while ensuring their own territorial and dynastic security. The outcome of the war was very unfavorable for the Spanish Empire, resulting in the signing of the Treaty of Utrecht (1713) and the Treaty of Rastatt (1714), which partitioned the empire between the European powers and forbade any future unification of the French and Spanish thrones. Thus, Spain lost its territories in Belgium, Luxembourg, Italy, Sardinia, and Gibraltar, and the Duke of Anjou had to renounce his claim to the French succession. He did, however, retain the throne of Spain and its American territories. The first Spanish Bourbon king, he reigned as King Felipe V until his death in 1746.

The arrival of the Bourbon dynasty to the Spanish throne with Felipe V in 1700 marked the beginning of a profound evolution in Spanish cuisine toward a more European approach to cooking and eating. This evolution was characterized by a number of long-lasting French influences, including new terminology used to name dishes and techniques, new dishes and new ways of presenting them, as well as new aesthetics and etiquette for serving and enjoying food at the palace. While the Habsburg kings had favored a relatively straightforward style of cooking—though excessive in both quantity and use of spices—the Bourbons introduced an array of new customs and tastes to the court that signaled a newly refined approach to cuisine. The nobility quickly imitated the royal family, making the French style and taste highly fashionable among the upper classes. French terms began to be used for many dishes and ingredients, such as *champiñón* (mushroom, from the French *champignon*), *béchamel* sauce, *consommé*, and *chaudeau*, and new professions—like sommelier, for example—started to become commonplace. Other influences also made their way into Spanish cuisine, as Alicia Ríos notes: "This new openness to contemporary, particularly French, influences from elsewhere in Europe had some flow-on effect on the direction of Spanish cuisine, which gradually adopted a more international character. Cookbooks, too, tended to reflect this new culinary direction."[16]

Some of these changes were quite abrupt, including the shortening of the royal menus, instituted by Felipe V early in his rule. The Habsburgs' over-the-top, multicourse menus were reduced to a more sensible number of items. Additionally, dishes were served in succession rather than presented all at once, as had been the custom. The everyday royal menu started to follow a set order with little variation: one or two soups at the beginning of the meal, an appetizer, between two and four dishes, and one or two types of roast, with two or three desserts to finish. Meat was still present every day in varied forms, from roasts to offal, and fish was still eaten only occasionally, given the difficulty of transporting it from the coast while maintaining its freshness (river fish such as trout and salmon were part of the monarchs' diets, though meat was definitely preferred). Vegetables were not prominently featured in meals until Isabel de Farnesio, wife of Felipe V, brought her Italian tastes to the court and requested that vegetables be served as garnish accompanying meat. Isabel also introduced pasta to the Spanish court, as well as cured meats, truffles, and cheese imported from Bologna and her native Parma to be served at banquets and other special occasions. At her request, *timbal de macarrones* (meaning "timbal or kettledrum-shaped macaroni pie") was served, a sort of macaroni casserole flavored with plenty of the Parmesan cheese she loved so much. Her fondness for macaroni and longing for other Italian foods was well known in court circles and was used by some astute noblemen seeking to win the king's favor, who procured for her some of her favorite foods. Everyone knew that a gift of Italian cheeses, pastas, cured meats, or sweets was the shortest way to the queen's heart. The cooking trends that began in the palace did have a trickle-down effect on the eating habits of the general population. Novelties were soon imitated by the nobility and the upper class and eventually made their way onto the more modest tables of common Madrileños. This was especially true of the French influences introduced by the Bourbons. This transformation peaked in the nineteenth century and can be considered the starting point of Spain's modern cuisine.

New World foods also started to appear in Spain around the mid-sixteenth century, slowly gaining acceptance and growing in popularity to end up becoming major staples of the Spanish diet. One of the key figures who helped popularize many of these new foods was Nicolás Monardes (1493–1588), a physician and botanist from Seville, Spain, who became known for his interest and experiments with plants brought over from America. The city of Seville was the official port of call for the fleets returning from the New World, a circumstance that helped Monardes gain access to newly arrived seeds, plants, and even firsthand testimonies about the use of plants in faraway lands like Mexico and Peru.

Monardes's most famous work, *Historia medicinal de las cosas que se traen de nuestras Indias Occidentales* (Medical study of the products imported from our West Indian possessions), published in three parts under varying titles in 1565, 1569, and 1574, details his research about the New World's plants that were arriving for the first time to Europe. His work focused mostly on the medicinal use of New World crops, gathering information about them from soldiers, merchants, Franciscan monks, royal officials, and anybody who had traveled to the Americas and could provide him with information or botanical samples. This botanist's fascination with the tobacco plant, for example, led him to believe that it possessed powerful medicinal properties, asserting that the use of tobacco could cure numerous conditions, from the common cold to poisoning to cancer. Partly due to Monardes's ideas, tobacco went on to be used as a medicine in Europe for some time before its pernicious effects became known and it was eventually abandoned as a medicinal plant. Monardes was one of the first to cultivate many New World foods in Spain, such as tomatoes, peppers, sweet potatoes, and potatoes, which would eventually become integrated into Spanish cuisine.

Another important figure was Dr. Francisco Hernández, court physician to King Felipe II and one of the most important physician-botanists of the sixteenth century, who composed a major treatise cataloging New World vegetables, fruits, herbs, and drugs, called *Historia de las plantas de la Nueva España* (Study of the plants from New Spain).

The most-consumed products by the popular classes in Madrid during the eighteenth century were bread, chickpeas, olive oil, lard, fresh or salted fish, eggs, chocolate, and wine. High-protein and high-fat foods were preferred over fruits and vegetables, which were consumed in lower amounts given their higher prices. Among these, asparagus, onions, garlic, cabbage, lettuce, chard, celery, and peppers were popular. Dairy was rarely available, except as a medicinal remedy or in the form of cheese.[17] *Cocido* was still eaten on a daily basis, and bread was extremely important for the population, which relied heavily on it for their sustenance; in 1772, there were 150 bread makers in the city. Fluctuations in the availability and price of bread and meat resulted in popular revolts in Madrid, as occurred in 1699 and again in 1766, in a revolt known as *Motín de Esquilache* (Esquilache riot). King Carlos III, very much aware of the importance of bread in keeping the population at bay, specifically ordered that the supply of bread to the citizenry was to be guaranteed. Meat was sold in the many markets throughout the city. The most commonly eaten kinds of meat were mutton (45 percent), cow (beef; 32 percent), and pork (23 percent).[18] The lower-quality and more affordable meats were sold at El Rastro, while better-quality products could be purchased at the Carnicería Mayor, the San Luis market, the Antón Martín market, and a few others throughout Madrid. Fish was somewhat costly, being brought from Alicante on the Mediterranean coast and Bilbao on the northern coast. Cod was the most popular and affordable fish, given that it could be preserved salted for a long time.

Generally speaking, Madrid enjoyed a steady supply of food during the eighteenth century, with considerably higher per capita consumption of bread and meat than in other parts of Spain. The city's many markets were well stocked with fruit; pulses, such as chickpeas and lentils; root vegetables; poultry; eggs; and chocolate and sweets, such as *turrón* (a traditional almond and honey nougat) and marzipan, with prices varying according to the market and the area of the city where the market was located, as well as the quality of the food. Nevertheless, a plentiful and varied diet was out of reach for many. According to David Ringrose, about 70 percent of incomes in eighteenth-century Madrid hovered around the subsistence level, with people surviving on a few staples such as wheat, wine, olive oil, and meat: "These were the apprentices, day laborers, *gente de librea* (servants), water carriers, sweepers, rag collectors, porters, refuse movers, washerwomen, and peddlers, [and] also those immigrants who entered the urban workforce because there was even less room for them in the countryside."[19] By contrast, about seven thousand households in the city enjoyed a much better economic situation, which allowed for "the bourgeois comforts of an apartment with several rooms; a diet including fruit, vegetables and sweets; and a cook, a houseboy, and two maids."[20] There is no question that class disparities were pervasive in Madrid's social structure, something that is even more evident when we consider the lifestyle of the royalty.

The Bourbons were very fond of sweets, a fondness that was by no means exclusive to them, as the Habsburgs also had relished the many confections that were part of Spain's culinary tradition from the time of the Iberian Peninsula's Arabic rule. Fruit jams, marzipans, nougats, sweet fritters, phyllo dough pastries studded with nuts, honey, and dried fruits were commonly enjoyed both within the palace's walls and around Madrid's boisterous streets.

When Felipe V arrived in Madrid, he brought with him a French cook—a novelty that initially did not sit well with the Spanish cooks of the previous monarch, Carlos II. The king's new cook made substantial changes to every aspect of the king's diet. Despite this, marzipans, *turrones* (almond and honey nougats), meringues, cakes, candied fruit, and honey-dripping phyllo dough pastries of many kinds continued to be present at every meal, accompanied by the latest sensation, chocolate, which was consumed at breakfast and at other times throughout the day. Both Felipe V and his wife, Isabel de Farnesio, were fervent enthusiasts of the dark beverage and would not go a day without it.[21]

Other novelties arriving with Felipe's French cooks included the use of cooked fruits in meat and fish dishes, resulting in creations such as sea bream with oranges, duck in quince sauce, and sausages with cardoons and oranges. More elaborate sauces were created using the meats' own juices, and the consumption of spices, although it did not disappear entirely, gradually declined in favor of fresh herbs used for aroma and flavor. Garlic, long shunned by the royalty and nobility as a commoners' food, began to lose its stigma and appear in the royal menus, and items like capers, anchovies, and aromatic herbs started to play a more important role.

The king's breakfast serves as a good example. In addition to a daily cup of chocolate, it usually included fresh eggs or some kind of soup. A breakfast menu for the king, dating from 1744 and preserved in the archives of the Palacio Real, describes it as consisting of "consommé or broth of some kind, without any water, cooked from the liquid juices from two hens, two quails, four pounds of veal and two of mutton."[22] A sweet and creamy soup called *chadeau* was also routinely served to the king, elaborated with egg yolks, sugar, and Burgundy wine, with a pinch of cinnamon added for fragrance. His son, who would rule as Carlos III from 1759 to 1788, also drank chocolate with breakfast every morning. A man of regular habits, Carlos III wanted little variation in his meals from day to day; his typical lunch consisted of a piece of roast—usually veal—one egg, a salad, and a glass of sweet wine from the Canary Islands, into which he would dunk pieces of bread.[23]

Doctors provided the eighteenth-century Bourbon kings with a long list of recommendations and prohibitions, many of them seemingly capricious and probably not very good prescriptions for a healthy life:

> Legumes and other greasy foodstuffs are forbidden, but vegetable soup can be eaten, as long as "hot" herbs such as cress, cabbage, garlic or turnips are avoided. . . . Meat must be from mutton, two years old at most, as well as veal, hen, capon, chicken and turkey, besides quail, lark, etc., but never pigeon, hare, rabbit, suckling pig or goose.[24]

Even in the nineteenth century, Spanish kings were still getting bad advice: Fernando VII, a king notorious for his bad temper and tyrannical reigning style, suffered from poor health and, among many other maladies, was often all but incapacitated by severe attacks of gout, an ailment that frequently plagued royalty during this time. The soup prepared for him by the famous French cook Marie-Antoine Carême for the purpose of alleviating his condition was probably not very effective in dealing with the disease. Carême had achieved great fame for his *grande cuisine*, an elaborate style of cooking loved by European royalty and aristocracy, and was perhaps the first "celebrity chef" in the modern sense of the term, even entrusted with creating Napoleon Bonaparte's wedding cake. Carême was clearly no medical doctor, though, as his recipe to help the Spanish king find relief from his gout symptoms shows:

> For 4 people.
> Ingredients: 6 large chickens, ⅓ lb. salted bacon, ⅓ lb. dried beans, 2 carrots, 1 celery stalk, 1 onion, 2 leeks, 1 splash sherry wine, salt.[25]

All ingredients were to be cooked together for about two hours, after which the sauce was strained through a sieve and added back to the dish. Even though chicken meat is not entirely a bad choice for gout sufferers, striking here is the meat-to-vegetable ratio and the use of bacon, making the soup heavy on protein, fat, and salt and an authentic nutritional bomb for anyone suffering from this ailment.

NO SMALL POTATOES: THE IMPACT OF NEW WORLD FOODS

In 1544, an envoy of Maya Indians traveled to Spain and presented future king Felipe II with sample offerings of the Mayas' most priced crops: cocoa, maize, sweet gum, sarsaparilla, and chilies.[26] Before that, in 1527, Hernán Cortés had already brought some items from the New World as gifts to Emperor Charles V (in Spain, King Carlos I), including cocoa beans, although apparently this first introduction of chocolate was not received with much enthusiasm. Despite this inauspicious start, cocoa became an instant sensation in Europe once it was prepared by mixing it with sugar and vanilla, so much so that in 1585 cacao beans started to be imported to Spain to be traded as a commodity. The Spanish Crown would profit from this crop by exporting it to all of Europe while retaining a monopoly over its commercialization up until the eighteenth century. The case of cocoa serves as an excellent example of how the discovery of the New World and the arrival in Europe of a number of foodstuffs from the colonies caused major shifts in Spanish cuisine. Even though the introduction and commercialization of American foods like chocolate, peppers, tomatoes, and potatoes did not happen rapidly, but rather over a period of two centuries, it did forever change European cooking. Beginning in the sixteenth century, the Old World's cooks started to encounter and experiment with completely novel products, many of which would eventually become embedded in the gastronomic repertoire of European countries. Most modern-day Madrileños would be incredulous if told that potatoes, tomatoes, peppers, or chocolate were all absent from the Spanish diet before the seventeenth century. In fact, many of today's iconic Spanish dishes feature these ingredients prominently and, in many cases, they are what "makes" the dish.

The Madrileños' revered *tortilla de patatas* is an excellent example. This thick, juicy, filling golden omelet is ubiquitous in Madrid's tapas bars, where it is enjoyed for breakfast, a midday snack, lunch, or dinner. It is worth noting here that, unlike in Mexico, the word *tortilla* always means "omelet" in Spain. The Mexican *tortilla*, made not from potatoes and egg but from corn or wheat flour, was originally called *tlaxcalli* by the Aztecs, but the Spanish conquistadors imposed the new name, referring to it as *tortilla*, or "small cake," from the diminutive of the Spanish word *torta*, meaning "round cake."

The traditional Spanish omelet is made with four basic ingredients: eggs, potatoes, salt, and olive oil. Its satisfying goodness owes everything to the humble Andean tuber, the potato, which arrived in Europe in the sixteenth century and received a lukewarm and apprehensive reaction, with most people not knowing *what* it was or what to do with it. Chestnuts had been used as a source of starch for centuries, and the potato seemed like an ugly and unpolished substitute, better suited for animals than for people. Even worse, the lumpy appearance and coarse skin of the potato made some believe that its consumption could cause leprosy. As a result, potatoes initially were used not for human consumption but to feed animals; it was only toward the end of the seventeenth century that the lower classes began using the potato as a source of sustenance.

The first mention of this tuber in a Spanish cookbook can be traced to the famed cook Juan de Altamiras in his 1745 cookbook, *Nuevo arte de cocina*, where he compares potatoes to *criadillas de tierra* (a type of truffle) and assures his readers that they are very similar to each other since they both grow under the soil and have a similar appearance and texture. Altamiras emphatically states that potatoes are delicious and highly nutritious once cooked, words of praise probably aimed at dissipating fears about this food, indicating how little they were known or appreciated: "If you eat many I warn you, you will have so much energy and be in such good spirits that with the wind you blow, you could set sail to go see the Pope, unless it's so strong that you rip your sails and have to repair them."[27]

Despite these mentions in the eighteenth century, the cultivation of potatoes had been taking place in rural areas of the Iberian Peninsula well before then. Locally grown potatoes were part of the patients' diet at Seville's Hospital de la Sangre—a building that today houses Andalucia's regional parliament—as early as 1573, and according to Hipólito Ruiz, potatoes were introduced in Madrid in 1662.[28] The so-called Spanish Road, a military route used by Felipe II's army while traveling across Europe to the Low Countries, passing through northern Italy along the way, served as a major vehicle for disseminating this edible tuber. Soldiers would eat off the land while en route instead of carrying their supplies, helping themselves to the grains and other foods stored by the peasants in the areas they passed through. Perhaps learning about them by word of mouth, peasants soon took to cultivating potatoes, realizing that by keeping the plants in the ground, they could have something left to eat after soldiers had taken the rest of their available food.[29] Potato farming would eventually spread throughout much of Europe and become a staple of vital importance to the dramatic population growth that the continent would see in the following centuries. Madrid's Real Jardín Botánico (Royal Botanical Garden), for example, was cultivating *Solanum tuberosum* in 1788, experimenting with seeds brought straight from Peru.[30]

Whether it was due to Altamiras's ardent defense of this crop or to its nutritious qualities and versatility, the potato did eventually become a part of Spanish cuisine and is still very much a part of it today. It is, however, amusing that such an essential ingredient of Spanish cuisine, present nowadays in hundreds of dishes and eaten in so many forms, was once despised so utterly that was considered nothing more than pigs' food.

A delightful Madrileño tapa involving potatoes that also owes its existence to the bounty of the New World is *patatas bravas*. Three ingredients hold the secret to its powerful draw: potatoes, tomatoes, and hot paprika (although some recipes omit the tomato). Potatoes are fried in olive oil (a European cooking technique) and smothered with a spicy sauce (hence the name "*brava*," or "brave") made from the chili pepper (*Capsicum annuum*) and the odd, red fruit we know as tomato (derived from its original Nahuatl name, *tomatl*). Curiously, all three ingredients happen to be members of the same botanical family, the *Solanaceae*. Eaten commonly as a tapa, *patatas bravas* are absolutely addictive, and today many places in Madrid compete fiercely for the claim of "best *patatas bravas*." Docamar, Bar Alonso, and

A tapa of fiery *patatas bravas*. Photo by E. J. Tepe.

Las Bravas are some of the most popular bars specializing in this tapa, and since some of them have been making it for more than fifty years, they must be doing something right. If you are in Madrid and feel "brave" enough, go out for a taste of this bold dish.

Tomatoes are a beloved ingredient in today's Spanish cooking and are found in many of Madrid's traditional dishes. However, as with potatoes, this wasn't always the case. First encountered by Spanish conquistadors in the markets of the great city of Tenochtitlán—today's Mexico City—tomatoes were very much part of the Aztec diet. Father Bernardino de Sahagún, a Franciscan priest who arrived in Mexico in 1529, provides a thorough description of an impressive Aztec banquet in his *Historia General de las Cosas de Nueva España* (General history of the things of New Spain). In Sahagún's account, tomatoes are mentioned repeatedly, along with red, yellow, and green chilies, maize, squashes, sweet potatoes, avocados, tamales, and tuna cactus fruits, plus several types of meat and fish, from venison to hare, turkey, duck, lobster, and sardines, along with some other more exotic sources of protein, such as winged ants, locusts, tadpoles, and salamanders.[31]

Spanish cooks were slow to accept tomatoes, though, and only started to use them in the eighteenth century, quite late when compared to other European countries like Italy and France, which had been using the fruit for some time. Antonio Latini's *Lo scalco alla moderna*, an Italian cookbook published in 1694, contains what is perhaps the earliest mention of the tomato as an ingredient in a European cookbook, but it would take more than fifty years before the fruit would make its first appearance in a Spanish cookbook. Again, it is found in Juan de Altamiras's *Nuevo arte de cocina* (1745). The book includes several recipes calling for tomatoes, among them a peculiar recipe for quails stuffed with sardines and cooked with abundant tomatoes; also found are recipes for *cabeza de ternera en guisado* ("beef head stew with tomatoes")[32] and for *abadejo con tomate* ("haddock with tomatoes").[33] It is unclear how long tomatoes had been used in Spain before their mention in Altamiras's book, but he refers to them as if they were a poorly known ingredient, even giving directions on how to best preserve them all year by submerging them in olive oil, suggesting that his readers perhaps were not familiar with them. A later cookbook, Juan de la Mata's *Arte de repostería*, published in 1747, also includes several recipes for tomato sauce.

. The spice known as paprika (or *pimentón*, made from peppers in dried and ground form), used in so many Spanish foods ranging from chorizo to sauces, is the result of drying and mashing the red chili pepper, a fruit first encountered by Columbus during his Caribbean exploits. Columbus brought back plants and seeds that he thought might have economic value if grown successfully in Europe. After all, his goal was to find a new route to Asia in order to secure a steady supply of the beloved and expensive spices Europeans used to flavor their food; it should not be forgotten that in the Middle Ages, black pepper was in fact more valuable than gold. The chili seeds Columbus brought back with him to Spain did sprout, and by the sixteenth century they were being cultivated in Spain's central region of Castile and other parts of Europe. This would be the start of what William Dunmire considers "a minirevolution in cuisine from Europe to Asia" since the use of paprika quickly spread as a substitute for black pepper, eventually becoming an essential ingredient in countless dishes around the world.[34]

Curiously, the purchase of *pimentón* (paprika) is documented in the inventories of Madrid's Palacio Real during the eighteenth and nineteenth centuries but does not appear in lists of purchases during the two previous centuries. Nevertheless, as Carolyn Nadeau notes, whole fresh peppers and paprika were well established in Spanish cooking by the seventeenth century.[35] Documents kept in Madrid's municipal archives show that in the year 1789, a staggering 59,326 pounds of paprika were consumed in the city, showing how widespread the popularity of this spice had become. However, as with other novel products coming from America, it is possible that peppers—both the hot and the mild varieties—had been incorporated into the diet of the lower classes long before royal cooks decided to use them in their cooking, since, generally speaking, even after the population got over their mistrust of these new foods, the upper classes and the royalty continued to resist their consumption, considering them fare for the poor. Jeffrey Pilcher notes that chili peppers raised suspicion among sixteenth-century physicians and naturalists, who were puzzled by their fiery effects. Spanish Jesuit missionary and naturalist José de Acosta, though he recommended them as a digestion aid, cautioned against their abuse, stating that "much use of it in the young is prejudicial to health, especially to that of the soul, for it heightens sensuality."[36]

These prejudices help explain why American foods were rarely included in royal menus until the nineteenth century, with the exception of chocolate, as mentioned earlier. This phenomenon once again underscores the gap between "low" and "high" cuisines, each evolving in separate directions. In addition, the exoticism of some of these products surprised many people who were perhaps not very adventurous in their eating in the first place. In a very telling anecdote, one of the first pineapple plants ever brought to Europe was presented as a gift—a costly and exotic one—to Carlos I of Spain. Intrigued by its thorny and alien-like appearance, the king touched and smelled the fruit, praising its odor, but absolutely refused to try it. Despite the king's rejection, the pineapple eventually became popular among the upper classes and with later monarchs and was even recommended by doctors as an appetite stimulant and digestion aid, though they also warned it was bad for the teeth.[37]

Fortunately, not all kings were this gastronomically conservative. Fernando VI was enormously curious about the natural world, and his inquisitive nature was decisive in launching the era of Spanish Enlightenment and the pursuit of scientific knowledge, resulting in the foundation of the Royal Botanic Gardens in Madrid in 1755. Conceived as a place to experiment with new plants from around the globe, many American species were first grown in Madrid's botanic gardens. The introduction of American crops to Europe was greatly aided by the work done by the naturalists of the time and the epic botanical expeditions that, under the auspices of the Spanish Crown, took place during the second half of the eighteenth century. Even though the goal of discovering and studying new plants from the New World was mostly motivated by the search for medicinal remedies to cure the many diseases of the time, many of these crops turned out to be fantastic edible discoveries. It is not surprising, then, that despite the rocky start of these foreign items, conflicting with the centuries-old European diets and prejudices, many American crops eventually became widely accepted among both the lower classes and royalty. Evidence of this is a breakfast menu from Madrid's Palacio Real, prepared for King Alfonso XIII, who ruled from 1886 until he was forced into exile in 1931. The menu reveals the fondness of the monarch for a particular ingredient, which, it seems, he ate on a daily basis:

Breakfast for Alfonso XIII

Four poached eggs and twelve biscuits.

HOT DISH:
One day, roast chicken and a plate of fried potatoes.
Another day, two veal chops with fried potatoes.
Another day, one large beefsteak with fried potatoes.
Another day, six mutton or lamb chops with fried potatoes.
Another day, three beef tournedos with fried potatoes.
Another day, four escalopes of veal with fried potatoes.[38]

Many of today's Madrid dishes include potatoes, tomatoes, and peppers among their ingredients. For example, the iconic *cocido*, an ubiquitous stew of medieval origin made with chickpeas and generous amounts of meat, has been enriched with the addition of the American potato. Another popular dish, *callos a la madrileña* (beef tripe Madrileño style), owes much of its flavor to the marriage of chili peppers and tomatoes, resulting in the rich sauce that makes the dish so unique. A similar sauce accompanies the classic *caracoles a la madrileña*, snails in spicy tomato sauce, and the list continues, as will be seen in more detail in chapter 7, which delves into the origins and ingredients of Madrid's most traditional foods.

CHOCOLATE, THAT DANGEROUS CONTROLLED SUBSTANCE

As previously mentioned, chocolate was first introduced commercially to Europe in 1585, and it would become, without question, one of Spain's most profitable imports from the New World. As Jesuit priest José de Acosta recounts in 1590 in his *Historia natural y moral de las Indias* (Natural and moral history of the Indies), "It [chocolate] is one of the rich businesses of New Spain, since it is a dried fruit than can be stored for a long time and will not go bad, and they bring ships loaded with it from the province of Guatemala."[39] Given how lucrative the trade of cacao was, however, Spain had to work hard to maintain a monopoly on the production and exploitation of this "new gold"—something it did until the eighteenth century—while fighting a contraband market run by other countries. Contraband cacao became rampant and supplied many European countries such as Holland, Britain, and France, despite the fact that it was a dangerous business punishable even by death.

References to the social importance of chocolate abound, with José de Acosta mentioning it as highly prized in both the Old and the New World. In pre-Columbian societies, cacao had a profound religious and social meaning and was even used as currency. The scientific name given to the plant by Carl Linnaeus reflects its religious significance: *Theobroma*, or "food of the gods." Bernal Díaz del Castillo, a Spanish soldier accompanying Hernán Cortés during the conquest of Tenochtitlán (today's Ciudad de México, or Mexico City), witnessed the ritual offering of this drink to the legendary Aztec emperor Moctezuma: "They would bring several cups made of fine gold, with a certain drink made from the same cacao, that they said was good for having relations with women. . . . What I saw was that they brought more than fifty big jars filled with frothy cacao, and he would drink from it."[40]

This and other similar testimonies may explain the mystique surrounding chocolate and its reputation as an aphrodisiac, though the marketing techniques of modern-day chocolate manufacturers have also helped keep this myth alive and well, as can be seen in chocolate commercials, most notably every year around Valentine's Day.

Chocolate, as drunk by the Aztecs, was a frothy, bitter, and spicy drink since it was flavored with chili peppers, and Cortés's soldiers found it disgusting at first given its bitterness, color, and texture. They also quickly noticed its energizing effects, however, and kept drinking it. Eventually, sugar and vanilla were added to make it more palatable, and by the end of the sixteenth century, the drink had

Ad for a Spanish chocolate brand, advertising its nutritious qualities. *Photo by the author.*

become wildly popular in Spain, especially among the aristocracy. The wealthy paid exorbitant prices to satisfy their cravings for chocolate, and this added to the drink's desirability, as it became a sign of economic status. From Spain, the consumption of this beverage spread to France, Italy, and other European countries, and its popularity continued to grow. Intrigued by its effects, doctors gave chocolate a close look, and some of them began recommending it as a remedy for numerous ailments, claiming that it could be used as an expectorant, diuretic, and aphrodisiac, as well as a cure for almost everything, from gout to hypochondria and even hemorrhoids. Others raised concerns about the safety of chocolate, warning that it would blacken one's teeth, cause stomach problems, and even cause pregnant women to miscarry. Within the Catholic Church, some voices raised the question of whether it was a sin to drink it too often due to its pleasurable effects and, since the drink was ingested in liquid form, whether it broke the fast imposed by the church.

Chocolate was at the center of many debates and rumors in seventeenth-century Europe. According to María Mestayer de Echagüe's *Historia de la gastronomía*, these controversies, along with an attempt at ending the spectacle of idleness created by the custom of getting together for a cup of hot chocolate, resulted in a law issued by the mayor of Madrid in 1644 banning the sale of chocolate and its consumption in public.[41] The law stated that "no one, neither in a store nor in a home or in any other part, is allowed to sell chocolate as a drink."[42] It could be purchased in solid form and the drink could then be prepared at home, but it was not to be sold ready to drink or consumed in a public establishment. The importance of the product and people's hunger for it was so great that between the years of 1663 and 1789, no fewer than 103 legal orders were issued in Spain to regulate cacao's production or trade.[43] The prohibition of its sale lasted only until 1664, however, when the church finally declared that it did not, in fact, break the fast. By this time, a flourishing black market had developed as a consequence of chocolate's prohibition, resulting in the appearance of adulterated chocolate and many instances of food poisoning. As is often the case, restricting the population's access to chocolate had the opposite effect of what was intended and ultimately did nothing to impede its sale or consumption.

Madrileños were in fact so taken with this dark drink that by the eighteenth century, during the reign of Carlos III, an estimated twelve million pounds of chocolate were consumed *each year* in the city of Madrid. It was so desired that it was often given as a gift to the monarchs as a way to gain their favor. Kings themselves used chocolate in the same way. When Carlos III ascended the Spanish throne, he sent a gift of cacao, vanilla, and *turrón* (almond and honey nougat) to Pope Clement XII, with whom he had an ongoing dispute regarding his legitimacy as king of Naples. Unfortunately, the gift was insufficient to solve the issue, which had complex political and territorial implications.

Chocolate con churros at San Ginés. *Photo by E. J. Tepe.*

Chocolate continues to be enormously popular in today's Madrid and can be enjoyed without breaking any laws at the many *chocolaterías* found in the city. It is still served in liquid form, thick and dark to suit the Spaniards' taste, and is accompanied by a batch of no-less-addictive *churros* (thin sticks of fried dough, crispy on the outside and soft in the inside) and *porras* (thicker and shorter than *churros*) for dunking. It is usually enjoyed either for breakfast or for *merienda* as a late afternoon treat. The charming Chocolatería San Ginés is the oldest *chocolatería* in Madrid still in operation, having opened its doors in 1894, and a taste of its *chocolate con churros* is an unforgettable experience.

Spain's chocolate monopoly eventually ended, illustrating how, over the next century, Spain would lose its status as a world power and see its wealth and influence diminish dramatically. As Ken Albala notes, "Spain in the seventeenth century could not bear the weight of its vast empire. The American colonies grew financially independent, costly wars depleted the royal coffers and a tax structure that supported nobles and the church kept the peasantry in permanent poverty."[44] The wars of independence that broke out in many of Spain's Latin American colonies between 1808 and 1829, sparked in great part by the Napoleonic invasion of Spain and the country's subsequent instability, added to the empire's troubles. Madrid was at the epicenter of the French invasion, and a terrible famine resulted from the French occupation and resulting resistance of 1812, with thousands of Madrileños refusing to accept food from the French and literally starving to death. Things were worse abroad. By 1833, Cuba and Puerto Rico were the only colonies still under Spanish rule, and they, too, would achieve their independence after Spain's swift and disastrous defeat by the United States in the 1898 Spanish-American War.

Ultimately, Spain's decline was the result of a number of factors: the successive bankruptcies of the Crown, unable to sustain a number of debilitating and poorly managed wars; a prolonged internal crisis; an unstable government run by a number of unfit monarchs and their power-hungry advisors; several internal succession wars; and the outright corruption of the government. Spain's 1898 military defeat and the resulting loss of Cuba and Puerto Rico were the final nails in the coffin of the Spanish Empire. Luckily, however, the culinary exchange between Spain and America remains to this day in the form of mutual influences, and it enriches many of the dishes that are enjoyed on both sides of the Atlantic, a reminder of the cultural impact of a shared history.

As will be seen in the next chapter, the nineteenth and twentieth centuries ushered in a series of dramatic ups and downs that would shape the country's identity and its cuisine. Madrid, being at the very center of many decisive historical events, would endure a difficult period, but the resilience, strength, and creativity of its people would combine to help the city rise from the ashes and prosper, paving the way for a multilayered and rich cuisine that is a source of much pride today.

3

A New Era of Creative Cuisine

LET'S TALK ABOUT FOOD: FRENCH TASTES VERSUS SPANISH TRADITIONAL COOKING

Grande cuisine. These two French words summarize the French-inspired cooking that invaded Spanish dining tables not only in Madrid but also in every city, town, and province of Spain during the nineteenth century. The invasion was more than merely figurative, as it resulted from the very real occupation of Spain by Napoleon Bonaparte in 1808 and the six years of war that followed. Even though Napoleon's conquest was ultimately thwarted, his stamp remained, and by the second half of the century, Spanish cooking had been overtaken by French influences. A love/hate relationship with France would become the norm in Spain for the next hundred years and, many would argue, continues even today in the form of a series of rivalries and neighborly disagreements. For the educated and well traveled of the nineteenth century, France was the model to imitate. Spanish intellectuals of the time praised everything French and pointed to France as the ideal example of an advanced nation, hailing its literary and artistic achievements and what they saw as a modern, organized, and civilized society. By contrast, they deplored the Spain's corrupted political class and the slow and inefficient bureaucracy that they believed impeded the country's progress. In the same vein, French food and hygienic cooking customs were also considered a model to follow, with Spanish cuisine seen as rudimentary, unsophisticated, and devoid of personality.

Not everyone shared this love of French culture, however, and accusations of being an *afrancesado* ("French lover") were commonplace. The term *afrancesado* implied betrayal of one's own country. In truth, however, *afrancesados* were Spaniards who longed for a better Spain and wished for changes to address the many problems weighing the country down. Many intellectuals preached the need for reform and progress and espoused various degrees of sympathy with France—for example, Mariano José de Larra (1809–1837), Ramón de Mesonero Romanos (1803–1882), Mariano Pardo de Figueroa (1828–1918), and Emilia Pardo Bazán (1851–1921), all of whom used their writing to spread their reformist message. Some of them, however, did emphasize the value of Spanish culture over foreign influences, and food was a central part of their argument. For instance, Emilia Pardo Bazán, a respected novelist and a feminist, wrote two cookbooks in which she compiled an exhaustive catalog of regional Spanish dishes and highlighted the importance of preserving the country's traditional cuisine as a cultural treasure. Mariano Pardo de Figueroa, better known by his pen name, Doctor Thebussem (which reads "em-bus-t[h]es," or "lies," if syllables are rearranged and read in reverse order, a sign of the author's trademark irony), wrote many essays calling for recovering and appreciating Spain's original cuisine and decried the use of French terms for dishes that already had Spanish names. It was in this context of debates about foreign influences versus national traditions that the conditions were created for a remarkable evolution in the role that food played in the everyday lives of Madrileños, going from hunger and survival cooking to an era of gastronomic splendor. It was an evolution not devoid of controversies and shaped by setbacks, as well as amazing breakthroughs.

The beginning of the century was challenging. The years 1803 and 1804 yielded very poor wheat harvests, creating food scarcity that had a great impact on Madrid's population. Barely recovered from this disaster, and still surviving on a very poor diet, the city was then faced with the 1808 Napoleonic invasion and the subsequent War of Independence, which lasted six years. The war gravely deepened the city's food crisis, resulting in the greatest famine that Madrid has ever seen. During 1811 and 1812, fields were devastated and abandoned, and any food coming into the city was either seized by French troops or intercepted by guerrilla fighters, rarely making it to Madrid's population.[1] Despite fighting heroically against the French invaders, Madrid's citizens suffered hard losses, with food shortages and fighting resulting in a loss of about 25,000 people from a population of 175,000 at the time.

This tremendous human tragedy during the French occupation and the famine of 1812 left a deep impression on the psyche of Madrileños for years to come. The writer Ramón de Mesonero Romanos, who endured these terrible events as a five-year-old boy, would never forget them, recounting in his autobiography many years later the devastating reality of death from starvation that he witnessed as a young child. For the rest of his life, he kept a stark reminder of this experience: a small piece of bread—dry, dark, and hardened by time—that he retained as an awful memento and still had in his desk drawer when he wrote his memoirs in 1880 at the age of seventy-seven. Painter Francisco de Goya (1746–1828), also in Madrid during the French invasion, famously portrayed the invasion's horrors with striking dramatism in his famous paintings *The Third of May 1808* and *The Second of May 1808* (also known as *The Charge of the Mamelukes*), as well as in the series of drawings he called *Disasters of War*. Today, the intensity and dark beauty of these paintings can be appreciated at Madrid's magnificent Museo del Prado (Prado Museum).

These difficult times did not spell the end for the resilient Madrid. After the Napoleonic troops were defeated and expelled with the aid of the English and Portuguese armies, Spain started to recover economically, and an incipient bourgeoisie began to flourish. The extreme hunger and destruction of the war gave way to a slow but steady economic recovery. The emergence of this new social class, with the means and curiosity to eat better, began to take hold, and the French concept of *gastronomy* was imported along with other French trends, including the use of terms like *menú* and *restaurante*. Many changes followed in the type of eating establishments found in the city, as well as in the food these establishments offered. The figure of the "gastronome," a *gourmet* intellectual who writes about food, was born, and several such figures would achieve social prominence in Spain, exerting considerable influence over the public and helping to change long-held culinary attitudes and opinions.

This new middle class had a cosmopolitan attitude toward food and used food as a way to show their worldliness and social status. Dining rooms in the upper-class houses of this period became the central part of the household, elaborate and ostentatious, with glass chandeliers, fancy silverware, fine fabric tablecloths and napkins, many different types of serving dishes and utensils, and a complex social protocol surrounding meals, even including a dress code. Dinner parties were ostensibly for entertaining, but they became more of a way to mingle with influential people and make social connections. Eating became a social event in which every element followed a rigid protocol and set rules adopted from other European countries, which were considered among the Spanish upper classes to be more sophisticated and "advanced" than Spain, with France being by far the biggest influence.

In Madrid, eating out was referred to as "*ir de fondas*," which meant going to several *fondas*, though these simple establishments did not have the refinement that characterized the newly opened French-style "restaurants." The first of these new establishments was Lhardy, inaugurated in 1839 by a French entrepreneur trained as a chef, Émile Huguenin Lhardy. Once it opened, it became the most refined place to eat in all of Madrid, with its golden-frame mirrors, elegantly decorated rooms, delicate china, fine tablecloths and silverware, exquisite service, and, above all, excellent French food; it caused quite a sensation. Still in operation today and retaining its aristocratic flair, this impressive restaurant is definitely worth a visit for its *cocido* or other specialties, such as the heavenly, delicate *pato a la naranja* (duck in orange sauce).

Having introduced fine French dining in Madrid, including the novelty of serving consommé at the beginning of every meal, Lhardy had little competition from other restaurants at the time. Options for upscale eating in the city were still few—namely, the now long-gone Fonda de Genieys, another restaurant called Farrugia, and the greatly praised Fonda Española. Fonda de Genieys became known in the city for its French-inspired dishes, like pork chops *en papillote*, its croquettes (some say this restaurant was the first to introduce this food in Madrid), and its roast chicken, which customers ate with their hands using a pair of gloves provided by the restaurant. Fonda Española opened in 1840 and quickly gained a reputation for offering much better food than the average *fonda*. It was owned by Perote and Lopresti, two Italians who, among other culinary contributions, introduced the fixed-price menu to Madrid.[2] Spanish novelist and food connoisseur Benito Pérez Galdós had only

Restaurant Lhardy, an absolute Madrid classic since 1839. *Photo by E. J. Tepe.*

words of praise for Fonda Española's dishes, extolling the virtues of its rice *milanesa* style, cod in tomato sauce, lamb with peas, the sea bream Madrid style, penne Italian style, and the many fish and seafood dishes that were cooked in Genovese and Provençal style. Pérez Galdós also asserted that the *fonda*'s *arroz a la valenciana* (rice Valencian style, the dish that would eventually become known as *paella*) was better at the Fonda Española than at any other Madrid restaurant.

Also noteworthy was (and is) Sobrino de Botín ("Botín's nephew"), also known as Restaurante Botín, which is, according to the Guinness Book of World Records, the world's oldest restaurant. This amazing establishment opened in 1725 and is still in operation today. It first opened as Casa Botín, not as an upscale establishment, but rather as a humble place serving simple fare. Today, however, it is a fine restaurant, still using the original cast iron wood-burning stove from 1725 and maintaining the decoration of its beautiful original tiles. Visitors can peek at the centuries-old oven and see a stunning number of suckling pigs lined up and ready to be roasted. From Francisco de Goya to Ernest Hemingway, a long list of celebrities have enjoyed the restaurant's *cochinillo asado* (roast suckling pig), *sopa de ajo* (garlic, egg, and sherry soup), and tender lamb roast.

Kitchen view of Restaurante Botín. *Photo by the author.*

Aside from these places, however, most establishments in nineteenth-century Madrid served hearty, decent fare, though it was criticized by some for its oiliness. Most places offered fare such as cod fritters, *cocido*, potato omelet, fried eggs in tomato sauce, cheese, cured pork products, gazpacho (a cold tomato soup very popular in the summer), and lots of Valdepeñas and Jerez (sherry) wines.

Spain's long tradition of producing wine, particularly sherry, deserves a side note: As mentioned earlier, the Arabs had introduced to Spain the technology required to fortify wine, and it is also believed that the grapes used to make sherry were introduced by the Arabs, the grapes having originated in Shiraz, Persia. Although there is evidence of wine making occurring in Spain as far back as 1100 BC, it was only when the process of distillation was introduced that fortified wines and brandies were created. The names "sherry" and "xerez" both come from the Arabic transliteration *Sherish*, the name of modern-day Jerez de la Frontera, where the drink was first produced. The popularity of sherry over many centuries is well documented, with Spanish Jerez being widely considered the finest wine available throughout Europe during the sixteenth century. Today, the name "sherry" is exclusively reserved for fortified wines produced in the towns of Jerez de la Frontera, Sanlúcar de Barrameda, and El Puerto de Santa María in the Andalusian province of Cádiz.

The arrival of train travel to Madrid, with the inauguration of the Atocha railway station in 1851, brought about many improvements to the Madrileños' diet. Not only did the capital begin receiving more visitors with discerning taste, seeking high-end establishments and luxury hotels, but, more important, train travel also cut down on the transportation time of fresh food to Madrid, allowing highly perishable products like fish to arrive quickly from the coast and then be served in Madrid's restaurants. Soon upscale hotels like the Gran Hotel de Paris and the Hotel de Embajadores opened and began catering to wealthy European visitors, which in turn raised the overall culinary standards in Madrid. This trend continued throughout the twentieth century, with the addition of the Ritz, the Palace, and the Florida Hotels. Boasting internationally trained chefs, these establishments set a new standard of quality and excellence and were true game changers for Madrid's cuisine, leading the capital to develop more sophisticated and better gastronomy.

The French influences that ruled cuisine during the nineteenth century extended beyond the dishes, the sauces, and the language used on the menus to the design of the meal itself and how it had to be served, with everything following what was fashionable in the land of Molière. Traditionally, each course at a banquet was presented all at once—in a way we would call buffet style today, though in steps, with soups first, followed by appetizers, meat dishes, fish dishes, and finally desserts—and guests could help themselves as they wished. Around mid-century, with Queen Isabel II, however, all this changed. Copying the French, she favored the adoption of the so-called Russian-style service (*servicio a la rusa*), consisting of serving guests only one dish after another, each dish being brought out in a set order as part of a fixed menu, without variations. This allowed for menus to be printed ahead of time on a card detailing the menu and the guest's name, as well as their place at the table.[3] A typical meal would consist of a number of small appetizers and a first course of soup, followed by a main dish of either meat or fish, finishing with dried fruits, pastries and jams, sweets, or cheese. Among the meats, *bistec* (a term derived from the English *beef steak*) and roast beef became quite trendy, imitating the English. With each dish, a different wine (sometimes imported) would be served: Spanish sherry with the soup and Burgundy or Rhine wines for the main courses. In these gatherings, certain conversation topics (such as death, disease, or politics) were off limits, while others were considered ideal. Dinner was usually followed by coffee, smoking—only for the men—and more conversation, although these took place in a different room, away from the table, where card games would be played for the remainder of the evening.

Having one's own cook was a status symbol; cooking—and manual labor in general—was considered "low class," and women of the upper classes wanted nothing to do with it. These aristocratic women abhorred the idea of having the smell of garlic on their hands, something they associated with servanthood. Middle-class families employed a *cocinera*—a female cook—who would go to the market to do the shopping and then cook the meal, and other help would set the table and serve dinner to the guests. The wealthy, however, had their meals prepared by a *cocinero*, a male cook. It is important to note that this was not a meaningless distinction, as male and female kitchen professionals were regarded very differently. While men had traditionally held prestigious positions as cooks for kings and the nobility and were the authors of all existing treaties on cooking, women were seen as intruders in the profession, incapable of doing a fine job in the kitchen, and were often treated with disdain in an arena dominated by men.[4] Therefore, the presence of women in the kitchens of upper-class households and fine restaurants was rare, and when they held such positions, they received substantially lower stipends than their male colleagues.

Obviously, not everyone in Madrid had the luxury of choosing what to eat and employing a cook to take care of the kitchen tasks. The majority of the population lived on a diet that was sustaining but neither fancy nor varied. Meals were repetitive, consisting of the humble *puchero* (stew) made with beans, vegetables, and whatever meat was available. This was a variation of the ever-present *cocido*, as was also the popular *olla podrida* (literally "rotten pot"), a stew that contained a combination of different meats (ham, poultry, and mutton, among others). Surprisingly, Queen Isabel II was a fan of this dish, and she even included it on the menu for official banquets at the palace. The stews eaten by the lower classes, however,

Casa Labra's famous cod croquettes and fritters. *Photo by E. J. Tepe.*

were much less rich than the royal version, and they often made up for the lack of meat by adding potatoes and whatever vegetables they could obtain. Their everyday meals were usually composed of some type of soup with legumes, cod, bread, cheese, and domestic wine—Valdepeñas being the preferred choice. Offal dishes, such as lamb's brains, pig's ears, or fried sheep intestines (called *gallinejas*), were also popular since they were cheap. Meat dishes copied from other cuisines—usually English, Italian, or French—were common in *fondas* and similar eating establishments. *Hojaldres*, puff pastry pies, were enjoyed widely. Empanadas and their smaller version, *empanadillas*, stuffed with many different savory fillings, from tuna and peppers to meat, ham, and cheese, are still hugely popular all over Spain.

Some other typical foods that were served at budget eateries and still survive today include the rich and flavorful *callos a la madrileña* (tripe Madrid style), as well as the delicious *croquetas* (croquettes), small balls covered in breadcrumbs and fried, giving them a wonderful and characteristic crunch on the outside, with an inside containing creamy *béchamel* sauce and small pieces of ham, cod, or *cocido* leftovers. *Croquetas* are immensely popular today and can be found in most Madrid bars; some are now made with innovative, gourmet ingredients. Today, traditional *croquetas* (made with *serrano*, a Spanish cured ham similar to Italian prosciutto) and *empanadillas* are available at Casa Manolo, a Madrid institution dating back to 1934, located across the street from the Spanish parliament building (Palacio de las Cortes) and next to the Zarzuela Theater and thus often frequented by politicians and musicians. Particularly well loved are the *croquetas de bacalao* (cod croquettes) sold at Casa Labra, a historic and peculiar stand-up-only establishment, which opened its doors in 1860 and is located near Puerta del Sol. This establishment is also of historical importance as the location where the Spanish Socialist Party was founded in 1879.

Street vendors were by far the cheapest sources of food throughout the eighteenth and nineteenth centuries. They sold all kinds of snacks, from cold drinks in the summer to roasted chestnuts in the winter, along with fresh fruit—oranges and watermelon were very popular—as well as sardines, cod, and other salted and dried fish; small meat pies; and sweets, among them the very traditional *barquillos* (rolled wafers). These vendors, most often women, could be seen in many of Madrid's corners, carrying a basket with their merchandise and appealing to hungry passersby. During hot summer months, these street vendors helped Madrileños quench their thirst with popular drinks like *agua de cebada* (a sweet drink made from barley), almond milk, *horchata* (initially made from the juice of the tiger nut and later from almonds), and *cerveza con limón*, a refreshing mix of iced beer and lemon juice.[5]

Earthenware wine jars in Bodegas Ricla, a traditional Madrid tavern that has been open since 1867. Its basement was used as a refuge from the bombs dropped over the city during the Spanish Civil War (1936–1939). *Photo by E. J. Tepe.*

Queen Isabel II's taste for *olla podrida* notwithstanding, Madrid's royalty lived in an altogether different culinary universe. The following menu for King Alfonso XII, dated June 17, 1875, written entirely in French, and composed exclusively of French dishes, is a good example of the preeminence of the *grande cuisine* that dominated the table of the rich at the time—a far cry from "rotten pot." Once again, for the great chefs cooking for the royalty and aristocracy, there just wasn't such a thing as Spanish cuisine, and the only acceptable style was French.

Menu

Potages	**Relevés**
Consommée à la Sevigné	Turbot à l'Almirale
Purée Pierre-le-Grand	Cuisseau de Chevreuil à la Pajarstki
Fritures	**Entrées**
Souffleé de Perdreaux à l'Ecossaise	Supremes de Chapons à la Thiers

Cotelettes de foies gras à la Charles trois	**Rôts**
Caisse d'ortolans à l'Isabel	Pulardes du Mans truffées
Aspic d'Homards à l'Espartero	Chaudfroid de faisans à l'Européenne
PUNCH A LA ROMAINE	**Entremets**
	Croustades à la Bourdaloue
Legumes	Glaces Sicilien
Mecedonie vert-pre	**Desserts**[6]

This menu illustrates well the breadth of the discrepancy between the cuisine of both the royalty and the nobility, who were deeply obsessed with emulating French *haute cuisine*, and the food of Madrid's lower classes. Some of these French influences had trickled down to the city's eateries, but in general there were two very different ways of eating in Madrid. This was, essentially, a continuation of the long tradition of "high" cuisine versus "low" cuisine, which had been the norm in Spain since the Middle Ages, and it would take more time for food to become more democratic and readily accessible, as it is today.

A CUISINE IN SEARCH OF ITS IDENTITY

Nineteenth-century Spanish intellectuals and foreign visitors criticized Spanish cooks' practice of imitating other countries' cuisines rather than emphasizing Spain's own traditional dishes. They also decried the country's lack of appreciation of its own regional cuisines and the failure to draw on the country's regionally produced products. For these intellectuals, the problem was clear: How could Spain's cuisine achieve any level of quality if it was just a bad copy of other cuisines? Spain's cuisine, they felt, needed to find its own identity, and they believed it had the potential to be excellent. Spain's meat, fish, produce, and wine were outstanding. There was also, they argued, a rich tradition of Spanish cooking represented in its many old, authentic, and original regional cuisines. The challenge was how to reclaim those cuisines and develop them. At the time, this theme pervaded many of the discussions about gastronomy, and eventually the thinking of these intellectuals caught on, and foreign influences started to be viewed negatively as impediments to the development of a true Spanish cuisine. Authors like Ángel Muro, Mariano Pardo de Figueroa (better known by his pseudonym, Dr. Thebussem), José Castro y Serrano (who signed his essays as "A Cook of His Majesty"), and Emilia Pardo Bazán championed the cause of a Spanish cuisine free of foreign influences. Dr. Thebussem, for instance, is credited with convincing King Alfonso XIII to change the language used in the menus for the banquets given at the Royal Palace from French to Spanish.

This newfound pride in Spanish cuisine and the desire to differentiate it sparked a desire to break free from foreign influences. Well-known intellectuals started to pay attention to food as a relevant social topic, highlighting its historical and political implications. The publication of cookbooks increased noticeably, catering to middle- and upper-class women who, even if unlikely to do the cooking themselves, wanted to be knowledgeable about what dishes were fashionable to serve at their dinner parties. A number of magazines aimed toward women began to appear, and both daily newspapers and popular "serious" magazines started to include recipes and essays on food. For instance, the weekly magazine *La ilustración española y americana*—which described itself as a publication devoted to "sciences, arts, literature, trade and useful knowledge"—published a column called *Sartén y pluma* (The cooking pan and the pen), authored by the above-mentioned Dr. Thebussem.[7] Many of these publications contained not only recipes but also guidance about social customs and, more important, tips on beauty, home remedies, household hygiene, and home economics, with the ultimate goal of educating women about their domestic roles; teaching them about what was considered "good manners," both at the table and in other social situations; and preparing young women for their future duties and family responsibilities. In 1892, a book called *La mesa española* (The Spanish table), by Mrs. Dolores Vedia de Uhagon, opened with a note from the author addressed to her daughter, where she dispensed the following advice:

> A good housewife must understand the art of cooking, so as not to be at the expense of the servants, who come and go, to be able to inspect the cleanliness and quality of the food, and to provide her husband and her family with a sense of well-being, a comfort that will make them prefer the simple cooking of their home over the greatest feasts anywhere else.[8]

She also added that well-prepared foods were essential to maintaining a healthy family and emphasized the importance of managing the household budget with austerity and good sense, something that, she concluded, was especially useful for middle-class families.

FOOD, POLITICS, AND A FAILED ASSASSINATION ATTEMPT

Madrid's long-standing existence as a "melting pot" destination, receiving a steady stream of immigrants from every corner of Spain since the sixteenth century, provided a perfect meeting point for the country's many regional cuisines. As a result, Madrid's cuisine was never a monolithic, fixed gastronomy, but rather one in constant evolution resulting from the combination of a wide variety of regional culinary traditions. Many classic eateries that still exist today opened in the second half of the century, and if their walls could talk, they would tell us about some of the extraordinary historical events they witnessed over the course of their long life. Great examples are the many cafés where writers, painters, and philosophers used to gather to discuss politics, literature, art, and everything in between. These establishments were the center of social life in Madrid during the nineteenth century, and politics and social issues were often ardently discussed within their walls.

The legendary Café de Pombo (once located in the heart of the city on Calle Carretas near the Puerta del Sol) and the Café Gijón (which still remains in operation at the beautiful boulevard Paseo de Recoletos) are both well known for the long list of intellectuals who have visited them over the years. Artists, writers, and poets like Federico García Lorca or Chilean Nobel Prize–awardee Pablo Neruda frequented Café de Pombo in the 1920s, which also attracted painters like José Gutierrez Solana, Pablo Picasso, Joan Miró, and a young Diego Rivera,[9] who lived in Madrid as a student in 1907 and who would eventually achieve fame as a muralist before marrying one of Mexico's most celebrated painters, Frida Kahlo.

Another café, Café de Fornos—nowadays home to a Starbucks—opened in 1870 on Calle de Alcalá and soon became renowned for its flamenco parties. Its clientele included some of the best-known Spanish authors of the time, such as Pío Baroja, Azorín, Miguel de Unamuno, and Gustavo Adolfo Bécquer; even King Alfonso XII visited the café. In 1904, a tragic event made this place notorious, when one of the owner's sons, heartbroken from a failed love affair, committed suicide by shooting himself in the head inside the café. His death, along with the frequent quarrels and other incidents that took place in these all-night establishments, prompted strict regulations about the types of clientele allowed in them and the hours they were allowed to keep; as a result, Madrid's governor ordered all cafés to close no later than midnight, keeping a tight watch on many of them to prevent any further disturbances.

Difficult memories linger within the walls of other establishments as well, reminders of the relatively recent historical struggles the city has seen: the basement of the Bodegas Ricla, a tiny but charming *taberna* located on Calle Cuchilleros, just a block off the Plaza Mayor, was used as refuge during the bombings of the civil war (1936–1939). Today, it provides visitors and locals with a friendly and quiet atmosphere, an excellent selection of domestic wines, and flavorful old-fashioned tapas.

A tragic event of a different sort struck the restaurant Casa Ciríaco on May 31, 1906. As King Alfonso XIII's wedding procession was passing through the Calle Mayor on its way back from the religious ceremony, an anarchist named Mateo Morral threw a bomb concealed inside a flower bouquet toward the royal carriage carrying the king and his bride, Queen Victoria Eugenia. The bomb, thrown from

Photo taken in Madrid's Calle Mayor on May 31, 1906, showing the explosion during the attempted assassination of King Alfonso XIII. *Photo by Eugenio Mesonero Romanos (public domain).*

one of the restaurant's balconies, apparently bounced on the streetcars' cables, missing its target and instead hitting the crowd that had gathered to see the wedding procession. Although the blast failed to kill the king, it caused the deaths of twenty-five people and injured a hundred more.

Other Madrid landmarks evoke happier memories, such as Museo Chicote, which opened in 1931 in the central Calle Gran Vía. Museo Chicote is, according to some, Spain's oldest cocktail bar, and it is famous for its scrumptious cocktails. This fashionable spot attracted many celebrities during Hollywood's golden age, among them Ava Gardner, Sophia Loren, Bette Davis, Rita Hayworth, Gregory Peck, Grace Kelly, and Frank Sinatra, as well as other public figures like the writer and bon vivant Ernest Hemingway. Museo Chicote has been a fixture of Madrid's nightlife for many decades, becoming a hot spot once again during the late 1970s and early 1980s, when a new underground cultural movement called the *movida* unfolded in Madrid after the death of dictator Francisco Franco. This countercultural movement of musicians, filmmakers—Pedro Almodóvar being the best known—fashion designers, and a wide range of creative types made

Museo Chicote a favorite haunt. An establishment with great character, it maintains its original 1931 furniture and style and is still very popular with Madrid's night crowd.

SURVIVING A CIVIL WAR: EGGLESS OMELETS, FRIED FLOWERS, AND A LOT OF SARDINES

"A good meal consists only of the indispensable."[10] These words by legendary French gastronome Anselme Brillat-Savarin in his *The Physiology of Taste* were the motto for many during the Spanish Civil War (1936–1939) and for a number of years after. The relentless violence suffered by Spaniards during the war was especially horrific in Madrid; the city was the target of numerous bombings and was under siege for a long time, subjecting the population to extreme food shortages. From the beginning of the war, these food shortages hit Madrid and Barcelona particularly hard due to the fact that they were both major targets for Franco's army. Additionally, big cities like Madrid depended heavily on bringing in products from outside the city—unlike the rural areas and smaller towns, which had the ability to produce food and were thus more self-sufficient.[11] As a result, the few cookbooks published during the war years and the years that followed instructed the population on how to endure the reality of food scarcity. These recipes emphasized making do with very little.

The old saying that "necessity is the mother of invention" sadly proved true for the citizens of Madrid. The amazing resourcefulness of the city's population, especially its women, who were ultimately the ones in charge of feeding their families, became decisive in these circumstances. They resorted to humble ingredients such as flour, eggs, milk, potatoes, sweet potatoes, chickpeas, and whatever could be found in the city's markets or even, if you could afford it, in the black market, the so-called *estraperlo*. Cooks learned to rely on just a handful of basic ingredients, aiming to maximize the amount of food available for the greatest number of people. For example, Madrid's *cocido*, the popular meat-and-chickpea stew, continued to be cooked during the war but contained little meat since meat had become scarce. This lack of animal protein and the prolonged state of undernourishment endured by the population soon resulted in serious health consequences. Hunger began to take its toll, and diseases caused by nutritional deficiencies proliferated, such as rickets, anemia, and the so-called war edema, caused by a deficiency of protein in the diet.

Lacking their usual basic products, cooks turned to others as substitutes. For example, *almorta*, or grass pea (*lathyrus sativus*), flour was used as a substitute for wheat or oats in a popular dish called *gachas*. As Paul Richardson notes, *gachas*, a sort of porridge made with *almorta* flour and somewhat similar to the corn grits eaten in many Southern US states, became very popular in Spain both during the war and in the postwar years: "In the years following the civil war, when its calorific and stomach-filling qualities were needed more than ever, this savory slurry became once more a staple of the national diet—along with other 'prehistoric' foods like migas, chestnut stews, milled acorns, and altramuces [lupini beans]."[12] *Gachas* with *almorta* were prepared with any meat available—the more, the better—combining all ingredients in the manner described below by Ricardo, a civil war survivor:

> You fry pieces of tocino [bacon], chorizo, and liver, and slices of sausage; and with the fat left over from the tocino you add the almorta flour; you toast the flour a little—and you add water, little by little. And you see how it begins to get thicker and thicker, and you keep on stirring, and you know when it's almost done when it starts to bubble, plup, plup, plup, like the lava in a volcano. It's at this moment that you add the fried things: the chorizo, the liver, the sausage and tocino, whatever you like. You can also add some caraway, some cumin, some parsley, ground up in a mortar and pestle with a little water. A little salt. . . . It's winter food, with plenty of calories. A bowl of *gachas* on a cold morning, and you'll be set up for the rest of the day.[13]

Unfortunately, *almortas* contain a toxin that, if consumed as the primary source of protein for a prolonged period of time, causes a neurodegenerative pathology called *lathyrism*, resulting in muscle weakness and paralysis of the limbs. This disease had already been a major problem in Madrid in the years of the Napoleonic invasion, gravely crippling many people who were unaware of the risks associated with consuming too much *almorta*. During the years of the Spanish Civil War, cases of lathyrism, as well as typhus, dysentery, and tuberculosis, once again reached epidemic proportions, especially in big cities like Madrid.

Food scarcity was portrayed in great detail by one of the most famous cooks of the time, Ignasi Doménech i Puigcerós (1874–1956), a cook who built his career working in Barcelona, Paris, London, and Madrid, working at the service of aristocrats and ambassadors. Doménech was the founder and editor of the legendary gastronomic journal *El gorro blanco* (The white hat) and also worked as a cooking instructor. He published more than thirty cookbooks, many of which became very popular and eventually were considered classics. In his 1941 book, *Cocina de recursos: Deseo mi comida* (Resourceful cooking: I desire my food), Doménech relates the dire situation endured by the populations of Madrid and Barcelona during the civil war. Many of the recipes he gives in the book call for substitutions and present ingenious ways to beat hunger. His recipes attest to the necessary creativity that people resorted to in their cooking. Some examples include "*tortilla sin huevo*" ("eggless omelet"); "*calamares fritos sin calamares*" ("fried calamari without calamari"), which were actually onion rings; "*mayonesa falsa*" ("fake mayonnaise"); "*selecto café de guerra*" ("select wartime coffee"), made from carob beans and roasted peanut shells; "*girasoles rebozados fritos*" ("battered and fried sunflower heads"); and "*chuletas de arroz*" ("rice chops"), made by forming a paste out of cooked rice that was then put into a mold in the shape of a pork chop, coated with breadcrumbs, and fried. These dishes were ingenious in that they substituted ingredients not available to the majority of the population—such as meat, eggs, or potatoes—for ingredients with a similar consistency, which pass more or less unnoticed, with the goal of filling the stomach with familiar flavors, textures, and shapes. Here, for example, are the chef's instructions for making "*tortilla sin huevo*" (eggless omelet):

> Take a few potatoes, onions, green beans, zucchinis and artichokes. Chop in small pieces. Place in a container that has been rubbed with garlic, add 1 tablespoon of finely chopped parsley, a pinch of paprika, 1 tablespoon of baking soda, 6 soupspoons of flour, some salt, 10 or 12 soupspoons of water, 1 tablespoon of oil. Let the mixture rest for 15 minutes, mix everything well and make the omelet.[14]

According to Doménech, this kind of omelet became extremely popular during the civil war; it was made by thousands of people and nearly replaced traditional omelets containing eggs. This creative chef took the idea a step further and came up with a recipe he called "*tortilla de guerra con patatas simuladas*" ("wartime omelet with fake potatoes"). In this recipe, eggs and potatoes are absent, instead replaced with flour, water, parsley, garlic, paprika, and a most surprising ingredient: orange pith. According to Doménech's instructions, after completely scraping the orange surface off the skin of the fruit, the pith is separated, cut into small squares, soaked in water for two to three hours in order to remove all orange flavor, and then dried and fried as if it were potatoes. The chef also recommends adding some onion for better flavor and texture.[15]

Aside from his recipes and commentaries on the harsh realities of war, Doménech also provides a thorough portrait of the overall gastronomic situation of Spain during the civil war years. The book includes his firsthand account of his 1938 visit to a number of eating establishments in Barcelona, ranging from the upscale to the very humble. As part of his research, he carefully recorded the meals he ate, their quality, and their price. Perhaps the best summary of his exploits is his advice against eating meat at any restaurant during this time, since, as he warns, "even though they would call it beef or ox, I knew that it came from horse, donkey or mule, which were then very often used for this purpose."[16] Likewise, rabbit meat was often, in reality, cat meat.

One of the few sources of protein still relatively easy to obtain during the civil war was sardines. This highly nutritious fish, still wildly popular in Spain today, was very affordable and sometimes plentiful, either fresh or canned, and for some it was a lifesaver since, when canned in oil, it provided a much higher caloric content than meat. Franco's Nationalist army relied heavily on canned sardines as a major protein source, and the food was transported by the thousands to the front to feed the soldiers. Both armies tried to get their hands on sardines as much as possible, as did the civilian population. Sardines were mostly eaten with bread as a sandwich, but if cooking them was possible, they were prepared in myriad ways. There was even a cookbook published during the war that focused exclusively on this fish, presenting sixty different ways to cook it![17]

Once the civil war ended, a long recovery period still lay ahead. Madrid, hard hit during the armed conflict, endured very strict food rationing, giving rise to an ever-stronger *estraperlo* (black market). According to historian Miguel Ángel Del Arco Blanco, high-quality products, in great demand during the postwar years, were most often traded through the black market:

> This meant that it was mainly low-quality items that were sold through the official rationing system at the much lower official prices. In this situation, the temptation for traders and foodstuff producers to adulterate rationed articles proved to be irresistible. Accordingly, it became extremely common for milk, a basic element for nutrition, to be sold after being diluted with a substantial quantity of water. For instance, in 1950, Madrid city council revealed that, at best, 40 percent of the milk consumed in the capital city was, in fact, water. This grim fact is borne out by other statistics which showed that, while 230,000 liters of milk entered the city of Madrid daily, actual consumption reached 400,000 liters.[18]

Anything could be bought in the black market. Women who engaged in such dealings could be seen carrying baskets of merchandise to sell in the local markets, "offering loaves of bread, bags of flour, and liters of olive oil, for either cash or barter," and the authorities mostly turned a blind eye to their activities.[19] Due to the continuing food scarcity, what that was being cooked in people's homes and in public establishments was simple, dull, and based on just a few staples. For the most part, only local products were used, and those who could grow vegetables to feed themselves and their families did so, selling their extra produce or exchanging it for other goods. Canned meat from Russia made its way to hungry Spain; cheap but satisfying dishes like *migas*, made with wheat flour, olive oil, and any cured meat available, became centerpieces of the diet for a big segment of the population, both in Madrid and everywhere else. Reusing leftovers by transforming them into something else and presenting them in an appealing manner at the table the next day became an art in itself. In reality, it was a necessity, and it was seen as a patriotic duty. Nothing could go to waste since rationing by the government became the reality for more than a decade after the civil war. Basic foodstuffs like sugar, milk, meat, bread, olive oil, eggs (an egg substitute called *huevina* was widely used instead), and wheat and other cereals, and even other quotidian articles like soap and tobacco, were rationed by the government. Chicken was a luxury item and so expensive that it was out of the reach of most families. Each family was issued a *cartilla de racionamiento*, a sort of coupon book that entitled them to receive a set amount of basic goods each month. Those who lived in the countryside were luckier since they often had the chance to cultivate a vegetable garden and raise chickens, and they were better fed than people in big cities like Madrid, who were unable to do so.

As a result of the rationing and severe shortages, the emphasis of cooking during the 1940s and 1950s was about stretching food as far as possible so as to feed the typically large families of the postwar years, when a high birth rate was encouraged by the Franco government as the basis of the patriotic Spanish family. Domestic cuisine was simple, traditional, and unsophisticated; as nutritious as possible, given the circumstances; and prepared exclusively by women. A number of cookbooks were published by the government during the 1960s through the Sección Femenina, an organization created to educate women to become the model housewives and mothers that the regime wanted, with the main goal of instructing women on feeding their families while staying within budget. Although these books occasionally included a few dishes adapted from French or Italian cuisines, their focus was on economically prepared Spanish dishes, many of them originating from regional cuisines, such as Basque, Galician, Asturian, or Catalan, and were for many years an essential reference for all Spanish women. Fortunately, as the country's economy improved, so did culinary tastes. Changes began taking place in the 1970s when an exciting cooking revolution began to unfold and continued at a steady pace during the 1980s, 1990s, and into the new century.

Although Spain did not undergo the kind of culinary revolution that took place in other countries during the nineteenth and beginning of the twentieth centuries, the origins of contemporary Spanish food culture can still be traced back to the culinary texts of a number of nineteenth-century authors.[20] Writers like Emilia Pardo Bazán, Dr. Thebussem, and Ángel Muro left an important mark, and their thinking about a Spanish national cuisine would be revisited by later authors during the 1930s, such as Dionisio Pérez (who paid homage to Thebussem by adopting the pen name Post-Thebussem), and in the 1970s, such as Néstor Luján. When looking at the progression of Spain's identity awareness through its culinary self, critic Lara Anderson concludes that "although the Civil War put an abrupt end to all types of cultural and social modernism in Spain . . . it is clear that the ideas at the heart of Post-Thebussem's culinary texts were taken up in the 1970s, when Spain once again started to emerge as a modern nation."[21] The renewed interest in Spanish regional cuisines resulted in a pronounced increase in the publication of cookbooks, a seminal step toward helping set in motion the cooking revolution that would finally happen in the 1970s when "professional chefs in Spain—In particular the Basque country and Catalonia—started to create an *haute cuisine* from traditional Spanish cuisine, which would quickly supersede the popularity of French cuisine."[22]

A DICTATOR'S LEGACY: FRANCISCO FRANCO AND THE CREATION OF THE *MENÚ DEL DÍA*

Walking around Madrid's streets around lunchtime reveals ubiquitous signs posted outside many restaurants that consists of a small chalkboard or a sheet of paper on the door advertising their *menú del día* ("the day's menu"). This set-price meal always consists of a first course, followed by a second course, plus dessert, bread, and a drink. For each of the three parts of the meal, there are several dishes to choose from. Coffee is sometimes included as well. Everything on the menu must be homemade, and the price usually ranges between €10 and €15. Nearly every restaurant in Spain is required to offer this on a daily basis as a remnant of the Francoist government's idea to boost tourism to the country, an industry that started in the 1960s and has since become vital for Spain's economy.[23]

During the 1960s and 1970s, Spain saw an unprecedented increase in the number of foreign visitors. In 1959, there were 2.9 million tourists, and by 1965 there were 11.1 million—a great leap. Aware of the importance of this new industry as a major source of income, Franco's officials came up with a mandatory "touristic menu," along with other new regulations that were put in place to help the industry grow and function. The *menú del día* was thus created in 1964, requiring every establishment that served food and drink to offer a daily three-course menu consisting of an appetizer or soup as a first course; followed by a dish of fish, meat, or eggs with salad; and a dessert course consisting of fruit, cheese, or a homemade dessert, such as flan. In addition, bread and a quarter liter of Spanish wine, beer, *sangría*, or another drink had to be included in the meal. Furthermore, the dishes offered had to change every day. The requirement was received grudgingly but was adopted by every establishment since compliance was not optional. An example of such a menu, advertised in the newspaper *La Vanguardia* in 1964, features a first course where the customer could choose from consommé, salad, Russian salad (potato salad), appetizers, or gazpacho (cold tomato soup); for the second course, paella or potato omelet, fish in tomato sauce, fried sardines, or baked sea bream; for the third course, escalope Milanese style, tongue, kidneys in sherry sauce, breaded liver, and Russian steak, plus bread, wine, and dessert.[24]

The fix-priced *menú del día* is still offered daily in nearly every eating establishment during lunchtime, which in Spain runs between 1 p.m. and 3 p.m.; dinner is a lighter meal and usually takes place around 9 p.m. or 10 p.m. Nowadays, however,

Signs outside a Madrid bar advertising the *menú del día*, as well as calamari sandwiches and a breakfast of *churros con chocolate*. Photo by E. J. Tepe.

every restaurant also offers a regular *carta* containing the complete list of dishes that the restaurant serves. A customer can order from the *carta* at lunchtime, but the *menú del día* constitutes the better-priced option. Most Spaniards take advantage of the *menú del día* during the busy weekdays and choose from the *carta* when eating out on weekends or at dinnertime.

NEW TASTES FOR A NEW CENTURY: THE RISE OF MOLECULAR GASTRONOMY AND FUSION CUISINE

By the end of the twentieth century, the tables had turned between Spain and France with regard to their standing in the gastronomical world. The end of a long era of insecurities and imitation in Spain gave way to the birth of a new era of self-affirmation and unprecedented creativity, a phenomenon quickly attracting the attention of food experts around the world. Interestingly, critics still compared Spanish cuisine with its French counterpart, but with a different conclusion. In 2003, after a visit to Ferrán Adriá's famed restaurant El Bulli, *New York Times* journalist Arthur Lubow declared that French cuisine had become stagnant and complacent and pointed to Spain as the epicenter of a new creative food movement, a way of cooking not bound by the rigidity of tradition but one that harmoniously combined the old and the new, resulting in an adventurous, original, and delicious cuisine. In a long, impassioned article, Lubow stated that "the effervescence that buoyed French nouvelle cuisine in the 1970's [*sic*] has somehow been piped across the Pyrenees. . . . Spain rising, France resting. The more attention I paid, the more I noticed everywhere this invidious comparison, between smug, stagnant France and innovative, daring Spain."[25] Lubow was not alone; shortly before his article appeared, the *Wine Spectator* had declared Spain "the new source of Europe's most exciting wine and food."[26] Other publications contributed to spread the hype about the excellence of Spain's new culinary trends, and soon everyone was talking about Spain's cooking revolution. Lubow's assertion that "Spain has become the new France" was earth-shattering for many, radically changing the world's perception of Spanish cuisine.

Spain's new status as a gastronomic powerhouse came in large part—at least initially—from a prominent figure. Hailed as "the most imaginative cook in all history,"[27] Catalan chef Ferrán Adriá spearheaded a creative revolution from his restaurant El Bulli, tucked away in a scenic cove near Roses, in the Catalonian Costa Brava. Adriá would soon become the central figure of a new culinary philosophy and technique known as *molecular gastronomy*. Molecular gastronomy uses scientific techniques to create inventive dishes, playing with textures, aromas, and flavors in an unusual manner. These chefs go beyond the traditional idea of satisfying the customer's appetite to provide a unique "experience" for the customer eating their dishes. Terms like *spherification* (a process by which a liquid is reshaped into a sphere), *deconstruction* (redesigning a traditional dish to rearrange its ingredients in a completely new manner), or *culinary foams* (delicate foams that encapsulate unexpected aromas or flavors) became part of every respectable chef's vocabulary. Perhaps the most famous example of Adriá's use of spherification is his creation of "liquid olives," which have the appearance of regular green olives but are in reality filled with olive juice that bursts into liquid in the mouth. Other creations include popcorn in the form of a large foam ball, which melts instantly when placed in one's mouth, and "melon caviar," pellets made of sphericated melon that have the appearance of fish eggs. These edible innovations are typical of Adriá's deconstructivist cooking philosophy. He seeks to transform a familiar ingredient or dish into a completely altered form, thus surprising the eater and forcing them to pay attention to all aspects of the dish: shape, color, texture, aroma, temperature, and flavor.

In reality, culinary innovation had actually been occurring in Spain for a while. *El País* food critic José Carlos Capel recounts the first signs of experimentation

in Spanish cuisine, which took place during the 1970s and 1980s, and the resulting sense of excitement that was in the air. The now legendary restaurant Zalacaín
opened in Madrid in 1973 and was awarded several Michelin stars over the following years; in 1987, it became the first Spanish restaurant ever to achieve the
top three-star category. Two years later, chef Juan Mari Arzak's restaurant, Arzak,
located in the northern Basque Country, would be the second restaurant in Spain to
earn such distinction. During the 1980s and 1990s, both the Basque Country and
Catalonia became hotbeds of gastronomical innovation, with two restaurants—El
Racó de Can Fabes and Adriá's El Bulli—receiving the three-star qualification in
1994 and 1997, respectively.

Capel recalls the 1980s as a very exciting—albeit chaotic—time for Spanish cuisine: "We had no idea where we were going; there was a sense of perpetual change
in the air."[28] In fact, as Pilar Bueno notes, the 1979 publication of the Spanish edition of Paul Bocuse's *La cuisine du marché*,[29] which included recipes from several
Spanish chefs who were experimenting with a new approach to cooking, signaled
the new direction in which Spanish cuisine was moving.[30] Until the 1990s, the
innovations put in practice by these chefs had mostly consisted of bringing Spanish traditional cooking up to date but still using the same cooking techniques that
had always been used. When Ferrán Adriá entered the culinary scene, he attracted
everyone's attention by using completely new cooking techniques and obtaining
amazing results. As Capel recalls,

> What happens in 1993, or 1994, is that we begin to hear about a new figure on the
> scene, a Catalan chef who is astonishingly innovative. He is creating a new cuisine
> with concepts and techniques that no one has ever thought of before. How should we
> cook shellfish? Should we cook them at all? In the old days, to make a French-style
> mousse, you needed some kind of fat, or whipped cream. He discovered that you could
> create a foam with carbon dioxide, and it would have a delicacy that no mousse had
> ever had.[31]

Adriá's influence in the world of gastronomy cannot be overstated. His take on
cooking has had a major impact and an enormous following. His success elevated
the status of Spanish cuisine around the world and gave Spain a renewed sense of
pride and much-needed faith in its own culinary potential. Chefs from all over the
world flocked to apprentice at El Bulli in order to learn Adriá's groundbreaking
techniques, and even though El Bulli closed its doors in 2011, its cooking style
continues to inspire a new generation of professional cooks who continue to search
for innovative techniques and experiment with new ideas, flavors, and textures.
Although it is still too early to estimate the long-term impact of the molecular
gastronomy movement, its influence is unquestionable, marking a turning point in
world cuisine, with "before" and "after" clearly noticeable. Molecular gastronomy

has a major following, with some of today's most sought-after chefs using many of its techniques and building upon them: David Muñoz, Sergi Arola, and Diego Guerrero in Madrid; Quique Dacosta on the Valencian coast; and José Andrés in the United States, along with many other chefs around the world, are pushing the limits of what a dish can be and developing a cosmopolitan cuisine that blends different culinary traditions from around the world. Terms like *author cuisine, fusion cuisine*, and *molecular gastronomy*, stemming from the trends that started to gain momentum during the 1970s and into the 2000s, have come to define the contemporary gastronomic scene the world over.

It must be noted, however, that molecular gastronomy does *not* represent mainstream Spanish cooking. In a fashion similar to what happened in the preceding centuries, there are two clearly differentiated cuisines in today's Spain. On the one hand, there is a cuisine for the elite, represented by the chef-driven style of cooking, which is highly sophisticated, very costly to produce, and available only to those who can afford the often-exorbitant prices of the restaurants that serve it. On the other hand, there is the popular cuisine, which is affordable and based on flavors, ingredients, and textures that are familiar and accessible to the majority of the population. Madrileños' favorite way of eating out continues to be enjoying the inexpensive tapas served in the majority of the establishments in the city. There is also a vast array of foreign cuisines available, which are enormously popular.

Popular cuisine sometimes takes its cues from the haute cuisine of the star chefs, a phenomenon that has been commonly recurrent for centuries. Other times, in contrast, it is these chefs who seek inspiration in the simpler, traditional popular cuisine. Regardless of this distinction—or perhaps precisely because of it—Spain continues to hold a prominent place in today's gastronomic world, with nine restaurants currently holding the Michelin top three-star rating. Admittedly, only one of them, Diverxo—spearheaded by the *enfant terrible* of Spanish cuisine, David Muñoz—is located in Madrid.[32] Of the remaining seven, four are located in the Basque Country, three in Catalonia, and one in Comunidad Valenciana. Nevertheless, aside from Diverxo, there are currently about a dozen other restaurants in Madrid that boast one or two Michelin stars: Ramón Freixa, El Club Allard (with chef María Marte as the notable exception in the male-dominated world of Madrid's chefs), La Terraza del Casino, Santceloni, and Sergi Arola have reached the two-star category, and DSTAgE Concept, Kabuki, Kabuki Wellington, Álbora, Punto MX, La Cabra, and Lúa have been distinguished with one Michelin star.

4

❖ ❖

Madrid, a Gastronome's Playground

Markets and Food Retailing through History

F ood vendors and food markets have long been a part of Madrid, dating back to the time of the Arab-built walled fortress of Medina Mayrit in the ninth century. In Muslim Madrid, the selling of food took place in three main spots: the souk, or open-air market, near the main mosque located at the end of today's Calle Mayor; the *alcaicería*, or enclosed market, found near today's Plaza de la Villa; and the *alhóndiga de trigo*, a wheat-storage facility built near the Puerta de la Vega, one of the main city gates, which has since been lost.[1] During the Middle Ages, Muslims and Christians lived in different parts of the city, and each group had its own markets. Christians established theirs around the city gates, and the Arabic souk was held at the Plaza de la Morería (Moors' Square), in the heart of the old town. After the Christian reconquest of the city in the eleventh century, the Plaza de la Paja (Straw Square) became one of the main marketplaces in the city and would retain that status for the next two centuries. Beginning in the fifteenth century, seasonal fairs featuring agricultural produce and meat, as well as horses and farm animals, were added to the existing weekly markets. Initially, these fairs took place twice a year—in May and September—and lasted fifteen days each, but given their popularity they began to be held on a weekly basis. The Plaza Mayor—the very heart of Madrid today—was called Plaza del Arrabal (Suburb Square) and fell within the outskirts of the city during the fifteenth and sixteenth centuries. It was used for commercial activities very early on, including a three-week-long agricultural fair that was held there each September. Most food-related commercial activity became concentrated in the Plaza Mayor, and permanent stalls for the sale of fruit, vegetables, meat, and fish were eventually established there and lasted until the eighteenth century.

After Madrid's designation as the capital of the kingdom in 1561, the city's population grew so rapidly that it doubled in a period of just thirty-nine years, from approximately twenty-eight thousand inhabitants to fifty-eight thousand by the year 1600. It is worth noting that compared to other European cities during the 1600s, Madrid was a tiny place, with a markedly smaller population than Paris (with 245,000 inhabitants at that time), London (200,000), Naples (224,000), and the much larger Istanbul (700,000). By 1750, the population of Madrid—the formerly agricultural town that had suddenly transformed into an administrative center and metropolis—had grown to 150,000, and forty years later in 1790, it reached 190,000 people.[2] This major difference is partly explained by the fact that Spain did not exist as a nation during the Middle Ages and was instead formed by several independent kingdoms, among them Castile, León, Aragon, Portugal, Navarre, Catalonia, Valencia, and Moorish Granada. It was only toward the end of the fifteenth century that a process of unification took place under the reign of Isabel and Fernando, who would start the enormously prosperous age of Spanish exploration and colonization of the New World. By the following century, Spain had become a powerful country, controlling large parts of the Netherlands and Italy, as well as numerous territories in the newly discovered Americas.

With the country's rise in political power and newfound wealth, an appreciation of new foods and new tastes quickly developed. As a consequence of the capital's rapid growth, importing food to Madrid became a pressing necessity, and a reorganization of the infrastructure for its commercialization and distribution became urgent. Food imported into Madrid was subject to taxes, a mandate that some merchants tried to avoid by sneaking into the city through clandestine openings in parts of the city's wall or by selling their merchandise just outside the gates. Plaza de la Cebada, a centrally located square in medieval Madrid, was initially designated as the place to sell grains, pork products, and legumes, although the Plaza Mayor (a remodeled and expanded Plaza del Arrabal) became the main commercial spot in the city with the 1619 construction of the Casa de la Panadería (Bakery House), where bread brought into the city from surrounding areas could be stored and sold. According to David Ringrose,

> Hapsburg Madrid possessed medieval señorial privileges that obligated the towns in its jurisdiction to provide bread to the city at regulated prices. . . . In the early eighteenth century this service obligation extended to towns 40–50 miles away. Even so, it quickly became a minor part of the bread supply, and in the 1660s this *pan de obligación* provided only a tenth of Madrid's annual consumption.[3]

The four-story Casa de la Panadería building can still be admired today on the north side of the Plaza Mayor, easily recognizable for its beautiful murals. On the south side of the square, the Casa de la Carnicería (Butcher's House) was built. These buildings became the principal locations for the storage and sale of bread and meats, staples the population relied on heavily.

The continued growth of Madrid during the sixteenth century, featuring new neighborhoods and quickly developing urban areas, called for further changes in the distribution of food, as well as storage. As the city's population increased and new regulations for the sale of food were put in place, more squares began to host ever-expanding markets, such as the Plaza de la Cebada, Santa Cruz, Antón Martín, San Miguel, and Santo Domingo, among others. During Christmas, both Santa Cruz and the Plaza Mayor hosted markets selling traditional holiday sweets such as *turrón* and marzipans. Harder to regulate, street vendors were numerous throughout the city, selling a vast array of foodstuffs year-round, from watermelon by the slice to many other kinds of fruits; vegetables; fish such as cod, sardines, barbels, and crabs from nearby rivers; meat empanadas; rolled wafers; pastries of various kinds; and drinks like *horchata* (almond milk), flavored ice, and even wine.[4] Fairs continued to occur throughout the year, attracting producers from nearby towns and even some from distant areas of the country. Typical products arriving in Madrid included veal from the city of Ávila, turkeys from Extremadura, olive oils from Andalusia, Castilla wines, garlic from Chinchón, strawberries and asparagus from nearby Aranjuez, honey from the Alcarria, and fresh fish from the northern coast of Spain, all of them much sought after items famed for their high quality.[5] The city's tariffs were of great importance, not only for highly desired products, which were otherwise unobtainable, but also because all items entering the city were taxed, translating into a significant source of revenue for the Crown. By the eighteenth century, taxes collected on food staples imported into Madrid amounted to a staggering 80 percent of the local government's total income.[6]

Meat was always a major staple of the Madrileños' diets. The first documented slaughterhouse in the city was located near the Puerta Cerrada (Closed Gate), one of the city's medieval gates, and dates back to the fifteenth century. Mutton, beef, and pork were the most commonly consumed meats. Starting in the eighteenth century, the area began to hold a market selling clothing, shoes, secondhand household items, and food (mostly offal and other inexpensive cuts of meat), as well as produce and bread.[7] Bread was by far the most important staple and by law had to be sold from raised platforms called *tarimas*, which were designed to prevent any contact of the bread with the ground. During the eighteenth century, bakers could sell bread from either their own house or a market stall, provided they paid all required taxes to operate it. The consumption of bread in Madrid decreased slightly during the nineteenth century, when potatoes began to be widely adopted by the lower classes as part of their diet, but for centuries the Madrileños' diet was characterized by the predominance of a few staples such as bread, meat, olive oil, wine, and legumes, as well as smaller amounts of higher-priced foodstuffs, like fish (mostly cod), fruits, vegetables, spices, and imported goods.[8]

Street markets continued to grow along with the population, becoming more established as time passed. Around the mid-nineteenth century, new ideas about hygiene and city planning began to take hold, pushed for by city architects, medical doctors, and scientists, who denounced the unsanitary conditions of many of the markets. The size of the markets also created traffic problems since they often spread out beyond the squares into adjacent streets. The number of stalls the markets housed provides an idea of just how big they had become: In 1853, the market at Plaza de San Miguel reached 304 stalls; La Cebada had 238; Plaza del Carmen, 219; Los Mostenses, 168; and the streets surrounding El Rastro were filled with 176 such stalls.[9]

Data from the *Matrícula de Madrid*, a census of all economic activities in the city, provides a snapshot of the volume of food-related economic activity in the capital in the year 1830: 254 *tiendas de comestibles y ultramarinos* (small grocery stores), 68 pastry shops, 41 *chocolaterías*, 46 stores that specialized in pork products, 80 bakeries, and 218 *albacerías* (shops that sold oil, vinegar, legumes, and *bacalao*, or dried salted cod), as well as 1,148 street vendors, who sold everything

Market at San Miguel Square in the nineteenth century. *La ilustración española y americana*, 1874. Author's personal collection.

from fresh fruit to roasted chestnuts, empanadas, and baked goods. Most impressive is the number of stores that sold wine or liquor, amounting to an astounding 1,063 according to this census.[10]

In the 1870s, the city began to address the demands of its rapidly growing commercial activity by building structures to house the street markets, with the intention of providing vendors with a permanent space and roofed structures. The goal was to create more hygienic conditions and safer storage while making inspections easier and preventing the sale of spoiled foods and illegal or adulterated goods. The markets of Los Mostenses (opened in 1875), La Cebada (1875), Chamberí (1876), and La Paz (1882) were built with this goal in mind. By this time, however, the population of Madrid was nearing half a million people, and these markets were still insufficient to meet the needs of the city's many residents. Thus, traditional street markets continued to exist alongside the new ones, although all were subject to stricter regulations aimed at improving their cleanliness and overall organization. Additional municipal markets were built in the following decades, during what came to be called the iron age due to the material used in their construction. The only original market structure from this era still surviving today is Mercado de San Miguel—constructed between 1913 and 1916—a favorite of Madrileños since it was built in the square with the same name.

Between 1940 and 1974 and coinciding with the city's post–Civil War reconstruction years, a total of forty-one additional covered markets were built, and eight more would open in the following decades. By 1991, there were a total of fifty-five municipal markets in operation in Madrid. This sustained expansion came to a halt, however, with the arrival of supermarkets and chain grocery stores in the 1990s, which resulted in customers shifting away from traditional markets, forcing some to close and others to be converted into a mix of retail and service space, offering options for shopping and eating at tapas bars, gourmet shops, restaurants, and the like.

Now, more than a decade into the twenty-first century, Madrid has seen a resurgence of its municipal markets, with forty-six currently in operation, coexisting with the many new supermarkets throughout the city. Many markets have gone beyond the traditional concept of the market as a place to buy and sell food and retail goods, becoming neighborhood cultural centers and devoting some of their space to activities such as concerts, art exhibits, children's workshops, and cooking classes, as well as community meetings, talks, and literary readings. Others have reinvented themselves as gourmet food marketplaces, combining shops that sell imports in addition to delicacies such as select seafood, organic produce, and high-quality meats, fish, and produce. In their manicured stalls, shops offering prepared and takeout foods intermingle with small ethnic restaurants, cafés, and tapas and wine bars. The resurgence of Madrid's markets has been such a success that the city has renovated many of them in recent years, and Madrid's City Council is now using social media to reach a new, young customer base, providing them with up-to-date information about activities taking place at each of the city's municipal markets.

TRADITIONAL AND HISTORIC MARKETS

Mercado de San Miguel

The beautiful and historic Mercado de San Miguel fills the space where once stood the church of San Miguel de los Octoes, a building dating back to the thirteenth century.[11] The church was destroyed by fire at the beginning of the nineteenth century and was never rebuilt, so the resulting empty lot soon came to be used as a public square. Eventually, an open-air food market opened there and soon became one of the most popular of its kind in Madrid, with vendors setting up stalls and using wooden crates as makeshift counters. In 1875, according to municipal rules, these crates had to be 1.33 meters wide (about 52 inches) and could be owned by the vendors or rented from the city, with owners even sometimes subletting them to other vendors.[12] Vegetables, fruit, cheese, fish, poultry, eggs, and meats were sold at the San Miguel market, including popular pork products such as ham, *morcilla* (blood sausage), and chorizo. In 1835, the architect Joaquín Henri designed a project for the building of a market at San Miguel; however, only the front facade was built, barely covering the unpleasant view of wooden boxes spread throughout the square. Another architect, Alfonso Dubé y Díez, designed a new building—partially building on Henri's—that was completed in 1916. Built in the glass-and-iron architectural style in vogue at the time, Dubé's Mercado de San Miguel is today the last surviving example of the so-called iron age and is considered the pioneer and most successful of Madrid's gourmet markets. It is by far the most visited, a foodie's paradise that was recently renovated in both appearance and philosophy, offering luxury items such as oysters, champagne, artisanal chocolate and pastries, *jamón serrano de bellota* (acorn-fed pig ham, the most expensive kind of Spanish ham), and other gourmet products, with numerous stalls offering food and drink in a "tapas bar" format. Located one block off the Plaza Mayor, the Mercado de San Miguel always buzzes with activity and is crowded with tourists. The highly photogenic glass-and-iron profile of this market highlights its historic charm, making it one of the most visited spots in the city. However, most Madrileños favor other *mercados* in the city for their daily purchases; San Miguel is not so much an everyday food market as it truly is a gastronome's playground.

The San Miguel market today. *Photo from www.mercadodesanmiguel.es/en/ press-room/.*

Mercado de la Cebada

Another large and more traditional market, the Mercado de la Cebada is located in the heart of La Latina district, one of Madrid's main neighborhoods in medieval times. The Plaza de la Cebada (Barley Square) began hosting a regular market during the eighteenth century, but commercial activity there dates back even further, with sixteenth-century merchants gathering at the spot, located by one of the city's main gates, to sell grains and legumes. Both the square and the market owe their names to the barley sold there and also to the fact that the square was where barley for the king's horses was separated from that of the knights' horses.[13] An enclosed market was finally built during the nineteenth century, a glass-and-iron structure designed by architect Mariano Calvo Pereira and inaugurated by King Alfonso XII in 1875. The architect modeled it after Les Halles, Paris's main market at the time, and even had the iron components made by the same French company and shipped from France. The building was demolished in 1956 due to structural problems and replaced by a new building two years later. Renovated again in 2011, the market is a popular destination today for La Latina residents. The Mercado de la Cebada has a distinctly "neighborhood" feel, and its eighty-six stalls feature a wide array of vendors, including butchers, fishmongers, poultry sellers, bakers, and fruit and vegetable stands, as well as watchmakers' and shoe repair shops and cafés serving breakfast and snacks.

Mercado de los Mostenses

Although it was designed by the same architect and inaugurated on the same day as Mercado de la Cebada, Mercado de los Mostenses was larger.[14] Built in the space previously occupied by the Premostratenses de San Noberto Convent, Los Mostenses market was a good place to buy fish and meat, especially fresh fish given its proximity to the north railway station, which brought fish directly from the northern regions of Galicia and the Basque Country. Sea bream was a particularly sought-after fish, and oven-cooked *besugo a la madrileña* (Madrid-style sea bream) soon became a popular Christmas dish and remains one of the city's traditional dishes even today.

The original market building was demolished in 1925 to make room for the extension of the Gran Vía, one of Madrid's central arteries, and the building currently hosting the market dates from 1946, though it has been remodeled several times over the years. It houses more than one hundred stalls and caters heavily to the city's immigrant community by specializing in foods from Latin America and Asia.

Mercado de San Antón

The historic neighborhood of Chueca, known as Madrid's gay district and famous around the world for its annual Gay Pride celebrations, drawing more than one million people each year, is home to the trendy Mercado de San Antón. This market is named for the nearby Church of San Antón, patron saint of animals, where every January 17 Madrileños bring their pets to the church to be blessed by the saint, following a centuries-old tradition. The original market, designed by architect Carlos de la Torre y Costa and built in 1945 as part of the postwar years' reconstruction effort, experienced ups and downs through the years, coinciding with the vicissitudes of its surrounding neighborhood. Attendance at the market declined in the 1990s, and the old building was demolished in 2007 and replaced by a new one in 2011, based on a mixed-services concept. Centrally located in the heart of the neighborhood, the Mercado de San Antón combines traditional food stalls on the first floor with sophisticated gastronomic eateries on the upper floors where customers can watch food being prepared. The market features an open-air terrace and an underground garage, complete with electric car recharging stations. The top floor is lined with Spanish and international restaurants serving tapas and small bites. Some stalls specialize in artisanal chocolate, others in baked goods and wines, while others serve Greek, Japanese, and Canary Island specialties, among others. A full-service restaurant serving food and cocktails until late hours of the night occupies the terrace on the third floor, allowing customers to enjoy the view. A full supermarket occupies the ground floor, and there is also space devoted to art exhibits and cultural events.

Chueca's central location, just a short walk from the Plaza Mayor, the Paseo del Prado—where the Museo del Prado is located—and other famous Madrid landmarks, wasn't always a desirable place to live. In the 1960s, it was neglected and suffered a slow decay, filling with abandoned buildings where drug dealers and their clients conducted business. Fortunately, in the 1970s both Chueca and neighboring Malasaña became the epicenters of Madrid's *movida*, an underground cultural movement emerging in the last years of Francisco Franco's dictatorship, which infused Spain's capital with a current of new creative energy. Music, film, fashion, and other arts found a home in these neighborhoods, and low rents encouraged young entrepreneurs to pursue their cultural projects. Drugs, crime, and prostitution were replaced by a new social dynamic, beginning with an influx of gay residents who bought and restored Chueca's old rundown houses, slowly transforming the area into the hip spot that it is today. Bars and saunas initially thrived and were later followed by sophisticated restaurants, coffee shops, and art galleries. Today, real estate prices in Chueca are some of the highest in Madrid. Modernity and tradition have found here a place to coexist, and the market provides residents and visitors with a friendly and convenient place to shop and interact. With the market's eclectic mix of spaces and functions, it serves as an apt reflection of the character of the neighborhood, home to a diverse alternative community in which gay and straight young couples intermingle with elderly residents who have lived there for decades.

Mercado de Antón Martín

Another example of this kind of harmonic coexistence between old and new is the Mercado de Antón Martín, located on one of Madrid's main arteries, the Calle Atocha, near the Atocha train station and close to several museums such as the Prado, the Reina Sofía, and the Thyssen-Bornemisza. With sixty-nine stalls today, the market has been in operation since 1941, although it occupies a space known to have been used as a marketplace since the sixteenth century. This is also the location where the *Motín de Esquilache*, one of the most serious riots against the Crown in Madrid's history, broke out in 1766. These riots were caused by growing discontent with the high price of staples such as bread, oil, and meat but also by a ban imposed by the Marquis of Esquilache, an Italian statesman and one of the king's ministers, on the use of long capes and broad-brimmed hats. The rioters' demands included the lowering of the price of food staples, expelling Minister Esquilache from Spain, requiring that the king's ministers be Spanish-born, and allowing men to wear the traditional garments that had been banned. The revolt over these issues quickly escalated, and several violent episodes took place before King Carlos III, fearing for his own safety and that of the Crown, conceded defeat and acquiesced to the rioters' exigencies. In the aftermath of the revolts, Esquilache was given the position of ambassador in Venice, where he died nineteen years later. The square eventually became a covered market kept in operation until the twentieth century.

In 1933, the city commissioned architect Gonzalo Domínguez Espúñez to design a building for the market, but the project's construction was halted by the 1936 Spanish Civil War and was not completed until 1941. After running into difficulties in the 1990s caused by the rise of supermarkets, the Antón Martín market was remodeled in the 2000s and is now experiencing a renaissance and thriving, having adapted to the needs of a new demographic: young customers with a discerning taste who seek fresh seasonal foods. In spite of the market catering to the young, cosmopolitan shopper, it also serves many older residents who shop daily for fresh products to cook at home. The key to this market's success is again a combination of both old and new: old-fashioned meat, poultry, vegetables, fruit, and fish and seafood stalls alternate with shops catering to a new generation of shoppers, with places like an oyster bar, a Japanese restaurant, a vegetarian and vegan eatery, a vermouth bar that also carries gourmet canned seafood—sardines, mussels, and octopus are wildly popular—an organic and fair-trade food store, an Italian-style pizzeria, and others. It is another great example of the rebirth being experienced by some neighborhood markets aided by the new foodie trends.

Mercado de San Ildefonso

The foodie movement phenomenon also explains the enormous popularity of the trendy Mercado de San Ildefonso. A recent addition to the list of Madrid's markets, it opened in 2014 in the historic Calle Fuencarral, at the heart of the Malasaña district. The *mercado* is located one block off Plaza San Ildefonso, which is named after the church overlooking the square and has hosted a market selling fruit, vegetables, and fish as far back as the eighteenth century. In 1835, a covered structure was erected on the square, but it was demolished in 1970 due to deterioration. The San Ildefonso church was built in the sixteenth century but was destroyed by Napoleon's troops at the beginning of the nineteenth century. The church standing on the square today dates from 1827, although it was fully restored in 1952. A plaque inside this small church notes that Rosalía de Castro, one of Spain's most prominent women poets, married there in 1858.

Strictly speaking, the Mercado de San Ildefonso is actually not a market. Closer in concept to the previously mentioned Mercado de San Miguel, San Ildefonso calls itself a "street food market," though "gourmet food court" might be a more fitting description. Small eateries lining each floor have a distinctly cosmopolitan feel, offering everything from Spanish *jamón ibérico* (Iberian cured ham), gourmet *croquetas*, and paella to sushi, ceviche, tacos, wood-oven pizzas, and grass-fed beef hamburgers. This modernly designed foodie's playground features bars on each of its three floors and an upbeat, hipster atmosphere. Art exhibits, workshops, and food tastings add to its appeal, attracting large crowds, especially on weekends. Drinks and food can be enjoyed indoors while sitting at a tall community table or outside on one of its two charming patios. The cosmopolitan and vibrant character of San Ildefonso is emphasized by the frequent events featuring various world cuisines that are open to the general public.

Mercado de Maravillas

With 178 stalls, Mercado de Maravillas is the largest and one of the most representative of all the municipal markets, as well as one of the biggest in Europe. Located in the Tetuán district, a very discrete exterior facade designed by architect Pedro de Muguruza in 1942 gives way to an open and bright interior, full of natural light. Its many stalls offer options to satisfy even the most demanding of foodies, and includes thirty-five butcher shops, thirty fruit stores, twenty fish stores, fifteen charcuterie and cheese stores, eleven poultry shops, seven bakeries, five pickle shops, and six bars. Several stalls specialize in foreign and exotic foods, such as sushi, rare fish, and products from every region of Spain and Latin America and far-flung places like Korea. One of the market's bakeries, Horno Atanor, is well known for its gourmet baked goods and the fifty different kinds of bread they bake there.

Mercado de la Paz

Another historic market that has been in operation since the nineteenth century is the Mercado de la Paz, one of the most popular in the upscale and historic Salamanca district. Built in 1882 in the "iron frame" style popular at the end of that century, the market's beautiful structure can still be appreciated today, as it still features its original classical iron arches, combining them with modern elements. Smaller in size than other markets, Mercado de la Paz caters to the wealthy Salamanca residents, with roughly fifty stalls carrying very select meats, fish, seafood, and produce, as well as imported cheeses and other gourmet items.

Mercado de San Fernando

The Mercado de San Fernando, known popularly as "*el mercado de Lavapiés,*" is located in the heart of what is considered by many the most multicultural neighborhood of the city. Lavapiés, a historic Madrid neighborhood, has become known in recent years for its diverse population, including a large number of immigrants from India, Africa, and Latin America. As always happens with immigrant

Fish and seafood stall at Mercado de la Paz. *Photo by the author.*

communities, their cooking traveled with them, as is apparent today in the streets of Lavapiés, which are dotted with myriad restaurants featuring the aromas and flavors of these cuisines. The San Fernando market opened in 1994 and its fifty-nine stalls are housed in a singular building designed by architect Casto Fernández-Shaw. Its imposing facade and welcoming, luminous interior features a variety of shops, including a wine store that specializes in natural wines, which are sold by the glass, bottle, or in bulk. There is also a bookstore that sells books by weight, oddly called La Casquería (offal shop). The market's tapas bars are enormously popular on the weekends, filling with hungry crowds trying the specialties of the different ethnic cuisines.

The story of the San Fernando market is truly remarkable and is a great example of how a neighborhood space can be repurposed to serve its community while remaining financially viable. The market reached a low point in 2010 when customers mostly switched to shopping at big supermarkets, and San Fernando was on the verge of shutting its doors, with many vendors having to close their shops for good. To avoid this prospect, shop owners opened up the process of buying or renting stalls and encouraged any interested neighbors to open their own businesses. This resulted in numerous young people opening new shops and developing projects intended to benefit the community by promoting sustainability, ecology, or craftsmanship. For many, this became an opportunity for self-employment, since running their own business allowed them to pursue their passions and put their skills to use. The success of this initiative infused new life into San Fernando, turning it into one of the most atypical—yet successful—of Madrid's municipal markets. The many community activities that take place there every week are part of the reason for its success. From music concerts to handcrafts workshops, poetry recitals, or talks on a variety of social issues, the market community's activities are inclusive to everyone and celebrate the multicultural and multiethnic spirit of Lavapiés's population. The majority of the stalls now feature bars, cafés, or small eateries, but there are also many traditional shops serving the needs of the neighborhood by selling meat, fish, fruits and vegetables, bread, and other staples. Currently, there are two fishmongers, four butchers, one poultry shop, a bakery, and three produce stands, one of which carries only organic items. Prepared foods and a wide array of other items, such as milk, eggs, legumes, rice, canned foods, cheese, and charcuteries, can be purchased at the market as well.

Many other markets throughout the city match the personality of their neighborhood. The Mercado de Diego de León, for example, located in the Salamanca district and in operation since 1939, features thirty-four stylish and spotless stalls offering meats, fish, and produce, as well as clothing stores, shoe repair shops, and cafés. Also well loved by Madrileños is the Mercado de Chamartín, a market easily recognized by its colorful facade and which has been open since 1962. The market boasts sixty stalls selling high-quality and gourmet foods, attracting some of Madrid's best-known chefs shopping for poultry, duck foie gras and imported cheeses, meat, fresh fish, seafood, and exotic fruits. Some of the market's merchants are known for their specialties, such as the marinated partridge and stuffed *poularde* prepared by Hermanos Gómez or the shisho leaves and pitahaya fruit from the Canary Islands sold at Charito's fruit stand.

El Rastro

Altogether different from these traditional markets is Madrid's oldest, largest, and most popular open-air flea market, the boisterous El Rastro, which holds up to thirty-five hundred stalls. Taking place every Sunday and public holiday in the streets around Plaza de Cascorro and Ribera de Curtidores in the La Latina district, El Rastro is known for its antiques, secondhand items, used and new clothing, and arts and crafts. It traces its origins to the eighteenth century, when the area became known as "El Rastro" ("the trail") in reference to the trail of blood that could be seen running downhill from the streets around Madrid's first slaughterhouse and the nearby tanneries.[15]

The flea market began as an unofficial gathering of purveyors of all kinds of goods, from food to shoes, clothes, and household objects.[16] Although no food is sold there nowadays, city records indicate that ten fishmongers were selling their products at El Rastro in 1732, and by 1756 there were four fishmongers and six fruit vendors. The number of food vendors rose continuously throughout the eighteenth century, with the number of fruit stalls alone increasing to twenty-three by 1776, making El Rastro the second-biggest fruit market in the city after the one at Plaza Mayor. By 1853, there were nineteen bread bakers and fifty-nine vegetable stands at El Rastro, while meat stalls were the most numerous, with forty-six of them specializing in *mondongo* (tripe) and an additional sixty-four stalls selling other types of meat products.[17]

Today's El Rastro is by far the most popular of Madrid's markets and attracts large crowds of both locals and visitors looking for unique items, rare antiques, or great bargains. Aside from El Rastro, the long tradition of street markets is alive and well today in Madrid, with about two hundred other street markets in the city and in nearby towns taking place once or twice a week, usually on Sundays. Fresh fruit and vegetables, as well as textiles and other household necessities, are sold there at popular prices.

Mercado de Barceló

Located in the Malasaña district, the renovated Mercado de Barceló (now called Centro Polivalente Barceló) goes beyond the idea of a food market, as it is part of an impressive and futuristic-looking complex that opened its doors in 2014 after the demolition of the original 1956 building and a six-year-long remodeling process.[18] The market is said to have housed Spain's first supermarket in 1937 during the Spanish Civil War, which was run by Madrid's association of food retailers, who joined forces to guarantee the supply of food for the city's population. The new space, renamed Centro Polivalente Barceló, boasts a large food-retail area, with more than one hundred stalls selling fruit, vegetables, meat, and fish, as well as a sports complex and a public library built into its three floors.

Centro Platea

Another recent addition to Madrid's food-retail landscape is the Centro Platea, which represents yet another model of food market, a combination of upscale food court and gourmet shopping center. Located in Plaza de Colón in the heart of the city, the Centro Platea is housed in a movie theater that was repurposed for this new use and inaugurated in 2014. Its large, sixty-four-thousand-square-feet interior has been exquisitely decorated, with the structure of the old movie theater filled with two floors of gourmet food stores, upscale restaurants graced by Michelin-starred chefs, a cocktail bar, and a patisserie area. The theater's stage features music shows and cooking demonstrations. The Platea bills itself as "the largest gastro leisure space in Europe," and this ambitious assertion shows the intent to exceed being a mere market or traditional food court; rather, the Platea is based on the concept of food as entertainment and caters to upscale customers in search of new culinary experiences:

> Platea is a unique gastronomic leisure space. A magical place, where the excitement never stops. A place to relax, enjoy yourself and meet friends in a setting where everything comes together and makes perfect sense. Platea is all about excellence and creativity. The culmination of a project that marries both entertainment and gastronomy in all their splendor. . . . [Platea] aims to become the reference point for gastronomy and leisure in Madrid and a landmark destination for both domestic and international visitors. . . . We are also all about performance, hosting a grand variety of live entertainment.[19]

Gastrofestival

The tradition of Madrid seasonal food fairs that took place in Madrid under Isabel and Fernando's rule continues into the twenty-first century, with several festivals taking place throughout the year in various spots around the city. One of the largest is Gastrofestival, held each January for the past seven years. Billed by its organizers as "the culinary event of the year," the Gastrofestival features cooking demonstrations, tastings, and culinary workshops, as well as gastronomy-themed exhibitions in museums and other events held at various venues. Described as a "world-class encounter between professional chefs," it involves restaurants throughout the city, which participate by offering menus especially designed for the occasion.

Food Trucks

This panoply of food venues would not be complete without a mention of the latest food craze, arriving in Madrid in recent years, as it has throughout the world; numerous specialty food trucks now roam Madrid's streets and sell their specialties at different events and places throughout the city. The MadrEAT group, for example, brings together more than twenty food trucks that gather at specific events, offering an "on the go" gourmet experience with bites from many different countries.

CENTENARY SHOPS AND MODERN SUPERMARKETS

In spite of the successful survival and reinvention of some traditional markets, there is no doubt that traditional and independently owned stores do face many challenges today. The unstoppable advance of chain supermarkets and *hipermercados* (giant retail stores à la Walmart) is an undeniable reality in Spain, and Madrid is no exception. According to a recent study, roughly 45 percent of Spaniards rely on supermarkets for their shopping, a trend also seen in the fast-paced capital, where busy supermarkets occupy thousands of corners throughout the city. Spanish companies such as Mercadona, Hipercor, or Dia compete with international chains like Lidl and Carrefour for the lucrative market of grocery sales.[20]

This new dynamic has brought about stunning changes, affecting how and where Spaniards purchase their food and the types of products they choose, a process that has accelerated dramatically in the past three decades. In 1985, there were 1,622 supermarkets and 72 *hipermercados* in all of Spain, but by 2016 these figures had increased to 19,554 and 450, respectively. Family-run business have been the first casualty of this trend, with independent grocery stores declining sharply during the last thirty years from ninety-three thousand to the current twenty-three thousand.[21] Lifestyle factors help explain the rise of the supermarkets, especially their convenience, ubiquitousness, and efficiency, featuring a wide array of products, flexible hours, and, perhaps most important of all, low prices. Modern-day customers pressed for time prefer one-stop shopping at these large stores instead of making several stops within a market, and small retailers cannot compete with the product variety and prices offered by large retailers, which are backed by multinational corporations with deep pockets. In addition, many independent stores are now being squeezed out of the central areas of the city because they are unable to afford the rising rents that result from neighborhood gentrification, a process that further paves the way for the big retailers to move in.

Despite this trend, there are still a number of historic stores in Madrid that have been in business for more than a hundred years. In addition to markets and food fairs, Madrid was historically home to many family-owned grocery stores, which peppered neighborhoods and supplied the population with needed commodities. *Mantequerías* ("butter stores") and *ultramarinos* (which literally translates as "products from beyond the sea") were abundant, and Madrileños relied on them to stock their pantries with items such as canned goods, cheeses, charcuterie products, baked goods, legumes, and produce. Even though the majority of these small stores have disappeared, a few are still in operation, having evolved into small supermarkets or gourmet shops specializing in high-quality artisanal products.

These shops are a major part of Madrid's history and landmarks of a bygone era, such as Bartolomé, which opened in 1837 and is the oldest food store still in operation in Madrid. Bartolomé originally began as a small shop that sold salted meats, hence its location on Calle Sal (Salt Street), where the city's salt deposits and various salt-related business were located. Bartolomé has recently become a gourmet store specializing in serrano ham, high-quality olive oils, cheeses, and other regional Spanish products, and it is owned and operated by the third generation of a family of butchers, the grandchildren of the family who owned it since 1931.

Spanish hams for sale at a traditional store in Madrid's Cava Baja. *Photo by the author.*

In operation since 1870, Mantequería Andrés is a gourmet *ultramarinos* shop that carries hard-to-find Spanish delicacies such as the sweet pastries *piononos* from Andalusian Granada, artisan cheeses from Asturias, and fresh milk from Madrid's nearby mountains. Another similarly historic shop, Mantequería A. Cabello—previously Casa Varona—first opened its doors in 1877, and its large window still features numerous kinds of canned goods, artisan oils and vinegars, pasta, fruit jam, legumes (both dried and in jars), sweets and artisanal pastries, and many other old-fashioned foodstuffs.

Another of the oldest food shops is Hijos de Lechuga, a butcher shop that has been providing fresh meats since 1840. This shop's excellent reputation during the nineteenth century made it a supplier of the Royal Palace, as well as high-end hotels such as the Ritz and the Palace and the houses of Madrid's aristocracy. Located in historic Calle Mayor, the store was remodeled in the 1960s, when its traditional appearance was replaced by a more contemporary one. Today, Hijos de Lechuga continues to sell top-quality meats, both fresh and cured, such as hams, chorizos, and *morcillas*, as well as cheeses and legumes, and to keep up with the times, the business has now expanded to allow online orders and even offer a home delivery service.

A seller of wine and liquor since 1895, Vinos y Licores Madrueño is a real Madrid institution. It was funded by the entrepreneurial Mariano Madrueño, who purchased a large commercial space on Calle del Postigo de San Martín across the street from the medieval monastery of Las Descalzas Reales. The space's large dimensions, roughly sixty-four hundred square feet, allowed Madrueño to build a shop, a wine cellar, and even a laboratory, as well as a spacious basement for storage. In his laboratory, he created new liquors, syrups, and vermouths using different wild herbs and artisanal techniques. He built a flourishing business selling his many flavors of syrups in bulk, in addition to the much-sought-after aromatic vermouth wines. The shop is still run by the Madrueño family and is now in its third generation of owners. It maintains its classic charm, with old wooden shelves, alembic stills, and barrels. The distillery stopped producing its own liquor in 1999, however, and began specializing in selling select Spanish wines and liquors from around the world, as well as hosting frequent tastings and wine and liquor appreciation classes. Unfortunately, the future of the store at its current location is uncertain given the building's precarious situation due to its age, lack of maintenance, and numerous structural issues.[22] The savvy Madrueño family, however, has opened a second location on Calle Calatrava to keep their robust business going, and they also sell their products online.

No review of Madrid's centenary stores would be complete without the inclusion of Los Ferreros. The great-grandfather and great uncle of the store's current owner arrived from León in 1898 and opened this *ultramarinos* store on a street adjacent to the Plaza Mayor, which at the time was the city's main commercial area; the store was later converted to a butcher and sausage shop. Los Ferreros has maintained its nineteenth-century aesthetics, with an elegant facade and window. Not to be missed are the paintings dating from 1900 that decorate the ceiling, which depict bucolic scenes of cows and pigs in a landscape of pastures and, curiously, a group of cherubs carrying hams, chorizos, and other cured meats. Given its proximity to the Plaza Mayor, Los Ferreros caters mostly to tourists visiting the city and specializes in typical Spanish items such as cheeses, serrano ham, and other dried meats, as well as wine, saffron, and other regional products.

The small but well-stocked Frutas Vázquez in the wealthy Salamanca neighborhood began selling produce in 1943 and is now run by the third generation of the Vázquez family. Despite its humble appearance and size, Frutas Vázquez exceeds the expectations of the average fruit shop, specializing in the best-quality produce from all over the world. The store supplies the Royal Palace, and members of the royal family and other celebrities are often spotted there while on a casual shopping trip.

Frutas Vázquez, the small but exquisite shop that supplies the Spanish royal family. *Photo by the author.*

CLASSIC PASTRY SHOPS

Madrid has a long tradition of bakeries and pastry shops dating back to the early nineteenth century, featuring both sweet Spanish specialties and many others from around the world. Many of these sweet treats are associated with specific religious celebrations such as the San Isidro Fair, Carnival, or the Christmas season. Some of the city's most traditional bakeries are still in operation today and are still making the specialties for which they became known a hundred years ago. In addition, a new generation of bakers now appeal to more modern tastes, selling macaroons, American-style cupcakes, and pastries aimed at specific niche customers, such as people with gluten sensitivity or diabetes. The nineteenth century can be considered the golden age of Madrid's patisserie industry thanks to the influence of French cuisine and the rise of an increasingly affluent middle class with refined tastes. During that era, the streets around Carrera de San Jerónimo became a hotbed for new shops, among them numerous pastry shops that featured trendy new items.

Some shops quickly developed excellent reputations, as in the case of Lhardy, Pastelería del Pozo, and Casa Mira, all of which are remarkably still in operation today and continue to make their traditional specialties. While Lhardy is best known now as a restaurant, it still maintains its pastry shop exactly as it existed in the 1800s. This beautiful and well-stocked store deserves a visit in order to admire its aristocratic golden-frame mirror presiding over the room, its wooden and white marble counters, and its silver-and-glass cabinets showcasing the many types of artisan pastries and cakes sold there, from *almendrados* (sweet biscuits made with almonds) and *empiñonados* (with pine nuts) to *biscuit glacés*, tea cookies, fruit jams, and chocolates. Canned old-fashioned delicacies such as beef tongue, hare meat pie, truffle-stuffed turkey, and duck foie are also found there.

The nearby Pastelería del Pozo maintains its original facade from 1830, beautifully decorated in wood and glass, and its interior retains all the character of an old bakery workshop, where the hundred-year-old artisanal method is still employed in making the pastries for which the shop is famous: *hojaldres* (phyllo dough pastries), empanadas (meat or fish pies, with tuna being one of the most popular), and especially *bartolillos* (triangular-shaped pastries of fried dough filled with custard cream, eaten on Easter). During the Christmas season, the Pastelería del Pozo's most popular items are their marzipans, their *turrones* (nougats made with almonds and honey), and the obligatory *roscón de reyes* (three kings' cake).

Madrid's best-known pastry shop for *turrón*, however, is Casa Mira. Luis Mira, its founder, was a native of the town of Jijona, a town in southeast Spain known as the birthplace of these nougats, where the prized *marcona* almonds used in these confections are grown. When Mira first arrived in Madrid, he sold *turrones* from a small stall in the Plaza Mayor, and their popularity eventually allowed him to open a shop in Carrera de San Jerónimo in 1855, which quickly earned a reputation for the quality of its *turrones*. Casa Mira now provides a wide variety of *turrones* with some variations on the traditional recipe, such as adding truffles and new flavors like tiramisu, chocolate, and rum. Even though *turrón* has traditionally only been eaten during Christmas, it can now be purchased year-round. The beautifully maintained 161-year-old store also sells other traditional sweets, such as marzipans, candied fruit, and a dizzying array of handmade pastries, including *polvorones* (made with ground almonds, butter, and sugar), *rosquillas de San Isidro* (small doughnuts made with flour, sugar, olive oil, and anise, eaten during Saint Isidro's festivities in the month of May), *marrón glacés* (a French confection of chestnuts candied in syrup and glazed), *glorias de Jijona* (made of marzipan and egg yolk, wrapped in sugar and rolled), and *yemas de nuez* (made with egg yolk and walnuts). During Christmas, Casa Mira is a Madrileño's favorite for buying the traditional *roscón de reyes*.

Another well-known pastry shop from the same era is Confitería El Riojano, an elegant establishment located in historic Calle Mayor that was founded in 1855 by Dámaso de la Maza, a pastry chef from the northern Rioja region who worked at the Royal Palace at the service of Habsburg queen María Cristina. The store has changed very little over its 160 years of existence and retains its classic and aristocratic look thanks to its original facade, Carrara marble counters, beautiful wooden shelves, and classic nineteenth-century-style round glass shop window. Aside from its aesthetics and historical value, Confitería El Riojano is a preserver of Madrid's culinary traditions, offering many of the city's sweet specialties that are eaten seasonally and during specific religious celebrations. This classic shop makes *panecillos de San Antón* (sweet bread rolls), *bartolillos* (cream-filled pastries), *torrijas* (the Spanish version of French toast, a typical Easter food in Madrid), *monas de Pascua* (Easter cakes), *huesos de santo* (cream-filled marzipan rolls), *mantecados* (butter cookies), *empiñonados* (pine nut cookies), and a dazzling array of phyllo dough pastries. Confitería El Riojano is also known for its *pastas del Consejo* (council cookies), lemon-flavored cookies shaped as a *C* that are said to have been made specially to help King Alfonso XIII stay awake when, as a young boy, he was forced by his mother to attend the long and tedious state council meetings.[23]

La Mallorquina's prime location facing Puerta del Sol at the corner on Calle Mayor makes it impossible to miss this classic pastry shop. Founded in 1894 by Juan Ripoll, a native of the island of Majorca who named the establishment after his city of origin, today it houses a small café in addition to the original shop, both of which are bursting with customers at all hours of the day. This is not surprising, as its windows showcase a stunning variety of goods, tempting passersby with scrumptious cakes, shortbreads such as *rosquillas* and *huesos de santo*, *bartolillos* (cream-stuffed pastries), *napolitanas* (chocolate- or cream-filled croissants), truffles, cream éclairs, *torrijas*, and cream puffs. Around Christmas and the New Year, La Mallorquina offers traditional *roscón de reyes* (three kings' cake), a round cake decorated with preserved fruit and stuffed with cream, chocolate, or *cabello de ángel* ("angel's hair," a sweet preserve made from pumpkin pulp and used in many traditional Spanish baking recipes).

Another notable pastry shop, La Duquesita (the little Duchess) opened in 1914 and stands apart for its elegant and refined creations. Currently run by renowned pastry chef Oriol Balaguer, the shop features a small area where coffee can be enjoyed while savoring their *piononos*, a traditional dessert, or a slice of one of the shop's many cakes. Chef Balaguer has earned numerous awards for his work, including the award of Spain's Best Pastry Chef and Baker in 2008 and the 2014 Award to the Best Artisan Croissant in Spain.[24] He has been described as an "auteur pâtissier" due to the personal style that underpins his work and award-winning cookbooks,[25] which include *La cocina de los postres* (2000, published in English as *Dessert Cuisine*), *Obsession* (2015), and the most recent, *Bake It Simple* (2016).

Located in the central Plaza Canalejas and open since 1915, Bombonería La Violeta is another Madrid institution and still maintains its original look of curved glass windows and antique wooden cabinets. Currently run by the third generation of the original owner's family, it specializes in candy made with violet essence. The aroma, color, and flavor of this unique confection, shaped in the form of flowers, are all truly remarkable and extremely distinctive. In addition to the candy for which it is famous, the shop also sells violet honey, candied violets and candied fruit, violet preserves, *marron glacés*, and the traditional *chocolate del músico* ("musician's chocolate," a chocolate fudge made with walnuts and raisins). It is rumored that King Alfonso XIII used to give the shop's famous violet sweets as a gift to his wife, Queen Victoria Eugenia, as well as to his mistress, Carmen Ruiz de Moragas.[26]

The highly successful Viena Capellanes was opened in 1873 by the entrepreneur Matías Lacasa to bake and sell Vienna bread, a novelty product for which he held the only licensed patent and exclusive rights in Madrid for a period of ten years. Lacasa had himself tried Vienna bread at a Universal Exposition while visiting the Austrian city, and he was so impressed by its delicate texture and flavor that decided to start his own Vienna bread business in Madrid. This type of bread was unknown in Spain, but after its introduction it became a highly sought-after luxury item among Madrid's wealthy class. Because Lacasa and his wife had opened their bakery near the residences of the Royal Palace chaplains, the shop began to be known as "*de capellanes*" ("by the chaplains"). Business was so good that the Lacasas ultimately opened sixteen branches throughout the city, counting the Royal Family and Madrid's best hotels among their patrons. They also opened the first of their cafés, Café Viena, in 1929. What started as a bakery selling a specialty product has grown today into a large company with several stores, a restaurant, a catering service, a hotel, and several cafés offering select coffee and their own line of high-end patisserie products served in an elegant environment. More recently, the brand has expanded into several new locations offering an even wider array of products, including breads for diabetics and other specialty items such as chocolates, coffee, and sophisticated pastries and cakes.

There are many other noteworthy pastry shops in Madrid, some of which have opened in recent years to great success, such as Mamá Framboise, Nunos, Venecia, Santa, Animari, Pareli, and Vinicius, to name a few. In addition, the changing market for these goods has led to the creation of bakeries specializing in gluten-free breads and cakes as well as lactose- or sugar-free desserts, such as Arte Diet, Celicioso, Confitería Marqués, Mordisquitos Sin Gluten, Singlutentaciones, Celikatessen, and Bye Bye Sugar, all of which offer cakes, pies, and other desserts for customers with specific dietary needs.

CLASSIC BAKERIES

As was the case during past centuries, bread continues to be an essential part of the Spaniard's diet, with stores selling bread on every corner of every city, big or small. The day commonly begins with bread, since breakfast most often consists of coffee and toast or sometimes a small pastry. In Madrid, however, the toast is occasionally replaced by a batch of fried *churros*. Every meal of the day in Spain is eaten with bread, whether lunch or dinner, and restaurants always serve a basket with a few slices or a small bun accompanying each meal. Spaniards purchase bread every day at their neighborhood bakeries and consume it within the day, since it becomes hard and dry within twenty-four hours. The number of bakeries has decreased in recent years, as more cost-conscious consumers have started to buy their bread at supermarkets, twenty-four-hour convenience stores, and even at gas stations. The quality of the supermarket bread is notably inferior to that of artisan bread, and although its price is hard to beat, there are important differences between the two: The dough used by supermarkets is produced in large amounts at a separate facility, then frozen and shipped to the stores, where it is baked and sold; artisan bread, by contrast, is made entirely at the bakery in small batches, using better-quality ingredients and without additives to artificially preserve freshness. As a result, artisan bread tastes better and has better texture, but, understandably, many Madrileños on a budget choose the bread from the supermarket due to its cheaper cost, as well as the convenience of buying it and other products in a single shopping trip.

Providing an alternative to low-quality bread, a number of artisanal bakeries cater to customers who prefer bread made traditionally. One such bakery, the century-old Panadería del Río, has been in operation since 1910 in its location near the Museo del Prado on Calle del Prado, occupying the space of another bakery that had previously been in operation there since 1891. Family-owned and -operated since it first opened, it is now run by the founders' grandson. Another bakery that has been serving Madrileños for more than a century is Museo del Pan Gallego, founded in 1887, and it is the oldest firewood-oven bakery still in operation in the city. The family who owns it has also opened several other artisan bread shops under the name Pandepi, in both Madrid and surrounding areas, and they take pride in making bread in the traditional manner, kneading it by hand and placing each piece individually in the oven using a wooden spatula. In addition to various kinds of bread, their stores also offer several typical Galician delicacies, such as meats, cheeses, wines, empanadas, and the traditional *tarta de Santiago* (Galician almond torte). Another traditional-style bakery, the Horno San Onofre—previously Horno de la Santiaguesa—has been making bread since 1972, and it has recently opened locations at several of the city's markets such as the Mercado de San Miguel and Mercado de Chamberí, where it sells its artisanal baked goods, as well as cakes, desserts, chocolates, *turrones*, and even ice cream.

MILK AND DAIRY SHOPS

Milk was traditionally bought freshly milked at Madrid's many *vaquerías* and *lecherías*, where cows were kept and milked daily. According to city's censuses, there were at one point fourteen thousand cows in the stables of the numerous *vaquerías* operating in Madrid. However, new health regulations put in place during the 1960s forbade keeping cows and other farm animals in cities with more than ten thousand inhabitants, and most *vaquerías* were replaced by *lecherías* that sold the milk brought in from farms outside the city. In 1964, a new law established that all commercialized milk must be pasteurized, packaged, and come from properly inspected industrial milk facilities. This forced most *lecherías* to also close their doors for good. The last existing *vaquería* in Madrid was La Tierruca, which survived into the 1970s by selling other goods such as bread and wine. La Tierruca's facade was decorated with beautiful early twentieth-century tiles depicting bucolic images of pastures and the milking of a cow—the work of Enrique Guijo, one of the best-known ceramic artists of the time—which can still be admired today at their original location on Avenida del Monte Igueldo.

CONVENIENCE STORES, SPECIALTY SHOPS, AND ORGANIC AND HEALTH FOOD

Besides the above-mentioned traditional markets, supermarkets, and traditional specialty shops, numerous convenience stores have opened throughout Madrid in recent years. Open twenty-four hours a day, seven days a week, they are popularly referred to as "*tiendas veinticuatro horas*" (twenty-four-hour stores). These stores carry a wide array of products, including bread brought in daily, newspapers and magazines, various kinds of snacks such as potato chips and candy bars, pizza and other similar frozen foods, and often beer and wine. Vending machines dispensing snacks, drinks, and hot coffee have recently started to appear in the city as well, as have a number of increasingly popular online-based food delivery services.

The locavore, vegetarian, and organic trend has arrived in Madrid as well, with many stores throughout the city specializing in local produce—referred to as "kilometer zero products" because of their low transportation carbon footprint—organic produce and meats, and health foods from all over the world. Places like Bio C'Bon, a French health-food supermarket chain, offers thousands of certified organic products, including fruits, vegetables, meats, breads, gluten- and dairy-free goods, and even cooking classes. Smaller stores, such as the locally owned Kiki Market, specialize in organic fruits and vegetables grown in nearby farms, as well as artisan cheeses and other dairy products.

Other modern shops specialize in organically and sustainably produced items, such as legumes, olives and other pickled goods, olive oils, dried nuts and seeds (very popular as snacks and generically called *frutos secos*), spices, and honey—a much-appreciated delicacy in Spain. La Moderna Apicultura, a store officially inaugurated by King Alfonso XIII in 1919, is the oldest honey and apiculture supply store in Madrid. Housed in a beautiful historic building, it carries more than twenty different kinds of honey, including the famed *miel de la Alcarria*, which is harvested in the traditional manner from rosemary, lavender, and other wild flowers from the nearby Alcarria region. Another independently owned shop, Miel el Colmenero, has been in the business of making organic honey since 1949 and today offers more than a dozen varieties of this prized delicacy, each made exclusively from one type of flower, from lavender to thyme.

5

❖ ❖

Historic Cookbooks

The history of Madrid's cuisine is woven throughout the pages of the numerous cookbooks that, dating as far back as the fourteenth century, have been composed by royal cooks, monks, noblemen, and, in recent centuries, even a few brave women. These classic texts tell the tale of trends, techniques, and modes of preparation, as well as the ingredients available or preferred, avoided or forbidden, over the many long centuries of Spain's culinary history. Because Madrid did not become a major city until the Spanish court moved there in 1561, it did not initially have a distinctive cuisine. Rather, Madrid's cuisine evolved and grew over time by incorporating the contributions and dishes of other parts of the country. By the time the city became Spain's capital in the sixteenth century, several major cookbooks had already been published in Catalonia, a region with a longer and richer gastronomic history than the new capital. Madrid would, however, eventually become an important center for the publication of cookbooks, as well as a gastronomic landmark in its own right. The food of Madrid is, in truth, the food of all of Spain, with dishes that have become associated with the capital after being part of its historic gastronomic repertoire for a long period of time, the most famous and perhaps oldest dish being the iconic *cocido*.

Many of the cookbooks examined in this chapter are invaluable treasures, amazing works of genius that chronicle, recipe after recipe, the centuries-old evolution of food and cooking in the Iberian Peninsula. These books hold Spain's complex gastronomic heritage within their pages, having left their mark on Spanish cuisine and therefore also on Madrid's, a city whose culinary identity is intimately tied to its role as the country's capital.

BOOK OF SENT SOVÍ (1324)

The *Book of Sent Sovi* is the first Catalan cookbook, but its importance extends to all of Spanish cuisine since it contains cooking techniques and dishes that survive to this day in modern Spanish cuisine. It is one of the oldest European cookbooks written in a language other than Latin, and it is, critics have concluded, a compilation of recipes taken from different sources that were then brought together into a single text. The *Book of Sent Sovi* contains recipes for soups, roasts, and desserts, bearing the mark of the Iberian Peninsula's Roman and Arabic heritages, but it also reveals the influences of French and Italian cuisines.[1] Arabic influences, for instance, are present in the use of spices like black pepper, cinnamon, saffron, and ginger, often found in Hispanic Muslim cooking manuals.[2] The Arabic legacy also explains the presence of dishes combining sweet and salty flavors and the use of onions and almonds as the base for sauces, as in the case of the traditional Madrid dish *gallina en pepitoria* (hen in a sauce made with ground almonds and saffron). However, Carolyn Nadeau emphasizes key differences between this book and previous Arabic cooking manuals, such as *Sent Sovi*'s inclusion of several pork dishes and the disappearance of cilantro, which is substituted with parsley. She also mentions the presence of hazelnuts in sauces and an unusual mushroom sauce, neither of which had been seen in previous cooking manuals:

> If you want to make a sauce of mushrooms that are boiled, pressed, and fried in oil, make the sauce like this: take onion, parsley, vinegar and spices, and mix it with vinegar and a little water. Make pieces of the mushrooms, to fry, or serve with a fried mixture, and then put them in their sauce, or serve them grilled with salt and oil.[3]

Another interesting recipe, "asparagus in a sauce," reflects the characteristic medieval preference for strong flavors and the combination of sweet and savory. The ingredients used in the *Book of Sent Sovi* are Mediterranean, as this recipe also shows:

> [Take] the tender part of the asparagus and boil it well; when cooked, squeeze out the moisture; chop it up and sauté in a pan with a lot of [olive] oil; cut up an onion finely and sauté it; and when the asparagus and onion are almost done frying together, add in a little wine syrup or honey. The sauce is made thus: get toast that has soaked in vinegar and good spices, and add a little hot water of bouillon; when the asparagus has fried, add in the sauce and boil it all together; stir constantly until it is off the fire and has stopped boiling.[4]

As Nadeau notes,

The flavors of Hispano-Muslim cooking traditions are found in early modern Spanish cooking and continue to be enjoyed today. Food stuffs such as rice, cous-cous, eggplant, spinach, bitter oranges, sugar, cinnamon, ginger and saffron that were introduced and/or enhanced by Arabs, Syrians, and Berbers when they came to the Iberian Peninsula continued in both the cooking manuals and the literature of the early modern period.[5]

ARTE CISORIA, BY ENRIQUE DE VILLENA (1423)

Originally written in 1423, this manual on the art of meat carving was not published until 1766, when a manuscript kept at the library of the Monastery of El Escorial was found. Virtually unknown until then, the book was the work of Enrique de Villena (1384–1434), also known as Enrique de Aragon and Marquis of Villena, a writer, theologian, and descendant of the royal house of Aragon who cultivated a variety of disciplines from mathematics to philosophy, alchemy, and astrology and translated the works of the classic authors Dante and Cicero. Considered by many historians as one of the first Spanish humanists, Villena composed his treatise on the art of meat carving at the request of Sancho de Jarava, *cortador* (official carver-at-table) for King Juan II of Castilla. The work, which can be described as a gastronomic treatise imbued with allegorical meaning, is a detailed manual about courtly manners.

The importance of the book, despite it not being, strictly speaking, a cookbook, comes from being the first text on a cooking-related topic written in Castilian Spanish. Authored by an expert in the field with years of experience, it is not merely a manual on carving but also a source of detailed descriptions and numerous drawings of the different kitchen and carving utensils used at the time, along with instructions on how they should be used, cleaned, and stored. Villena emphasizes the connection between the art of carving and healthy eating, reflecting commonly held beliefs of the time, noting which parts of the animal were beneficial and which parts might be dangerous to eat or hard to digest. The book is a valuable source of information about medieval eating, as it details the sophisticated rituals and ceremony that accompanied royal and noble banquets of the time.[6] It also describes the origins of the art of carving and details the duties and privileges of those working as carvers in the royal court.

Structured in two main parts, the book reflects the cultural mind-set of medieval Spain, with the first section, "Tiempo Carnal," presenting the food to be eaten on regular days, when meat consumption was permitted, and the second for "Tiempo de Cuaresma," Lenten days, when dietary restrictions needed to be followed. The book's twenty-four chapters include detailed instructions on a variety of courtly topics, ranging from how to set the table to the obligations of the different court professionals, from cooks to servants, as well as detailed instructions on carving meat, poultry, fish, and even fruit.[7]

As Rafael Chabrán points out, "By listing the specific items to be carved, the author inadvertently provides us with a detailed catalog of foodstuffs found in the medieval and early modern pantry."[8] It is an impressive list, though it must be kept in mind that this is what was served at the royal court and by no means shows what was within reach of the majority of the population. Nevertheless, the author's list of the many delicacies served at the royal table includes pheasants, partridges, game hens, doves, quails, chickens, capons, geese, ducks, sparrows, oxen, cows, buffalos, deer, rabbits, goats, pigs, sheep, camels, otters, whale, grouper, eel, turbot, salmon, sole, cuttlefish, octopus, tuna, dolphin, sardines, oysters, shrimp, sea snails, clams, hake, and ray, as well as a variety of fruits, nuts, and vegetables.

LIBRE DE COCH, BY RUPERTO DE NOLA (1520)

Originally published in 1520 in Catalan as *Libre de Coch* by Mestre Rupert di Nola, this work and its 1525 Spanish translation, published in the city of Toledo as *Libro de guisados, manjares y potajes intitulado Libro de Cozina*, would have a major influence on later Spanish cooking manuals. Not much is known about the author, whose name appears as Mestre Robert or Rupert de Nola, and some scholars even question his very existence.[9] Scholars agree that the book dates from at least a century earlier than the first-known publication year of 1520 given that it provides recipes for dishes referring to Lenten dietary restrictions that had already been abandoned by that date.[10] Without question the most interesting text preserving Catalan medieval cuisine, it was one of the greatest editorial successes of the sixteenth century and was reedited three times in Spanish (in the years 1525, 1529, and 1538) and at least five times in Catalan (in 1520, 1535, 1560, 1568, and 1678), with both the Catalan and the Castilian Spanish versions being enormously popular.

Nola's work is a very detailed manual full of practical information that was clearly meant to be consulted and used often. Writer Néstor Luján called the book "an Epicurean catalogue of Mediterranean cooking,"[11] containing French, Italian, Catalonian, and Arabic recipes, as in the case of this "Berengenas a la morisca" ("Moorish eggplant") recipe. Eggplant had been introduced into the Iberian Peninsula by the Arabs in the twelfth century and had become very popular, prepared in many different ways. By contrast, this vegetable would not be known in the rest of Europe until the sixteenth century:

Hull the eggplant and cut into four quarters: when they are well cooked, take them off the stove and then press them between two wooden blocks to get rid of all the water, then chop them up with a knife, and put them into the pot and fry them very well with good bacon fat or with oil which is sweet, because the Moors do not eat bacon, and when they are well fried, cook them in a pot with a good thick broth, and the meat fat, and finely grated cheese, and ground cilantro [coriander] with everything, and then stir them as if they were squash, and when they are almost cooked, put the yolks of beaten eggs to them as if they were squash.[12]

The book also contains an early recipe for *escabeche de conejo* (marinated rabbit), an Arabic cooking technique used in the Iberian Peninsula for centuries to cook and preserve food—fish or meat—by marinating it in vinegar. This dish is still served in Madrid's restaurants today using this ancient cooking technique:

Roast the rabbits; cut them along the joints and take in a skillet two parts of vinegar, if it were weak vinegar, and one of water; and if it were strong, equal parts; and put salt to it until it has taste; add the salt in parts, not all at once, or it may become too salty; add oil which is sweet, whatever quantity you think fit, because some like it a little, and some a lot; and boil it all without the rabbits; and put it all afterward together in a pot; and let it go cold; and put to it ginger, and cloves, and saffron; and this marinade will last a great many days.[13]

LOS QUATRO LIBROS DEL ARTE DE LA CONFITERÍA, BY MIGUEL DE BAEZA (1592)

Cookbooks on baking and the making of sweets have been published in Madrid as far back as 1592, when *The Four Volumes on the Art of Confectionery* was published in Alcalá de Henares, the birthplace of Miguel de Cervantes and just a short distance from Madrid. Authored by Miguel de Baeza, it is a work composed of four volumes, of which only one copy survives today, kept at the library of the Monastery of El Escorial, near the city of Madrid. Not much is known about the book's author except for what is provided in the book when the author identifies himself simply as a baker in the city of Toledo.

The book is one of the first Spanish cookbooks focusing exclusively on pastries and sweets, and it contains the first study in a Spanish book on the sugarcane production process. Most of Baeza's book is devoted to describing the elaboration of the different sweets that existed at the time, such as fruit preserves, jams, marzipans, *turrones*, and cakes. Sugar, however, occupies an important place in the work, with the author enthusiastically extolling its virtues: "Among the things that God has created for the good of men, sugar is one of them, being so soft and sweet and very useful for many things, since many preserves and jams can be made with it, medicines and syrups for both the healthy and the sick."[14]

Baeza's work seems to be guided mainly by an educational purpose, having the goal of compiling and sharing his knowledge to make it accessible to anyone interested. To this end, he provides detailed explanations about the technique to clarify sugar with egg and to make sugar candy using round pitchers made in Seville and by cooking the sugar until its weight is reduced by half. The author elaborates at length about the different types of sugars produced in both Spain and the colonies, comparing the ones made on the coast of Granada and in the town of Gandía, on the southeast coast of the Iberian Peninsula, to the ones produced in the Canary Islands, which he considered to be the best in quality.[15] Baeza's work is of great interest to contemporary food historians since it unites the medieval Christian tradition of conventual pastry-making with the inherited contributions of Arabic and Jewish confectionery.

LIBRO DEL ARTE DE COCINA, BY DIEGO GRANADO (1599)

Diego Granado's *Libro del arte de cocina* (1599) is a controversial work, since, as modern scholars have pointed out, Granado incorporated many materials from other texts without citing any of his sources. For example, he seems to have copied entire sections of Rupert de Nola's 1525 *Libro de guisados* into his own work without crediting or making any reference to Nola or Nola's work. As Juan Cruz Cruz notes, Granado omitted some sections from Nola's book that he perhaps did not deem interesting or relevant and altered the order of the chapters, either to conceal his plagiarism or to maintain the coherence of his own book. In addition, he changed the order of the recipes that he took from Nola and alternated them with other recipes from different sources.[16] Granado's book is considerably more extensive than Nola's, containing 755 recipes compared to Nola's 242. However, Granado also included material taken from a second work, again without citing it, Bartolomeo Scappi's 1570 *Opera dell'arte del cucinare*, which Granado translated from Italian into Spanish. It has been established that more than five hundred of the recipes included in Diego Granado's *Arte de cocina* are translations from Scappi's work. As with Nola's book, Granado seems to have tried to conceal his plagiarism by eliminating seasonal references that appeared in the Italian work, adding or deleting ingredients, and sometimes changing the order in which the information is provided.[17]

Despite these obvious shortcomings, Granado's book enjoyed moderate success among readers for about a decade. But this came to an end when a royal cook by the name of Francisco Martínez Montiño published his own cookbook in 1611, harshly attacking Granado's work. Although he did not mention Granado by name, Martínez Montiño is clearly referring to Granado in the prologue to his book, *Arte de cocina*, when he describes the need for good books on the subject of court cooking and specifically mentions that he had read one that was "so flawed that whoever uses it will be ruined. It is composed by an official that hardly anyone at this Court knows," and of the recipes it contains, "not only are they not good, nor should they be made but furthermore it was impertinent to write them at all."[18] After Martínez Montiño's scathing criticism, Diego Granado's prestige vanished, and his *Libro del arte de la cocina* was quickly forgotten.

For today's readers, it is difficult to objectively evaluate Granado's true intentions when composing his book, especially when taking into consideration that the concepts of imitation and originality were more fluid during the sixteenth century and the notion of plagiarism was not clear-cut, with authors commonly "borrowing" elements from previous texts as part of their own creative process. Ultimately, perhaps Diego Granado's best contribution to Spanish culinary history may in fact be his translation of Bartolomeo Scappi's great work and the resulting introduction of the Italian author's innovative cuisine to Spain, with dishes and ingredients previously unknown in the Iberian Peninsula.

LIBRO DEL ARTE DE COCINA, BY DOMINGO HERNÁNDEZ DE MACERAS (1607)

Domingo Hernández de Maceras was the cook of the Colegio Mayor de San Salvador de Oviedo at the University of Salamanca, where he worked for forty years before publishing his cookbook. The *colegio* was a university residence for students of very limited means who were given a scholarship that included room and board. Hernández de Maceras's book is unique in that it provides valuable information about the cooking done at an institution like Salamanca's Colegio Mayor, which, since the goal was to feed students on a budget, tells us a great deal about the everyday cooking of the time.

The book shows how cooking was done when using economic ingredients to make the most of what was available. Hernández de Maceras is not concerned with the food of the royal court, portrayed by so many other books of the time; rather, he presents the cuisine of the masses, made with simple, yet nutritious, ingredients assembled in practical ways. He also includes meals appropriate to the season, providing heavier dishes for the winter and lighter fare for the summer, even detailing meal times and how they changed according to the seasons.

A very complete work, the book includes recipes for meat, fish, desserts, eggs, and stews, as well as many specific recipes for Lent. There are also traditional

Castilian recipes, some of which are still eaten today, such as rice pudding or roast lamb, though others have been forgotten, as in the case of lettuce stuffed with lamb or pigeon pie. The author also provides a recipe for the classic dish *olla podrida* (a rich stew that literally translates as "rotten pot"), made by slowly cooking several kinds of meat, such as lamb, beef, pig's feet, even hare, together along with chickpeas, turnips, and garlic. As Ken Albala notes, *olla podrida* is one of the few recipes that is found, with some variation, in almost all European cookbooks from this period.[19]

ARTE DE COCINA, PASTELERÍA, VIZCOCHERÍA, Y CONSERVERÍA, BY FRANCISCO MARTÍNEZ MONTIÑO (1611)

Martínez Montiño (or Motiño), author of the *Art of Cooking, and Making Pastry, Biscuits and Conserves*, worked as a cook at the court of King Felipe III. His book, which was reedited profusely during the seventeenth, eighteenth, and even the nineteenth century, has been called "the *summa teologica*" of baroque cooking[20] and was enormously influential in Spanish cuisine. In Ken Albala's view, "Aesthetically, Montiño appears to be focusing and refining Spanish cuisine, giving it an energy and directness that is not unlike Spanish Baroque Painting."[21] The *Arte de Cocina* not only includes recipes but also discusses matters related to how food should be served at the table and includes great detail about the ideal composition of royal menus. Martínez Montiño shows great awareness about the material benefits and prestige that cooking as a profession could yield at the time, providing access to circles of power and the opportunity to gain the esteem and confidence of monarchs and influential members of the court. In truth, the benefits for a valued and socially well-placed cook were countless. Martínez Montiño's book was meant for those wishing to make cooking their profession, assuring them that they, too, could become highly regarded professionals if they followed his example and the teachings of his book.

In his prologue to the *Arte de Cocina*, the author states his motivation to write the book, noting that

> there are no books by which those who serve the kitchen can turn to for guidance, and everything is entrusted to memory. . . . And what has encouraged me to write is to have served so many years to His Majesty the King, and to have been charged with the greatest things my art can produce, which have been offered in the royal palace, to the satisfaction of my chiefs; and because I am very inclined to teach, and great officials have developed under my tutelage.[22]

Martínez Montiño's cooking was intended for the court and was aimed at pleasing the palate of kings and cardinals. Even though he declares in one instance that he is not fond of "fantastic dishes" and that most of the dishes he presents are fairly simple, others are sophisticated and even outlandish, as in the case of following recipe for "young deer antler tips":

> The antlers of the deer when they are covered with hair have very tender tips. These must be cut in a manner that the tender part is toward the tip, and peel them in hot water, and they will turn very white, and they have to be prepared like the gut of the deer, except that they do not get roasted, but instead cooked with a little broth, and seasoned with pepper and ginger, and throw a little bit of fresh butter; and with this they cook for an hour; and it is not to be curdled with eggs, nor is it to be added any vegetables. It is a very good dish, only its name is bad.[23]

Martínez Montiño includes numerous recipes for cooking a variety of meats, some not commonly accessible to the majority of the population, such as boar, capon, duck, turkey, Cornish hens, lamb, pork, and even frogs and pigeons. There are also numerous recipes for empanadas stuffed with meat or fish, as well as a recipe for *alcuzcuz* (couscous), an Arabic dish that would disappear from Spanish cooking manuals in successive centuries. The variety of dishes compiled by Martínez Montiño provides for interesting contrasts, ranging from the humble *sustancia de pobres* ("sustenance for the poor") to *albondiguillas Reales* ("royal meatballs"), a dish no doubt better suited to the tastes of the royal court.

NUEVO ARTE DE COCINA, SACADO DE LA ESCUELA DE LA EXPERIENCIA ECONÓMICA, BY JUAN DE ALTAMIRAS (1745)

Juan de Altamiras's *Nuevo arte de cocina* (New art of cooking) is one of the most important works of Spanish conventual cooking and for centuries was an important resource for both cooks and cookbook authors. The name Altamiras (sometimes spelled "Altimiras") is actually the pseudonym of Raimundo Gómez, a Franciscan monk who was chef for the convent of San Diego in Zaragoza. Because the Franciscans were a charitable order that worked to help feed the poor, this book provides an insightful portrait into eighteenth-century popular cooking, removed from the sometimes-extravagant cuisine found in other cookbooks of this period.

For the most part, Altamiras's books presents simple dishes, such as stews and stuffed vegetables, drawn from the author's own experience, as mentioned in the title, and with an emphasis on frugality and affordability. As Altamiras states in his prologue, "It is not my intention to write about exquisite ways to cook, since there are already many books given to light by the cooks of the monarchs, but the execution of their teachings is costly, as if dictated by a silver tongue; rather, in this one the golden tongue of charity can be heard."[24] This distinction made by the author between the cooking style of the court and that of monasteries is significant since it emphasizes the distance that existed between the two. The cuisine of the royalty and the nobility, referenced here by the mention of the "golden tongue," was clearly not that of the commoners. Instead, Altamiras presents simple, inexpensive dishes, making the *Nuevo arte de cocina* a most valuable source of information on the dietary habits of the general population in eighteenth-century Spain, not just within the walls of convents and monasteries but also outside them. As María de los Ángeles Pérez Samper points out, contrary to court cuisine, which was out of reach for the majority of people, the products and cooking methods used in religious institutions were a much better reflection of those used by popular classes.[25] This is exemplified by Altamiras's own admonitory words, when he reminds his audience to "always think about how to employ what is left over, because it is often useful for something else, and the poor (following Christ's example, who after having fed five thousand men, asked to gather what was left) must make use of everything."[26]

The book's many references to monastic life and the precepts of different religious orders, as well as the numerous dishes for Lent, leave no doubt that the book was written by someone living in a cloistered religious environment. Nevertheless, the book's personal style reveals its author to be a most intelligent and kind person with a deep knowledge of not only culinary matters but also human nature. The book is full of warnings and advice about the cleanliness, good sense, and honesty required of a good cook, especially in a monastery. Altamiras also exhibits a wonderful sense of humor in his comments, such as when giving the formula for a drink made from barley, he shares the following advice and thoughts: "It is good for those who study a lot, because it is fresh, according to the opinion of many. Good reward for studying, to eat barley, and food of a rare quality, to be common to both wise men and asses."[27] Another example of this wit can be seen in the comments accompanying a peculiar recipe for "Almondiguillas de ranas" ("frog meatballs"):

> You will remove the meat from the legs, and chop it finely with parsley and some yolks from hard-boiled eggs, so that they bulge. Then you will take some breadcrumbs, and cheese, in a small proportion, not so much that it is too noticeable. You will mix the chopped meat with raw eggs, season with salt, and all the spices, and you will make the meatballs, without touching them with your hand. You will have a mold to make them, and if it is easier [use] a vessel, wetting it in warm water from time to time. You will take the meat in the amount you want inside the cup, and moving it, the meatball will be made perfectly, and not even the tidiest nun is excused from this diligence, even if you have the cleanest: keep an eye on the flies, you will not have little to do, do not let the dough grow with them; I hope my warning does not bug any of them. You will prepare a broth, if possible, made of fish or at the very least with chickpeas; throw the meatballs in the boil, and with a couple of boils they will be cooked. Make a sauce with egg yolks or hazelnuts, and serve the meatballs with a little broth.[28]

Altamiras's book is a product of its time, and as such it illustrates the gastronomic legacy to which it belongs as well as the variety of influences that give Spanish cuisine its unique character. The Arabic influences, for example, are evident in the frequent use of spices such as cinnamon or saffron. New World products also appear, with several dishes using chocolate, potatoes, or tomatoes—a somewhat novel ingredient in Spain at the time—and there are even some brief instructions on how to preserve tomatoes all year by submerging them in olive oil. Among the recipes featuring tomatoes as an ingredient is the following peculiar one that combines poultry and fish, where Altamiras also recommends removing the skin of the tomatoes by roasting them:

Roasted partridges with sardines

After cleaning well the partridges, put two sardines inside the body of each one, in a manner that they don't come out, roast with good pork lard, and if you do not have any, fry bacon and throw it on the partridges, with some tomatoes without skin; to remove it, throw them into the coals. If you do not have tomatoes, add some lemon juice, or orange, with a bit of pepper, salt, a little parsley; and when they are roasted, take out the sardines: serve the partridges, which will always keep the taste of the sardines.

ARTE DE REPOSTERÍA, BY JUAN DE LA MATA (1747)

The Art of Confectionery, by Juan de la Mata (or Juan de Mata), was published in Madrid in 1747 and features on its first page the official approval of Domingo Fernández, the king's pastry chef at the time. Juan de la Mata's cookbook features not only traditional Spanish specialties but also those of French, Portuguese, Flemish, and Italian origin, with the author acknowledging the influences of these countries and their importance as confectionary trendsetters at the time. The *Arte de repostería* appears to borrow heavily at times from Francois Massialot's *Nouvelle instruction pour les confitures, les liqueurs et les fruits* (1692), although it also contains original work such as its chapter on gazpachos (cold soups).[29] Among de la Mata's recipes is the following recipe for gazpacho, which is very different from the modern cold summer soup that is typical today of Andalusia and known throughout the world. As de la Mata's recipe shows, in its early forms gazpacho did not have any New World ingredients such as tomatoes or peppers:

Take the crusts of a one-pound loaf of bread, without the crumbs, toast them and soak in water: afterwards put them in their sauce, composed of anchovy bones, and a couple of cloves of garlic, well ground, with vinegar, sugar, salt, and oil, all thoroughly mixed, letting the bread soften in the garlic. Then put it all on the plate, adding all or some of the ingredients and vegetables of the royal salad.[30]

Arte de repostería is a more specialized and comprehensive work than previous cookbooks and focuses on confectionery and cake making, as well as on recipes for a variety of sweets popular at the time. The book includes no less than twelve different recipes for marzipans and twenty-eight for biscuits, along with instructions to make preserves with many kinds of fruits, as well as pickles, sauces, and even salads.[31] Numerous foods from the New World are mentioned in this work, such as citrons (*"cidras de Indias"*), chocolate, and tomatoes, showing how the red fruit had slowly become popular in European cuisine, going from being a botanical curiosity to a commonly eaten food. Interestingly, the first written recipe for a sauce made from tomatoes had appeared in 1692 in *Lo Scalco alla Moderna*, by the Italian author Antonio Latini, a recipe for tomato sauce he called *"alla espagnuola"* ("Spanish style"). Latini lived in Naples, which was ruled by Spain at the time, where he worked at the service of Cardinal Antonio Barberini and the first minister to the Spanish Viceroy of Naples, Don Stefano Carillo Salcedo. More than fifty years later, Juan de la Mata published this first recipe for tomato sauce in a Spanish cookbook, *"salsa de tomates á la Española"* ("tomato sauce Spanish style), to be prepared in the following manner:

> After baking three or four tomatoes, and removing their skin, chop them on a table as finely as possible, then put them in the sauce boat and add a little parsley, onion and garlic, also chopped very finely, with a little salt, pepper, oil and vinegar; when everything is well mixed together, it may be served.[32]

This basic sauce is still used in many of Madrid's dishes, accompanying such foods as snails, potatoes, and cod. De la Mata also includes a second recipe (titled *"Otra manera,"* "another way"), featuring different spices—cumin and oregano—and stating that there are many other types of tomato sauces widely used, according to people's tastes. He claims that this is so common in fact that he does not deem it necessary to even include them in his cookbook.[33]

De la Mata describes the common custom of dying fruits using flowers and vegetables,[34] exhibiting great familiarity with fresh fruits, their growing conditions and season, and how to best use and preserve them, as well as providing many recipes for fruit jams. He writes at length about apricots, praising their suitability for being made into preserves:

> Nobody is unaware of the shape, size and color of apricots: it is one of the least respected Fruits; but in the use of preserves, both liquid and dry, it rightly occupies one of the highest places. They are excellent for garnishing and decorating a dessert, with their colorful variety, particularly those which come in bunches. The early apricots, which last from June until the end of July, have white flesh; but not because of this are they better than the yellow ones, which do not come until the middle of this latter month. Make them into compotes, and like this they are at their best. The fire and sugar lend them a gentle fragrance, which is not there when they are uncooked.[35]

LA COCINA MODERNA, ANONYMOUS (1875)

This book, as well as augmented editions published in the following years under the title *La cocina moderna perfeccionada* (Modern cuisine improved), was extremely popular during the nineteenth century, with at least fourteen editions published in relatively few years. It is a work of very wide scope, although as was common during this period and as the fact that it is an unsigned work suggests, it was probably created by copying from other sources, most likely some of the many French cookbooks in circulation at the time. *La cocina moderna* provides recipes for numerous dishes, from soups to eggs, meat, fish, and vegetables, as well as pastries and confectionery. It claims to include recipes by "the most famed cooks, Spanish and foreign,"[36] as well as advice on topics like household economics and gardening.

It appears to be a typical work of the time, heavily indebted to other Spanish and French works. Encyclopedic in scope and length, it is a substantial volume with hundreds of recipes, sections on food preservation, methods to make ice cream and liquors, descriptions of kitchen utensils and how to use them, and information on how to properly set a table and how to carve different kinds of meats, from poultry to lamb and beef, as well as numerous drawings. The augmented, or "perfected," edition of the book adds a long list of home remedies for everything from burns to hair loss, removing stains, and even instructions for making invisible ink, catching mice, and a section on the care of domestic plants—so detailed that it even incudes their scientific names.

Among the many dishes listed in this volume we find this early recipe for Valencian paella, a dish that was becoming popular beyond its region of origin and throughout the country, popularized even further in places like Madrid by cookbooks like this one. This particular recipe lists some notably unusual, if optional, ingredients:

Valencian Paella

Place a frying pan on a stove that has a charcoal or firewood fire; pour oil or a proportionate amount of lard, and when it is very hot fry a few peppers in it, and remove them after frying. Immediately fry some pieces of chicken, duck, pork loin and sausage, and when they are golden, put three or four cloves of garlic, cut and diced, tomato, parsley, red pepper, salt, saffron and a little pepper. Stir all this until well fried, then put artichokes, green peas or green beans, stir everything well until it is cooked, and then add broth or hot water and allow to boil until everything is cooked. Turn up the fire and increase the amount of broth, and when it is boiling, add the rice and bring to a boil, adding the peppers, pieces of eel, other types of fish, or frogs, if desired. Bring to a medium boil and let cook without touching or stirring. When it is ready, remove from the fire, let rest for a few minutes, and serve. It should be noted that the rice should not be undone, nor fully cooked. Some also add a few well-washed snails when they put the eels in.[37]

EL PRACTICÓN, BY ÁNGEL MURO (1894)

A Madrid-born engineer, gastronome, and journalist, Ángel Muro Goiri (1839–1897) became well known in Madrid as a journalist and a gourmand and for his writings combining his interests of food and cooking. A friend of other writers also interested in food, such as Emilia Pardo Bazán and Benito Pérez Galdós, Muro first achieved notoriety for a series of newspaper articles under the title "*Conferencias culinarias*" (Culinary essays), which he published monthly between 1892 and 1895. They were enormously popular at the time and remain of interest to readers today, as they contain a wealth of information about tastes and cooking trends in nineteenth-century Spain. In 1892, he published *Diccionario general de cocina*, a two-volume gastronomic dictionary containing thousands of entries on different dishes, ingredients, and other food-related topics. Muro's best-known work, however, is without question *El practicón*, a cookbook of more than eight hundred pages first published in 1894 but so successful that by 1929, it had been reedited thirty-five times, becoming a classic of Spanish cuisine and the main reference for Spanish chefs, both professionals and home cooks, until the 1930s.

Muro's knowledge of Spanish cuisine and his specific influence on the gastronomy of Madrid are undeniable, as was his passion for the subject. In the prologue to *El practicón*, he criticizes what he views as his fellow Spaniards' attitude of "eat to live," as opposed to "live to eat," and emphasizes the need to set aside French influences to appreciate instead the "sober" Spanish cuisine: "Our beloved Spain, with its variety of terrains and climates that make its territory fertile in excess, is the country that offers the greatest products to provide its people with the best diet."[38]

Muro believed that Spain's autochthonous cuisines had great potential in their own right, and he made it his mission to encourage his fellow citizens to embrace the many treasures of the Spanish culinary heritage. With that goal in mind, he composed his *Practicón*, a book containing hundreds of recipes but also a wealth of practical information—hence its title—about food and cooking. It is written in a humorous and sometimes opinionated tone, with the author often interspersing personal opinions on a variety of topics, such as when he decries "the disrespectful and dirty habit of smoking at the table while you are eating. . . . I find it rude that some will fill the room where food is being enjoyed with smoke and cause the delicacies to soak the smell of tobacco, which is generally very bad."[39] The book is a well-structured and very thorough work, following the style of preceding classic Spanish cookbooks such as Martínez Montiño's *Arte de cocina* and Enrique de Villena's *Arte cisoria*. Muro's book contains sections on how to carve different types of meat and fish, appropriate table manners, the proper ways to serve food and use silverware and napkins, and which foods are acceptable to eat with your hands—and which are not—among other etiquette topics. The author also comments on the quality of the products available in Madrid, complaining about the sale of fraudulent meat in the streets of the city and calling for better government control on such foods:

> In Madrid, all of us, unknowingly, eat, or have eaten, or will eat, donkey passing as beef, and when I say donkey, I say also mule and horse, but not in the conditions in which all this is eaten abroad, out in the open and under the inspection and guarantee of the authorities, but in a sneaky way, fraudulently. . . . Because there is no doubt; in Madrid, Barcelona and in other large centers of population, healthy horses die daily by accident or are killed, whose meat is not going to be thrown to the garbage pile, and it is not, having so much consumption of cheap salchichón [sausage] in these places that it would be impossible to manufacture it with the meat of all the pigs from five slaughters put together.[40]

LA COCINA ESPAÑOLA ANTIGUA, BY EMILIA PARDO BAZÁN (1913)

La cocina española antigua (Traditional Spanish cuisine) and *La cocina española moderna* (Modern Spanish cuisine), published five years later in 1917, were both written by one of Spain's finest novelists, Emilia Pardo Bazán (1851–1921). Born to a Galician noble family, she inherited the title of Countess of Pardo Bazán, and she received a progressive education, unusual for women at the time but encouraged by her father, who believed in the rights of women and allowed her access to his extensive library from an early age. Pardo Bazán attended a French school in Madrid and became fluent in English, French, and German, as well as being well versed in numerous matters from the humanities to the sciences. A frequent visitor to France, where she met other European writers of the time such as Victor Hugo, Pardo Bazán is credited with introducing Émile Zola's naturalist movement in Spanish literature. A true intellectual, she was also a feminist and in 1892 founded the Biblioteca de la Mujer (Women's Library), a publication series aimed at spreading in Spain the feminist ideas already taking hold in the rest of Europe. In 1913, however, disappointed by the poor reception of these ideas and the blatant indifference of Spanish society toward feminist issues, she decided to publish a cookbook, *La cocina española antigua*, cleverly reflecting on the irony of her choice in the book's prologue. Nevertheless, she produced a remarkable cookbook that is, on the one hand, a comprehensive catalog of all the regional cuisines of Spain and, on the other, full of erudition and a reflection of her vast knowledge. Pardo Bazán's intellectual approach to food is evidenced by her emphasis on the importance of cooking as a discipline connected to anthropology, stating that eating habits can reveal more about a culture than "other inquiries of a scientific nature" and adding that "there are dishes in our national cuisine that are no less interesting or historical than a medal, a weapon, or a tomb."[41]

La cocina española antigua and its sequel, *La cocina española moderna*, were important books that became very well known in their time. They contain a vast array of Spanish recipes and provide invaluable information on Spain's eating habits and traditions at the beginning of the twentieth century. The first of the two volumes is by far the superior work, where the author shows her remarkable knowledge of both the Spanish and foreign culinary bibliography, referring to classic cookbooks such as Martínez Montiño's *Arte de cocina* but also to those of her contemporaries, such as Ángel Muro's *El Practicón*, Picadillo's *La cocina práctica* (Practical cuisine), and a very popular Basque cookbook of the time, *La mesa vizcaína* (The Biscayne table) by Mrs. Dolores Vedia de Uhagon. Pardo Bazán also includes recipes from some of the most renowned Spanish chefs at the time, such as Melquiades Brizuela and Ignasi Doménech, as well as others taken from novels and old cooking manuals. She even includes several recipes given to her by other well-known writers, as in the case of her friend Benito Pérez Galdós, who often incorporated scenes in his novels portraying Madrileños' eating habits. She borrows this classic recipe for cooking cod from Pérez Galdós:

Desalt good, white and thick codfish for six hours. Clean it well and instead of cutting it into pieces, cut into thin strips. Oil the inside of a silver or metal kettle that can be taken to the table, sprinkle it with breadcrumbs and place the fish strips in the dish. Cover with breadcrumbs, chopped parsley and some oil. Repeat the operation creating another layer and until forming a kind of cake of some thickness. Finish with another layer of breadcrumbs, soaked in oil, and cook the cake in the oven at medium temperature for one hour.[42]

La cocina española antigua includes recipes from literary works, from *Don Quixote* and other texts by Miguel de Cervantes to Tomás de Iriarte's *Fables*, from which Pardo Bazán copies a recipe for eggs, to works by the Golden Age playwright Calderón de la Barca. Perhaps one of the most unusual recipes in Pardo Bazán's first cookbook is this one for *Guisado particular* (peculiar stew), which lists seventeen different birds among its ingredients. A seemingly impossible dish to put together, the author herself declares it a decadent and "barbaric" dish, reminiscent of the most extravagant banquets of ancient Rome:

Guisado particular [Peculiar stew]

Stuff a good olive with capers and chopped anchovies, and after marinating it in oil, place it into an oropendola or any other small bird whose delicacy is known, and place it later into another big bird, like an ortolan. Then take a crested lark, removing its legs and head, so that it serves as cover for the others, and cover it with a slice of very thin bacon, and put the crested lark inside a thrush, hollowed in the same manner; put the thrush inside a quail, the quail inside a lapwing, this in a sparrow or plover, which will be put in a bird-shot, and this in a woodcock; this in a teal, which goes inside a guineafowl; the guineafowl inside a duck, and this in a cock; the cock in a pheasant, which will be covered with a goose, all of which will be put into a turkey, which will be covered with a bustard, and if by chance you find any empty space to fill, resort to some testicles, chestnuts and mushrooms to make a filling, and everything is put in a pot of sufficient capacity with chopped onions, cloves, carrots, chopped ham, celery, a bundle of fresh herbs, ground pepper, some slices of bacon, spices and one or two heads of garlic. All this is cooked over the fire for twenty-four hours, or better in a hot oven. It is then degreased and served on a plate.[43]

Emilia Pardo Bazán's cookbooks were written with several goals in mind, perhaps most important that of contributing to the development of the concept of a Spanish national cuisine by preserving and extolling the value of its traditional dishes while rejecting the French influences that, in her opinion, had long "contaminated" Spanish cuisine. Although both of her cookbooks include dishes from every region of Spain, they appear under the wider label of "*cocina española*" (Spanish cuisine). In doing so, Pardo Bazán was vindicating the need for a sense of national pride in an era when Spain still suffered from a certain inferiority complex with respect to neighboring France. As the author vehemently states, "Each nation has the duty to preserve what makes it different and what is part of its own way of being. It is all well and good to know how to cook in French, Italian, and even Russian and Chinese style, but the basis of our table, by natural law, has to fall on what is Spanish."[44]

LA NUEVA COCINA ELEGANTE ESPAÑOLA, BY IGNASI DOMÉNECH (1915)

La nueva cocina elegante española (The new elegant Spanish cuisine), by Catalan author Ignasi Doménech i Puigcerós (1874–1956), is just one of the more than thirty cookbooks published by this prolific author over the course of his career. Doménech was a professional cook who acquired extensive work experience cooking fo· diplomats and members of the nobility in Madrid, such as the Dukes of Medinaceii and the Marquise of Argüelles, as well as in other European cities like Paris and London; for members of the European aristocracy, such as the Prince of Wrede, the Baron of Wedel, and English diplomat and conservative politician Sir Henry Drummond Wolff; and for the embassies of England, Norway, and Sweden. His influence on other cooks in both Madrid and other parts of the country is unquestionable.

Aside from his work as a chef, he was an indefatigable teacher, editor, and cookbook author. Doménech seemingly wrote about every possible aspect and style of cooking, becoming one of the most respected Spanish cookbook authors of his time. Among his many works are *Arte del coctelero europeo* (Art of the European cocktail, 1911), *La cocina vegetariana moderna* (Modern vegetarian cuisine, 1923), *Un festín en la edad media* (A medieval feast, 1913), *La cocina vasca* (Basque cuisine, 1935), *Cocina de recursos: Deseo mi comida* (Resourceful cooking: I want my food, 1941), *160 platos de arroz* (160 rice dishes, 1930), *El cocinero americano* (The American cook, 1917), and *La guía del gastrónomo y del maître d'hotel* (Guide for gastronomes and head waiters, 1917). His books introduced Spaniards to exotic ingredients and dishes from all over the world, but they also reveal his deep knowledge of Spain's own regional cuisines. While living in Madrid, Doménech ran a professional cooking school for several years while also funding and directing two cooking magazines: *La cocina elegante* (The elegant cuisine), which was only published from 1904 to 1905, immediately followed in 1906 by the longer-lived *El gorro blanco* (The white hat).

His 1915 *La nueva cocina elegante española* is a major work that provides a fascinating portrayal of haute Spanish cuisine at the beginning of the twentieth century. Almost five hundred pages long, the book's comprehensive nature is reminiscent of the classic recipe manuals of previous centuries. As the author states in the prologue, this was not "just one more cookbook—and please forgive the lack of modesty of this assertion—it is the minimum product of thirty years of consecutive work."[45]

Opinionated and extremely proud of his work, Doménech writes at length about the importance of culinary arts and the long history of his profession, emphasizing the value of cookbooks as major contributions to the progress and well-being of humankind. He includes sections on "culinary vocabulary," "general ideas on the good government of a kitchen," and "directions for a kitchen and the proper way to set the table," in which he explains different cooking techniques and gives advice on proper dining etiquette, ranging from wine pairings to the order in which dishes must be served and even to the decoration of the dining room and table, specifying that

> the dining room must have high ceilings, have good lighting and be ventilated. That the views you have are pleasant, and that you should avoid that your windows look west so that the sun does not disturb the diners when you eat in the afternoon. . . . In the places where the ladies sit, cushions will be placed so they can support the feet.[46]

As this much attention to detail suggests, the recipes included in the book are highly cosmopolitan and sophisticated, reflecting not the popular cuisine of Spain at the time but the high cuisine enjoyed by the aristocracy of Madrid and other

European cities. The following menu, which Doménech designed and served at a banquet for the Baron of Wedel, ambassador of Sweden and Norway in Madrid, shows the type of meals fashionable among the European upper classes at the beginning of the twentieth century:

Menu of a Great Meal

Oysters with lemon
Chicken Consommé à la Princess
Crab Bisque Cream
Small Game Puff Pastries Cumberland Style
King Prawns à la Neva
Steak a la Richelieu
Foie-Gras à la Victor Hugo
Artichoke hearts à la Mornay
Roasted *pulardas* (fattened hens) garnished with woodcocks
Goyesca salad
Ice Cream Puerto Rico
Savarin Singapore*
Chester cake
Candies
Desserts

*yeast cake moistened with syrup[47]

GUÍA DEL BUEN COMER ESPAÑOL, BY DIONISIO PÉREZ (1929)

Dionisio Pérez was a writer and historian who signed his gastronomic books under the pseudonym Post-Thebussem in reference to Mariano Pardo de Figueroa, a nineteenth-century Spanish gastronomic writer who used the pen name Thebussem (*embuste*, or "lie," spelled backward). Pérez worked for the Patronato de Turismo (Spain's tourist office) and was named honorary president of the Asociación Profesional de Cocineros de Cataluña (Professional Cooks' Society of Catalonia). The Spanish government commissioned his *Guía del buen comer español* (Guide of good Spanish eating) as a tourism promotional tool, and it provides a fairly complete panorama of Spain's regional cuisines, presenting the traditional dishes of each region of the country—always with a tone of high praise and in advantageous comparison to French cuisine. He also includes historical information about the origin of many dishes, though unfortunately these details are often inaccurate and unsupported by references.

Pérez's lack of objectivity about Spanish cuisine, pervasive throughout the entire book, is perhaps the book's biggest weakness. The author occasionally launches into ill-informed diatribes against French cuisine, attributing to Spain the creation of many of France's best-known dishes, such as consommé, duck foie, or the use of truffles in poultry dishes. He provides no proof or documentation for these assertions, and in some cases he seems to be merely echoing false myths without checking their veracity.

With regard to Madrid's cuisine, Pérez characterizes it as clearly divided into two different types: on the one hand, a high cuisine of the court and aristocracy, with strong French influence, and, on the other, the cuisine "of the people," which he considers authentically Madrileño. As an example of typical dishes of this "genuinely" Madrileño cuisine, he mentions *cocido,* garlic soup, dry beans *"a lo Tío Lucas,"* roasted suckling pig, roasted lamb, and marzipan from the nearby town of Toledo.[48]

LA COCINA COMPLETA, BY MARÍA MESTAYER DE ECHAGÜE (1940)

A fascinating figure and author of several books on cooking and gastronomic history, María Mestayer de Echagüe (1878–1956), better known by her pseudonym of Marquise of Parabere, was born in the northern city of Bilbao, the daughter of the French consul in Spain and granddaughter, on her mother's side, of a prominent Bilbao banker. Although Mestayer de Echagüe did not have any aristocratic titles, she was given permission to use the title Marquise of Parabere as a pen name by the real Marquis of Parabere, who was her husband's cousin. An excellent cook and avid entrepreneur, Mestayer de Echagüe opened two restaurants in Madrid during her time; though both were successful, they were doomed by their ill-fated historical circumstances, which eventually forced their closing. The first closed when the Spanish Civil War broke out in 1936. Parabere, her second business venture, opened in Madrid in 1941 and quickly became considered one of the best restaurants in the city, but its great reputation was not enough to survive the rough postwar years, when Spain was hard hit by food shortages and economic hardship.

Despite these setbacks, Mestayer de Echagüe, or the Marquise of Parabere, is a major star in the world of Spanish culinary literature. Her best-known cookbook is *La cocina completa* (The complete cuisine), a volume of more than nine hundred pages first published in 1933 that became highly popular and was reedited numerous times over the following decades. Given its popularity, the editions since the 1940s added *Enciclopedia culinaria* (Culinary encyclopedia) to the title, soon becoming the essential cooking reference book of its time. In the book's opening pages, the author declares that *La cocina completa* is the product of more than twenty years of work compiling and testing all its recipes. She also mentions receiving the approval of other important Spanish and French cooks of the time. The book is indeed a monumental and well-developed work, described by critic Manuel Martínez Llopis as "without question, the most complete book on cooking of this period."[49]

This tremendously successful book continues to be republished today with considerable success. Among its long catalog of recipes, it includes many that are genuinely Spanish, as well as others heavily influenced by French cuisine, as is the case with this peculiar way to prepare frogs' legs:

Ranas [Frogs]

Since frogs are considered for the effects of the vigils as fish, they are admitted, therefore, during the days of precept. Your best time is the months of March, April and May. Only the frogs' legs are edible, and since they are usually sold already stripped of the skin and strung on sticks, we will not detail here the disgusting operation of their vivisection. They have to be very fresh. If their skin is wrinkled and discolorated they should be discarded, as it is a sign that they are not fresh. How to prepare them: The nails or little claws are cut off and the legs are soaked, for an hour, with water and milk: for each liter of water, half of milk. After this time they are drained, dried with a cloth and put in a marinade, for another hour, with a little fine oil, lemon juice, chopped parsley, one crushed clove of garlic, salt and ground white pepper. From time to time they are turned so that they soak the marinade well. They are then well drained and dried with a dry cloth, because they do not fry well if they are wet.[50]

Mestayer de Echagüe's first cookbook, *Confitería y repostería* (1930), dealt exclusively with sweets and desserts and was also a best-seller; by 1964 it had reached its eleventh edition. In 1940, she published two more books: *Entremeses, aperitivos y ensaladas* (Hors d'oeuvres, appetizers, and salads) and *Conservas caseras: Hortalizas, fruta, pescados, carnes, caza, etc.* (Homemade preserves: Vegetables, fruit, fish, meat, game, etc.). In 1958, she published what would be her last cookbook, *Cocina vasca* (Basque cuisine). It is, however, in her 1943 *Historia de la gastronomía* (History of gastronomy)—not so much a cookbook as a treatise on the history of food and cooking—that her passion and vast knowledge on the subject become clear, citing classic authors, numerous cookbooks, and treaties on the topic of food, from Apicius to Martínez Montiño, from Brillat-Savarin to Escoffier and even her own contemporaries. Mestayer de Echagüe does not shy away from discussing controversial issues, such as the hypothetical superiority of male cooks over female ones or the role of foreign influences in Spanish cuisine. As for her vocation, Mestayer de Echagüe states:

This book is the result of my two passions; History and Gastronomy. I will say at once how I became fond of the latter: by the desire to dominate it. Without previous studies, with no practice whatsoever, using only good gastronomic publications, I went into the kitchen. . . . I built myself a good gastronomic library, collecting and preserving all the data, historical anecdotes and cookery studies that fell into my hands.[51]

She also declares the primacy of food against any questions or doubts that anyone might pose: "Many poets have sung the virtues of wine, but none of them has praised food, and if they have written about it, they did with a satirical purpose: *Trimalcion's Banquet*, by Petronio; *Gargantúa*, by Rabelais; *Wedding of Camacho*, by Cervantes." Showing indignation with regard to what she considers a hypocritical attitude, she adds, "In order to live, one must *eat*. By contrast, neither wine nor music are indispensable for it."[52]

RECETARIO DE LA SECCIÓN FEMENINA (1962)

The 1936–1939 Spanish Civil War marked the beginning of a dark era, characterized by the scarcity of basic supplies and food shortages, but when the economy eventually started to recover, the recovery ushered in some changes in eating habits. The publication of cookbooks by religious and political institutions under the Franco regime became an important vehicle for the government's efforts to indoctrinate women about their role in Spanish society. Cookbooks provided a subtle education tool, training women to become content and devoted mothers and housewives by instructing them on how to successfully run a household and prepare nutritious and economic meals for their families. To this end, the Francoist government published a number of cookbooks aimed at women through an organization called Sección Femenina, the women's section of Franco's political party, Falange Española, specifically in charge of maintaining the values that Spain's traditional Catholic society instilled in all women.

The role of women in Spain during the 1950s and 1960s was restricted to being "the angel of the home"—that is, the family's caregiver. The *Recetario de la Sección Femenina* (Sección Femenina cookbook) was a useful propaganda tool, containing hundreds of recipes to feed large families on a budget. For decades, it was found in virtually every household, and several generations of Spanish women learned to cook with it, hence its long-lasting impact on Spanish home cooking. The dishes included in this and other similar cookbooks were simple yet filling, with recipes that relied heavily on bread and flour, rice, pasta, potatoes, eggs, milk, and legumes such as chickpeas and lentils. It also contained numerous fish and meat dishes, with vegetables as sides. Above all, despite their propagandistic nature, Sección Femenina cookbooks emphasized the importance of thriftiness, showing ways of skillfully using leftovers and stretching small amounts of food to feed the typically big families of postwar Spain.

1080 RECETAS DE COCINA, BY SIMONE ORTEGA (1972)

The cookbook *1080 Recetas de cocina* (1,080 cooking recipes) was published during the final years of Francisco Franco's dictatorship (his death would occur in 1975, marking the beginning of a political transition to a democratic monarchy), the work of Simone Ortega Klein (1919–2008), a French-born woman who married into the family of the renowned Spanish philosopher José Ortega y Gasset. This unpretentious yet amazingly complete work delivers on what its title promises, listing the 1,080 recipes, as well as daily and weekly three-course menus to be adapted to each family's needs and preferences. This enormously successful cookbook has been republished numerous times since 1972 and continues to enjoy best-seller status, having sold more than two million copies. The reasons behind *1080 Recetas de cocina* becoming a classic cookbook owned by nearly every Spanish family include its simplicity, the vast number of recipes it includes, and the clarity of its explanations. According to Simone Ortega's daughter, Inés, her mother spent three years trying out every recipe from the book, making sure that each one turned out perfectly when prepared. This thorough attention to quality no doubt contributed to the success of the no-fuss cookbook, which is a straightforward work that contains no photos but dozens of different ways of preparing numerous ingredients, ranging from the basic to the complex. Ortega's cuisine occasionally reveals her French upbringing, though she definitely adapts it to Spanish tastes. Published in the 1970s, it is aimed primarily at middle-class housewives, always striving to offer economical ways to feed large families. All of this explains why Ortega's cookbook was considered for decades to be the "bible" for Spanish cooks and for a long time was commonly given to young newlyweds facing the daunting task of cooking for the first time in their own home in the absence of their mothers. In 2007, *1080 Recetas de cocina* was translated into English and published by Phaidon as *1080 Recipes*, with the assistance of both Simone Ortega and her daughter, Inés.

GASTRONOMÍA MADRILEÑA, BY JOAQUÍN DE ENTRAMBASAGUAS (1954)

Books focusing specifically on Madrid's cuisine began to appear during the second half of the twentieth century. Most of them approach the topic from a historical point of view, but some include references to specific dishes, as well as recipes for them. All acknowledge the debt that Madrid's food has to other Spanish regions and the city's character as a "melting pot," absorbing specialties and food traditions from every region of the country given the major role played by immigration in the growth and development of Madrid over the centuries.

A good example of such a cookbook is *Gastronomía madrileña*, published in 1954, one of the first books to give an account of the city's gastronomic history, accompanied by a list of genuine Madrid recipes. Its author, Joaquín de Entrambasaguas (1904–1995), was a university professor of Spanish literature and a native of Madrid. His book emphasizes Madrileños' passion for good food, something that he says has been greatly aided by the continuous arrival of people from every region of Spain. He also points out how the majority of products consumed in Madrid were brought in from somewhere else, with the exception of wine, for which he mentions several kinds produced in nearby towns within the Madrid region, among them the wines from Navalcarnero, Villa del Prado, and Getafe, as well as Chinchón's anisette, which is still produced and sold in Madrid today. Entrambasaguas mentions the high quality of all the products coming from every corner of Spain to the markets of Madrid, arriving "at the peak of their freshness and quality . . . as in a classic still life painting of all of Spain."[53]

Written as a historical work, *Gastronomía madrileña* contains abundant information about traditional dishes and restaurants from earlier periods, especially the nineteenth century. Restaurants such as Casa de Botín and Lhardy are mentioned, as are numerus typical dishes long associated with Madrid, for which Entrambasaguas provides recipes, including *cocido*, *soldaditos de pavía* (cod fritters), sea bream, trout, fried fish from the Jarama River (a delicacy impossible to obtain nowadays), white beans from Tío Lucas's tavern, *gallinejas* (fried sheep intestines), snails, and sweets such as custard-stuffed *bartolillos*, *churros*, and *buñuelos* (fritters). One of the most interesting recipes he provides uses two ingredients produced in small towns near Madrid, the "*Melón de Villaconejos al Chinchón*," consisting of combining melon from the town of Villaconejos with anisette from Chinchón in the following fashion:

> Choose a good melon from Villaconejos, wash the skin well and cut off the end on the less pointy side, so that it can stand upright on that end. Cut a hole on the other side to extract the seeds and "guts," but not the juice. Pour in Chinchón anisette, sweet or dry, according to taste, and let it cool in the refrigerator for at least two hours, shaking it occasionally so that the whole interior is evenly coated with the liquor. When it is cold enough, present it standing on its base on a glass dish. Bring to the table, cut into slices from top to bottom, and serve. It is best paired with a glass of sweet wine from Getafe, and it is excellent either to start a meal or at the end of it.[54]

OTHER BOOKS

Many other cookbooks were published in Spain during the nineteenth and twentieth centuries, though most focused on Spanish cuisine as a whole, certain regional cuisines such as Basque and Catalan, or a specific thematic approach. Some were more popular than others, such as *El cocinero español y la perfecta cocinera* (The Spanish [male] cook and the perfect [female] cook), by Guillermo Moyano, a work published in the southern city of Málaga in 1867 that became popular throughout the country. Another popular work with a number of editions was *Manual del cocinero* (Cook's manual), by Mariano de Rementería y Fica, published in 1837. *La cocina de la madre de familia* (A mother's cooking), by Matilde García del Real (1908), was written with the purpose of educating young women about household duties. Writer Carmen de Burgos also published three cookbooks, though they were commissioned works and were not especially original. None of these cookbooks was as popular as *Carmencita o la buena cocinera* (Carmencita of the good cook), by Eladia de Carpinell, published in Barcelona in 1899 and republished numerous times, becoming a favorite with cooks everywhere.

In 1987, José del Corral published *Ayer y hoy de la gastronomía madrileña* (Past and present of Madrid's gastronomy), a historical study and one of the first books to focus specifically on Madrid's cuisine. Other valuable works include *La cocina típica de Madrid* (Madrid's typical cuisine), by Manuel Martínez Llopis and with recipes by Simone Ortega, published in 1987, and one of the few books on this topic written in English, *Cocinando la historia: Curiosidades gastronómicas de Madrid / Cooking History: Gastronomic Curiosities of Madrid*, a bilingual book by José María Escudero Ramos published in 2011. This book features beautiful photos of Madrid's traditional establishments, accompanied by brief texts on the gastronomic history of the city. Lastly, in 2014 gastronomic historian Ismael Díaz Yubero published *Gastronomía de Madrid* (Madrid's gastronomy), a book of historical essays that includes a selection of recipes from Madrid. Many more cookbooks and historical works about the food of this fascinating city have appeared in recent years, portraying the strong ties of Madrileño cuisine to its past and rich legacy and its exciting evolution during the twenty-first century.

6

❖ ❖

Historic Restaurants, *Tabernas*, and Cafés

EATING IN MADRID: CLASSIC RESTAURANTS AND CONTEMPORARY POPULAR EATERIES

Madrid offers a vast array of culinary options ranging from traditional dishes to modern, trending cuisine. The city has welcomed people from all regions of Spain and numerous other countries for centuries. Madrid's cuisine today is the product of serving as Spain's cultural "melting pot," combining numerous influences, tastes, and cooking trends. As a meeting place for people from all over Spain, specialties from every region of the country may be enjoyed. The variety of eating establishments in the city is dazzling, ranging from *gastrobars* to *tabernas*, tapas bars, and restaurants, both traditional and avant-garde.

Spain's capital boasts a number of eating establishments more than one hundred years old, with some even nearing two centuries of existence. These classic locales are popular with both Madrileños and visitors, and they have become de facto custodians of Madrid's traditional cuisine, existing alongside newer restaurants led by energetic young chefs who have traveled the world and brought back cutting-edge techniques and brand-new ideas, combining the best of Spain's cuisine with a vast array of international influences. These traditional eateries strive to maintain Madrid's traditional cooking style, to successfully preserve old-fashioned dishes. Unfortunately, they are sometimes overlooked in favor of new locations practicing an inventive cuisine of modern influences and world fusion. Foodies and the media, constantly looking for new places and innovative dishes, often disregard older establishments that have managed to survive in a difficult market by offering consistent quality. These restaurants and taverns have been fixtures of Madrid's social life for years, and many key events in the city's history have taken place within their walls. In order to increase their visibility and promote appreciation for Madrid's "old-fashioned" cuisine, Madrid restaurants that are at least one hundred years old have founded an association, the Restaurantes y Tabernas Centenarios de Madrid (RCM),[1] which aims to increase awareness about the gastronomic assets of these unique establishments.

Food historians have noted how the Spanish Civil War marked a decisive "before" and "after" in the culinary history of Spain's capital. For example, after the war and the initial years of food rationing, a new type of gastronomic space emerged in Madrid called *cafeterías*. These were places that served coffee and quick bites but were very different from the cafés popular before the war, where customers would linger for hours over just one cup of coffee. *Cafeterías* were fast-paced and convenient, although the food they served was not particularly good. Taking inspiration from the concept of the American diner, a number of establishments with American-evocative names opened during the 1950s, such as Cafetería California and Cafetería Nebraska. The latter was so successful that several other locations opened throughout the city, which are, remarkably, still in operation today, offering American fare such as hamburgers, fries, and old-fashioned ice-cream sundaes.

While the postwar years were in general characterized by food scarcity and rationing, a small, privileged class of people with means and access to goods became customers of the few high-end restaurants in existence in Madrid at the time. The opening of Jockey, an upscale restaurant whose owner had worked at the Ritz hotel for more than twenty years and who had also apprenticed at some of the most prestigious restaurants in Europe, such as Maxim's in Paris and the Mayfair in London, was a major event in Madrid, quickly attracting a discerning clientele. Jockey became a legendary venue and was in operation from 1945 until 2012, catering for many decades to Spain's elite, counting King Juan Carlos among its regular customers, as well as numerous members of Spain's aristocracy. The restaurant also hosted glamorous visitors such as Grace Kelly and Frank Sinatra, as well as foreign dignitaries such as Richard Nixon and the shah of Iran. Styled as a traditional English gentlemen's club and recognized with a Michelin star, the restaurant catered the wedding of the current Spanish king—who was at the time crown prince—Felipe VI and Queen Letizia in 2004. Other than Jockey, there were few other truly upscale places in Madrid during the 1950s, with the notable exceptions of restaurants like Lhardy and Sobrino de Botín.

Many eateries that were affordable by the middle class opened during the 1940s and in the following decades. Rodilla, a popular restaurant chain specializing in sandwiches, got its start in 1939 when entrepreneur Antonio Rodilla opened a confectionery shop in Callao and ended up deciding to specialize in sandwiches, making his own English-style bread—which was different from the baguette-style bread commonly eaten in Spain. His shop quickly became popular, with new locations soon opening throughout Madrid. Today, Rodilla is still successful, boasting a total of seventy-two restaurants, which are very popular for breakfast or a midday coffee and snack, in different Spanish cities.

The 1960s saw a major wave of immigration from all over Spain to Madrid. This urban influx favored the rise of eating establishments catering to the working class at a time when eating out was becoming more common than ever. From business lunches to weekend dinners with a spouse or friends, Madrileños began eating out much more frequently. This new trend resulted in the opening of many restaurants, though for the most part the food served was plain and not of high quality. Some iconic places opened during this decade and the following one, however, such as El Lacón, which is beautifully decorated with hand-painted tiles and has served traditional Castilian food since its inception; today it is considered one of the best places for tapas in the city. Quality improved during the 1970s when several new, excellent restaurants opened, offering dishes made with high-quality products and better attention to detail. For example, in 1975 iconic Madrid restaurateur Lucio Blázquez opened Casa Lucio, a place known for a few simple but hearty dishes like *huevos rotos con chorizo* (broken fried eggs with chorizo). Casa Lucio has since become one of the most famous eateries in Madrid, a favorite with people from all walks of life, where it is not uncommon to spot celebrities from around the world, as well as members of Spanish royalty. Other restaurants of great reputation during the 1970s and still in operation today include Zalacaín (open since 1973 and still considered one of the best and most select places in the city), Horcher (a German restaurant that actually opened in 1943), and Viridiana (the brainchild of chef Abraham García and a reference to Madrid's fine dining for the last forty years). Historic restaurants from this era like El Amparo, El Bodegón, and La Dorada have sadly closed their doors in recent years.

The 1980s saw the arrival of American fast-food restaurant chains such as McDonald's and Burger King, many of which can be found today on Madrid's main streets and prominent tourist spots. In general, international restaurants were still uncommon in Spain until this decade, though some had opened timidly in the 1960s. One such place was a Chinese restaurant called House of Ming, which opened its doors in 1965 in the central Paseo de la Castellana at a time when Chinese food was considered exotic and was viewed as an exciting gastronomic adventure. For decades, House of Ming was one of the most refined restaurants in

Madrid, often frequented by the Spanish royal family and also by Hollywood stars of the 1960s, such as Ava Gardner and Anthony Quinn, during their visits to the city. This Madrid landmark closed its doors in 2007, and by then Chinese food was no longer exotic.

Among the most historically significant restaurants of Madrid today are Lhardy and Sobrino de Botín, institutions well known in Madrid, as well as on an international level. Together with Madrid's other centenary restaurants, they are the jewels of this food-obsessed city, featuring its most iconic dishes and keeping its traditions alive. Besides these historic restaurants, however, Madrid offers a multitude of eating options, ranging from the casual to the sophisticated featuring contemporary to avant-garde cuisine. Some feature Spanish fare, while others focus on world fusion and international dishes.

Every neighborhood has something interesting to offer in terms of food: The streets of the Cava Baja, in the La Latina neighborhood—one of the oldest parts in the city—are one of the most popular spots in Madrid for tapas and drinks and are especially lively on weekends; Calle Huertas and adjacent streets in the Las Letras neighborhood are filled with restaurants to please every taste and suit any budget; Calle Ponzano in the Chamberí area is currently one of the trendiest spots for cutting-edge cuisine at affordable prices; and the multicultural Lavapiés neighborhood is home to eateries from dozens of different nationalities, from Mexican to Senegalese to Indian. Other areas of the city, such as Malasaña, Chueca, the upscale Salamanca neighborhood, and the Gran Vía—at the very heart of Madrid—all offer an impressive array of great eateries to fit every budget. Places like the picturesque Museo del Jamón, with several locations in the center of the city, provide a great option for an affordable and delicious meal and the opportunity to try the famed *jamón serrano* in a unique atmosphere, surrounded by hundreds of cured hams hanging from every corner of the ceiling. Other Spanish chain restaurants, such as 100 Montaditos and Lizarrán, also offer quick bites at any hour of the day in the form of small slices of bread stacked with cheese, ham, or some other type of meat.

American fast-food chains are also ubiquitous in Madrid, from McDonald's and Burger King to Subway, Domino's Pizza, and Kentucky Fried Chicken, offering their regular fare but also serving beer. During the summer months, rooftop bars and restaurants are popular, with some of them, such as Azotea del Círculo on Calle Alcalá, offering beautiful views of the city to go with their chef-created menus. Finally, a number of restaurants are located in and around the historic Plaza Mayor, with outdoor seating, typical dishes, and, by virtue of being right on the busy square, fantastic opportunities for people watching.

HISTORIC RESTAURANTS

Lhardy

At the beginning of the nineteenth century, a young pastry chef named Émile Huguenin de Montbéliard, after learning this trade at Besançon, improved his cooking skills in Paris and then moved to Bordeaux, where he befriended French writer Prosper Mérimée, who apparently suggested that Huguenin open a restaurant in Madrid. It is not clear how Huguenin was renamed "Emilio Lhardy"—perhaps it was inspired by the name of a famous café in Paris, Café Hardy—but in 1839, Huguenin moved to Madrid and opened a pastry shop named Lhardy in the Carrera de San Jerónimo, then "the busiest street in the city,"[2] as novelist Benito Pérez Galdós wrote, though the street was not paved yet and at that point had no more than fifty houses.

According to different written accounts, at the beginning of the nineteenth century, the *fondas* of Madrid did not favorably impress international travelers (or even many countrymen). As the witty writer Mariano José de Larra pointed out, the gastronomic offerings were poor and the service was lousy: "A waiter for each room and a room for every twenty tables."[3] As previously noted, in the eighteenth century it was not customary for Madrileños to eat out often, and the meals served in most places were usually heavily seasoned with oil and garlic, not to the liking of foreign visitors; hence, for the international traveler, the opening of Lhardy was a welcome alternative.

The pastry shop eventually became a restaurant, catering to some of the most prominent personalities and events in Madrid, such as the inauguration of the Palace of the Marquis of Salamanca on the Paseo de Recoletos in 1858, the inauguration of the rail section of the Aranjuez-Alicante train, the inaugural banquet of the trams in Madrid in 1871, and the lunch offered in 1880 to the king Alfonso XII and his wife, Maria Cristina, in the Hall of Councils of the archbishop's palace of Alcalá de Henares.[4] Queen Isabel II was a regular at Lhardy, and it is rumored that she would often sneak out of the palace to secretly meet a romantic interest there. King Alfonso XII ate at the establishment so often that the phrase "I just saw the king; he was walking into Lhardy" became a common joke among Madrileños. Numerous Spanish writers frequented Lhardy over its long history, from Benito Pérez Galdós, Emilia Pardo Bazán, and Juan Valera to Ramón Mesonero Romanos and Nobel Prize–awardee Jacinto Benavente.

In 1885, Lhardy became one of the first establishments in Spain to install a telephone—Madrid had a total of forty-nine telephone home lines at that point—and this would mark the beginning of the idea of making reservations and ordering food for home delivery, a novelty at the time. Lhardy was ahead of the times also with regard to women's rights, being the first eating establishment in Madrid that allowed women to visit unaccompanied, unlike everywhere else, where women were required to be escorted by their husband or father.

Lhardy was the first true French-style "restaurant" in the capital, introducing both refined French confectionary and a catering service, the latter of which was a novelty that came to be in high demand among Madrid's wealthy class in the late nineteenth and early twentieth centuries. At the beginning of the twentieth century, aerostation had become a popular competitive sport for wealthy Spaniards, with several pilots in Madrid offering rides to wealthy customers as entertainment, giving them the opportunity to enjoy the thrill and excitement of flying over the city while admiring the views. On February 18, 1906, a balloon named *Cierzo*, manned by famous sportsman, automobile, and air pilot Jesús Fernández Duro, flew over the city carrying three passengers: Mr. Procopio Pignatelli, his sister Mrs. Natalia Lanz, and Mr. Alfredo Escobar y Ramírez, director of the newspaper *La Época* and Marquis of Valdeiglesias.[5] The marquis later wrote a detailed account of the event, relating how the balloon departed from Madrid and flew over a number of nearby towns such as Valdemoro, Getafe, Carabanchel, Villa del Prado, Navalcarnero, Parla, Fuenlabrada, and Torrejón, finally landing about five hours later near the town of Illescas, about twenty-two miles from Madrid. After reaching an altitude of two thousand meters (about sixty-five hundred feet), the pilot offered his passengers the opportunity to eat their lunch in flight, and they accepted. The food provided by Lhardy was exquisite, according to the marquis's account:

> Lhardy prepared the lunch with much care. The turkey in gelatin is tasty; the partridge cake, perfectly cooked; the roast beef bloody but marbled, and the ham flavorful. The Riscal wine and the Munn champagne pair well with the viands. And while the orange peels slowly fall, and the wrappers from the Marquise chocolates flutter around the balloon, Pignatelli has raised his glass to pronounce his customary toast "may the Spanish nation soon recover the prestige and preponderance which, they say, it had in former times."[6]

Embedded in Madrid's history like no other place, Lhardy hosted historical figures such as the renowned spy Mata Hari, who was in Madrid in 1916 conducting a secret mission and who, shortly after her stay in Spain, would be arrested and executed. Important political agreements and decisions took place within Lhardy's walls, especially in the beautiful "Japanese" dining salon, the favorite of Miguel Primo de Rivera, a dictator and military officer who was Spain's prime minister from 1923 to 1930 and who often met there with other government officials. It was in this salon that on November 2, 1931, the decision to offer Niceto Alcalá Zamora the position of president of the Spanish Republic was made.[7]

Today, Lhardy maintains the same style and decoration that has always set it apart and continues to host prominent visitors while still welcoming everyone. The restaurant still offers traditional and sophisticated specialties, such as *callos* (tripe), *cocido*, duck in orange sauce, and *riñones al jerez* (kidneys in sherry sauce).

Sobrino de Botín

What do seemingly disparate historical figures like the painter Francisco de Goya and the writers Ernest Hemingway, Benito Pérez Galdós, and Truman Capote have in common? In addition to their genius, the four frequented or mentioned in their works Sobrino de Botín, which is the world's oldest continuously operated restaurant according to the *Guinness Book of World Records.*[8] Founded in 1725, Sobrino de Botín is the essence of old Madrid and traditional Castilian cuisine. It was founded by the Frenchman Jean Botin, who married an Asturian woman and moved to Madrid. When they died without descendants, the business was inherited by their nephews, and the name Botín was changed to "Sobrino de Botín" ("Botín's nephew"). In 1930, the ownership of the premises passed to the González Martín family, which runs the restaurant to this day.

Sobrino de Botín remained open during the challenging years of the Spanish Civil War, run by a determined "grandfather Emilio," and on the outside one of the balconies even shows remnants of the battles that took place in the city, with one of the balcony's bars bent and damaged by shrapnel. The main witness of the continuity of the restaurant is its original oven, which, despite its many years, continues to roast the exquisite meat of suckling pig and lamb with oak wood in the traditional manner. The oven has never been turned off since the restaurant's beginning, with its embers lit twenty-four hours a day, seven days a week.

The restaurant, known to locals today simply as Botín, boasts four floors, with wooden beams spanning the ceilings and classic Spanish tiles decorating the floors. A converted wine cellar is now a dining room area, lined with arching brick walls, giving diners the opportunity to eat underground in a cave-like space. Located next to the steps of Arco de Cuchilleros (Cuchilleros's Arch), which lead to the Plaza Mayor, the city's main square and for centuries the commercial center of the city, Botín started out as an inn, similar to the many inns clustered around Plaza Mayor that provided food and lodging to visitors. The famous painter Goya is said to have worked there as a waiter and dishwasher in his younger days, and the inn became popular in the nineteenth century among bohemian and literary figures such as writer Valle-Inclán and painter Julio Romero de Torres. Botín appears in the novels of many authors, such as Benito Pérez Galdós and Ramón Gómez de la Serna, and in the plays of Carlos Arniches. Later, the English author Frederick Forsythe and American writers such as Graham Greene, James A. Michener, and

Ernest Hemingway would become frequent visitors and include the restaurant in their works. In particular, Hemingway described Madrid as "the most Spanish of all cities, the best to live in," and the one having "the finest people, month in and month out the finest climate."[9] He made frequent visits to Botín, even setting the last scene of his 1926 novel, *The Sun Also Rises*, in its main dining room: "We lunched up-stairs at Botin's. It is one of the best restaurants in the world. We had roast young suckling pig and drank *rioja alta*. Brett did not eat much. She never ate much. I ate a very big meal and drank three bottles of *rioja alta*."[10]

A frequenter of numerous Madrid taverns and restaurants, "Don Ernesto"—as Hemingway was known in Madrid—attracts such interest among tourists that some establishments now humorously distinguish themselves by hanging a sign on their door that reads "Hemingway never ate here." True fans of the American writer, however, can sign up for a "Hemingway tour" and visit the author's favorite haunts in the city, including places where he did eat and drink, such as Sobrino de Botín.

La Taberna de Antonio Sánchez

The history of La Taberna de Antonio Sánchez is steeped in the Spanish tradition of bullfighting, beginning with its founder and first owner, a picador—a bullfighter aide who rides a horse during the bullfight—named Colita ("pony tail"), who opened a small tavern in 1830. The tavern's name changed when Antonio Sánchez Ruiz became its owner in 1884, naming it after his son, Antonio Sánchez, a bullfighter who had been gored by bulls more than twenty times by the time he retired in 1929. During the first half of the twentieth century, the tavern was frequented by writers such as Nobel Prize–winner Camilo José Cela and renowned poet Gloria Fuertes, as well as painters such as Ignacio Zuloaga, a close friend of Antonio Jr.'s who would regularly meet there with other intellectuals for drinks and debates and whose paintings hang on this tavern's walls. One of the oldest and best-preserved taverns in Madrid, it is unique in that it still maintains its original bullfighting ambiance and decoration. An imposing bull's head mounted on a wall, impossible to miss, belongs to Fogonero ("Fiery"), the very first bull fought by Antonio Sánchez in 1922 as part of his *alternativa*, a ritual bullfighting ceremony that validates a bullfighter's passage from being a *novillero*—an apprentice or junior bullfighter who only fights young bulls—to becoming a full *matador de toros*.

Not surprisingly, bullfighting is the theme of the many paintings and drawings on the walls of the *taberna*, but its decor also features many original and interesting antiques, such as a hundred-year-old cash register, old gas lamps—still being used—and beautiful original marble tables and wooden seats. La Taberna de Antonio Sánchez takes pride in its reputation as a keeper of Spanish traditions, offering live flamenco shows while both local and out-of-town customers sip homemade

The centenary Taberna de Antonio Sánchez in the vibrant Lavapiés neighborhood. *Photo by E. J. Tepe.*

vermouth and enjoy traditional Madrid fare such as hearty chickpea *cocido,* ox tails cooked in red wine, snails in tomato sauce, or the ubiquitous *callos a la madrileña,* Madrid-style tripe stew. The tavern is best known, however, for its extremely popular *torrijas* (Spanish-style French toast). During the nineteenth and early twentieth centuries, customers would line up daily to buy up to two thousand of these sweet treats, made from slices of day-old bread dipped in milk and sugar and fried in a large pot of boiling oil. At the height of its popularity, this establishment had two women in charge of slicing and frying bread, and despite working nonstop, they could barely keep up with the demand; the process eventually was made easier and faster with the acquisition of a bread-slicing machine.[11] *Torrijas* are still popular today at La Taberna de Antonio Sánchez and throughout Madrid, and although they are in peak demand during Easter, they are available year-round, usually enjoyed with a glass of sweet wine or vermouth.

La Casa del Abuelo

La Casa del Abuelo (Grandpa's House) is a wonderful place to experience the charm and traditional flavors of old Madrid. Like many traditional businesses in Madrid, the ownership of La Casa del Abuelo has been proudly passed from generation to generation within the same family since being opened in 1906. First opened as La Alicantina (The Girl from Alicante), this establishment was known for selling sweet wine from Alicante, a city in the southeast of Spain. Because the wine they carried was aged and tasted sweet, it became known popularly as *el abuelo* (grandpa). Eventually, people started to refer to the establishment as the place to get *abuelo*—aged wine—and the tavern eventually changed its name to La Casa del Abuelo, meaning "grandpa's house" or "grandpa's place."

Four generations of the same family have run this charming and old-fashioned establishment, which did not close even during the difficult years of the Spanish Civil War (1936–1939). During that time, the owner had difficulties finding food to serve at his establishment and resorted to cooking whatever he could find. Since the most affordable and plentiful food item at the market was shrimp, he began preparing them in any way possible in order to serve his customers. When he prepared them *al ajillo* (sautéed in garlic), a famous tapa was born.

Today, La Casa del Abuelo continues to serve its famous sweet wine and to be known for its popular shrimp tapas, which are prepared in a variety of ways, from crunchy *con gabardina* (which literally means "in a raincoat"—that is, battered and fried) to *a la plancha* (grilled) and the crowds' favorite, *gambas al ajillo* (garlic shrimp). This 110-year-old establishment is a great example of a classic Madrileño eatery, from the food to the decor and the atmosphere, which have been preserved with many original elements such as the wall tiles, the old wall clock, and the large windows advertising the restaurant's specialties written by hand, the old-fashioned Madrid way.

Malacatín

Founded in 1895, Malacatín first opened as a simple wine bar, with a sign hanging over the door that laconically read *Vinos* (wines). Julián Díaz, the owner, had arrived in Madrid two years earlier from the town of Cuenca and had saved his money after working as an errand boy for his family's small shop. The wine bar had very humble beginnings, opening at six in the morning to cater to a blue-collar clientele, and added a kitchen only in the 1950s. Malacatín is now a traditional restaurant, run by the fourth generation of the same family and well known for its generous *cocido*, Madrid's traditional meat-and-chickpea stew. The servings of this dish are so generous, in fact, that the restaurant claims no customer has been able to successfully finish an entire dish.

Restaurante La Bola

Picturesque La Bola (The Ball) has served as the stage for at least a dozen films over the course of its existence since first opening for business in 1870. Its founder, an Asturian woman named Cándida Santos, opened the restaurant with *cocido* as the main dish, but then she decided to adapt the menu to her customers' budget and started offering three kinds of *cocido* at three different prices. These three versions were cooked and served throughout the day, varying from the most basic, aimed for blue-collar workers and employees and consisting of the basic broth, chickpeas, potatoes, and cabbage; a more expensive version for students, containing chicken; and the most expensive, which contained beef and pork in addition to the chicken, was prepared for members of the royal family who regularly patronized La Bola, such as Alfonso XII and his sister Isabel, as well as members of the nobility and other wealthy people. Today, everyone at La Bola gets this last rich and hearty version of the stew—after it has been slowly cooked in individual clay pots over coals for eight hours. It is a delicious dish, full of flavor and quite filling, although definitely a winter dish.

Run by the Verdasco family for four generations, La Bola has received the Alimentos de España award for the preservation of traditional Spanish cuisine. The decoration and appearance of La Bola make it unique, from its bright-red outside walls featuring the restaurant's name in golden letters with a golden ball underneath to its interior, which features classic nineteenth-century furniture complete with hat racks and a marble bar counter. Adding to the charming historic atmosphere, the restaurant's walls are decked with original artwork made for La Bola by famous illustrators, as well as with signed photographs of celebrities who have visited the restaurant to try its famed *cocido*.

La Bola, a historic restaurant specializing in the typical *cocido. Photo by the author.*

Posada de la Villa

What once was a wheat mill located on Calle Cava Baja in medieval Madrid became in 1642 the Posada de la Villa, an inn for travelers coming to the city. One of the numerous inns sprouting up at entry points to the city, such as Plaza Mayor, Calle de la Cava Alta, and Calle Cava Baja, as well as Calle de Toledo, Posada de la Villa offered lodging and food to travelers and their horses, as well as to merchants, workers, and visitors who came to Madrid after the royal court was established there in 1561. Over time, such establishments became aged and obsolete, and Posada de la Villa and others such as La Posada del Dragón and La Posada del León were neglected and fell to ruins. In 1918, however, the Posada de la Villa was rebuilt by entrepreneur Félix Colomo and was turned into a classic upscale restaurant.

Popular today with both Madrileños and visitors, the restaurant offers a classic menu and a decoration that re-creates a 1700s inn, complete with wooden beams, stained-glass windows featuring coats of arms, a central fireplace decked with antique pots and pans, large wooden tables and chairs, and an engraved wooden map of seventeenth-century Madrid on one of its walls. La Posada de la Villa specializes in traditional Madrid cuisine, offering the ubiquitous *cocido*, cooked in ceramic pots over straw and holm oak ashes, and roasted young lamb prepared in ceramic pots in an old Arabic-style oven.

La Cruzada

The oldest, though not continuously operating, *taberna* in Madrid, La Cruzada first opened in 1827 and quickly became known as a meeting place for Madrid's artists, writers, and socialites due to its privileged location near the Royal Palace and Royal Theater and as the favorite tavern of Alfonso XII, whose glass cup is still kept there. La Cruzada closed for a few years but is now back in operation and is popular with Madrileños, who go there to enjoy a glass of wine or vermouth to accompany their tapas. This establishment offers dishes like *cocido* and cod and tapas such as croquettes, fried chickpeas with eggs, potato *empanadillas*, bone marrow on toast, and gourmet Galician canned seafood; it is also known for its homemade desserts. The decor is reminiscent of an old tavern, with an early twentieth-century bar made from hand-carved Spanish walnut, and it has a charming vintage aesthetic, down to the characteristic red door that during the nineteenth century served as a way to distinguish Madrid's eating establishments from other types of businesses.

Taberna La Carmencita

With a name evocative of a famous Spanish cookbook, Taberna La Carmencita first opened in 1854 and has seen ups and downs over the years, with different names and owners, closing for several years before finally reemerging in 2013 with its original name. The "new" Carmencita aims to re-create the "old" Carmencita as much as possible, preparing many of the same traditional dishes straight from the classic cookbook *Carmencita o la buena cocinera* (Carmencita or the good cook).[12] The book, first published in Barcelona in 1899 by Eladia Martorell, was an instant best-seller, being reedited profusely in the following decades and reaching its fiftieth edition by 1974. This tremendously popular book was written by a humble housewife and became the cooking "bible" for women all over Spain, outselling those published by famous male chefs of the time. *Carmencita o la buena cocinera* offers hundreds of recipes, presented with clear and simple directions, and includes dishes for every occasion from an array of world cuisines, ranging from Spanish to Catalan, Cuban, American, French, and Italian. The author states in her book's prologue that she put great care into making sure that her work was "within reach of all intelligences."[13] A visit to Taberna La Carmencita is thus a rare opportunity to step back in time and try the homemade-style cuisine that was the norm in Spanish households many decades ago, such as squid in its own ink, meatballs, *callos* (tripe), hake cheeks, beef ox tail stew, veal tongue, hen *pepitoria* style (with an almond and saffron sauce), and *hojaldre de la Reina* (queen's pie, a puff pastry filled with sweetbreads, liver, and mushroom sauce), all providing a unique glimpse into Spanish cooking at the end of the nineteenth century and the beginning of the twentieth.

Casa Alberto

Occupying the ground floor of a building where *Don Quixote*'s author, Miguel de Cervantes, once lived and wrote, Casa Alberto opened in 1827 and to this day retains the distinctive classic air of Madrid's old taverns. Customers hang out along the long, curved zinc wet bar, where vermouth from the tap—a favorite aperitif wine for Madrileños—is served along with accompanying tapas. The establishment's long history and the celebrities who have visited it over the years are illustrated by the many paintings and photographs hanging on the walls, giving it the aura of a museum. Aside from being a *taberna* serving drinks and tapas, Casa Alberto is also a full restaurant that serves classic Madrid dishes made following old recipes.

Casa Ciríaco

This restaurant, well known and loved for its traditional homemade-style dishes, such as *gallina en pepitoria* (hen in a wine and almond sauce), opened in 1929, but their wine cellar is documented dating as far back as 1887. It is located in the same building on Calle Mayor where on May 31, 1906, an anarchist named Mateo Morral threw a bomb hidden in a bouquet of flowers into the wedding procession of King Alfonso XIII, failing to kill the king and queen but causing the deaths of several bystanders. For decades, Casa Ciríaco was frequented by a famous journalist and writer from the northern region of Galicia named Julio Camba (1884–1962). Camba was the author of *La casa de Lúculo*, a book that portrayed in a humorous light Spaniards' food obsessions and dogmatic traditions, as well as Madrid's own cuisine: "Spanish cuisine," he asserted in what is, perhaps, his most famous quote, "is full of garlic and religious concerns."[14] After Camba's death in 1964, a monthly gathering of renowned writers and artists honored his memory for several decades. Casa Ciríaco, among the city's oldest and most revered restaurants, is still known today for its old-fashioned cuisine, represented in traditional Madrileño dishes, prepared from recipes that are more than a hundred years old.[15]

Casa Paco

Established in 1890, this humble tavern sold wine almost exclusively until being purchased in 1933 by Francisco Morales, known informally as "Paco," who renovated the space and changed its name to the current Casa Paco (Paco's House). He turned the venue into a tavern serving food and drink to a highly diverse neighborhood crowd that included bullfighters, cattle dealers, jewelers, coalmen, plumbers, writers, and antique dealers from the nearby El Rastro market. These antique dealers are said to be the originators of a tradition that began in the 1950s, in which Casa Paco served as the starting point for the traditional Carnival celebration known as *el entierro de la sardina* (the burial of the sardine), a festive, make-believe funeral procession taking place on Ash Wednesday and signaling the end of Carnival's festivities and the beginning of Lent. This popular celebration, in which a big papier-mâché sardine is paraded around in a coffin and then burned to music, dancing, and fireworks, was masterfully portrayed by Francisco de Goya in his famous 1814 painting *El entierro de la sardina*.

Over the decades, the *taberna*'s clientele has included Hollywood actors such as Charlton Heston and Ava Gardner, bullfighters such as Palomo Linares, and Spanish actors such as Paco Rabal and Fernando Fernán Gómez, among many others whose signed photographs hang on the tavern's walls. Closed during the rough years of the Spanish Civil War, Casa Paco reopened right after, offering *cocido*, served in individual clay pots, for the low price of 25¢. The tradition of serving *cocido* in small clay pots continues to this day, with the popular dish being offered every Tuesday. Casa Paco also specializes in grilled meats, which are served on hot stones.

Ceramic-tile decoration advertising the traditional *cocido. Photo by the author.*

Casa Pedro

In 1702, Pedro Guiñales opened a small inn serving basic food and drinks, naming it Casa de la Pascuala (Pascuala's House) after his wife. In its beginnings, Casa de la Pascuala was a simple establishment serving visitors to the city. Given its location on a road outside the city, it was a convenient stop for muleteers and cattle breeders passing through Madrid on their way to France. Ownership of the inn was eventually passed on from Pedro to his son and later to his grandson (also named Pedro), who in 1796 began producing and selling wine using the family's own *garnacha* grapes. The family's next generation continued to develop the business, with Juan Guiñales Soriano changing the name of the inn to Casa de Silvestra, after his own wife. He continued to make wine from the *garnacha* grapes grown in the family's vineyards but also added new varieties, such as *moscatel* and *pardillo*.

The inn became popular with Madrid's high society in the early twentieth century, including with a young King Alfonso XIII. In 1940, the inn changed its name once again when Pedro Guiñales López, son of Juan and Silvestra, changed it to its present name, Casa Pedro, in honor of both his great-great-grandfather and his grandfather. He turned the inn into an upscale restaurant specializing in traditional Castilian cuisine, serving dishes such as roast lamb, lamb chops, suckling pig, game, and rabbit.

During the 1960s and 1970s, Casa Pedro became a popular upscale choice and was frequented by Spanish and foreign celebrities alike, from King Juan Carlos I to actors such as Anthony Quinn and Alain Delon and actresses such as Sofia Loren and Sara Montiel, as well as many well-known Spanish singers, artists, bullfighters, journalists, and influential politicians, many of whom left their signatures on the walls. The restaurant is, remarkably, still run today by the same Guiñales family, now in its sixth generation. Pedro Guiñales Valle, the great-great-great-grandson of the original Pedro Guiñales, has added his own trademark by restoring and expanding the old wine cellar and creating "Bodega Pedro."

La Taberna del Capitán Alatriste

Despite being opened in 2006, La Taberna del Capitán Alatriste deserves to be mentioned among Madrid's historic eateries, as it is housed in an eighteenth-century house palace built over a series of caves—now part of the restaurant. In actuality, La Taberna del Capitán Alatriste is not really a tavern, but rather an upscale restaurant that remarkably re-creates the atmosphere and decoration of a seventeenth-century tavern. The "Captain Alatriste" to which the establishment owes its name is the hero of numerous novels by famous writer Arturo Pérez-Reverte, whose adventures have sold millions of books that have even been adapted to the big screen.

A remarkable peculiarity of this establishment are the caves on which it is built, dating from the sixteenth century but perfectly maintained and excavated right up to Madrid's exposed medieval wall. The caves were built in the sixteenth century from materials salvaged from Madrid's ninth-century Arab wall, and those same materials were also used to build neighboring houses and fill the city's old defensive moat after it was no longer needed. The layout of the walls and moats are now lost, and only a few segments survive today. However, the current names of nearby Calle de la Cava Alta and Calle Cava Baja (*cava* meaning "moat" or "underground cave or tunnel") hint at the rich past of this part of the city.[16]

La Taberna del Capitán Alatriste's decor closely resembles that of an old tavern, complete with noble woods and real antiques such as daggers, swords, and armors. Its menu, replete with fire-roasted meats such as lamb or piglet, *olla podrida,* and partridge-meat pie prepared according to a medieval recipe, aims to be historically accurate. In Pérez-Reverte's fictional universe, this tavern occupies the very space where, in the eighteenth century, a tavern called Taberna del Turco (Turk's Tavern) existed, later run by Caridad la Lebrijana, a female character who maintains a romantic relationship with the novels' protagonist, Captain Alatriste. Both taverns—the fictional and today's real one—are located in the heart of the area known as "El Madrid de los Austrias" (or Austria's neighborhood), the center of Madrid under the Habsburgs' rule. The old stone-and-brick walls from the ground floor of the original eighteenth-century building are still intact. Its current owner, Félix Colomo, also owns two other historic restaurants, the picturesque Las Cuevas de Luis Candelas (open since 1949, occupying the caves on Cuchilleros's Arch, which are located on one of the entrances to Plaza Mayor and said to be the hiding place of famous nineteenth-century bandit Luis Candelas) and La Posada de la Villa, mentioned earlier.

Bodega de la Ardosa

The word *bodega* translates as "wine cellar" or "wine bar," and many of Madrid's wine bars kept the word *bodega* in their name even when they began serving food. Food at *bodegas,* however, consists mostly of tapas, which are usually eaten standing up. Bodega de la Ardosa, one of the oldest and most legendary *bodegas* in the city, was opened in 1892 on Calle Colón by Rafael Fernández, a native of the nearby town of Toledo who moved to Madrid and brought with him the wine he produced in his own vineyards in La Ardosa (Toledo). Bodega de la Ardosa opened locations throughout the city, and four remain today, though each is now independently owned. The original location on Calle Colón maintains its beautiful antique facade and interior, featuring shelves lined with old wine bottles and antique mirrors.

Always crowded, walking into Bodega de la Ardosa is like stepping back in time, and it is a favorite place for today's Madrileños to enjoy vermouth, which is made on the premises; *tortilla de patatas* (potato omelet), the bodega's best-selling tapa; and *croquetas* and *mojama*, dried salt-cured tuna loins, a delicacy of Arabic origin popular in the Mediterranean region of Spain. Both drinking and eating are very casual affairs at this historic spot and are done standing up near the counter or at one the few tall tables available, since there is almost no seating and space is tight.

Taberna Oliveros

Founded in 1857 under a different name, of which no record has been found, Taberna Oliveros changed ownership several times over its long life before finally being purchased by the Oliveros family in 1921, who have owned it since. The tavern has long been frequented by people of the bullfighting world and is known for its characteristic tile decor. In 1921, the owner commissioned an advertisement containing the clever rhyming slogan "Para comer bien y barato, San Millán 4" ("To eat well and cheap, go to San Millán Street, number 4"). The advertisement, a mural made with hand-painted tiles, portrays a cook cutting slices off a ham leg. Apparently, during the years of food scarcity following the Spanish Civil

Taberna Oliveros, San Millán Street, Madrid. *Photo by Sergio Esteve.*

War, guards had to cover up the sign because it made people hungry and was too disturbing an image for the famished Madrileños. Today, these decorative tiles are displayed proudly on the wall of the Taberna Oliveros, which is well known for its homemade dishes, such as *chabaza*, a mix of chickpeas, tripe, and white broad beans.

MADRID'S OLD CAFÉS

During the eighteenth century, three products, each bearing the aura of being miraculous substances, were introduced in Europe, with varying degrees of acceptance in different countries. These substances were chocolate, coffee, and tea. Of these three, the first two were received enthusiastically in Spain, though coffee was introduced in Spain much later than in other European countries, due perhaps to its geographic location at one end of the continent but also due to competition from the much more popular chocolate. Coffee eventually became quite popular, and Madrid's coffee, made with beans from plantations in the Dominican Republic, Cuba, Guatemala, and Puerto Rico, gained a reputation for its high quality. The first work devoted to this drink was published in Spain in 1693, a diatribe by Fernández Matienzo against what he considered the pernicious effects of the drink, warning of its many alleged health risks. The debate about whether it was safe to consume coffee became a controversial topic at the time, with some ardently opposed and others passionately in favor. The first Spanish cookbook to talk in detail about coffee and how it should be prepared is Juan de la Mata's 1786 *Arte de repostería.* De la Mata explains in his book that it is "a type of grain that comes from Persia and other countries of the Levant, similar in appearance to our beans." He then describes in great detail how the beans should be dried, roasted, and ground before being added to boiling water and allowed to rest for a while, and finally, after discarding the grounds, adding milk and sugar to taste. Coffee, he tells us, "dissipates and destroys the vapors of wine, helps the digestion, comforts the spirits, and prevents excessive sleep."[17]

The eighteenth century saw the proliferation of coffeehouses and *botillerías* (refreshment parlors also selling alcoholic drinks) in Madrid, where customers could go for tea, coffee, chocolate, French pastries, preserves, and liquors of various kinds—though no card playing or smoking was permitted at either type of establishment.[18] In his portrait of eighteenth-century Madrid, Charles E. Kany mentions *botillería* Canosa in the Carrera of San Jerónimo as one of the best known, though "it was not customary for women to enter the well-known establishment of Canosa. They therefore remained seated in their coaches outside the door, where the cold beverages were brought to them."[19]

Botillerías progressively disappeared and transformed into cafés, and Madrid joined the trend already taking place in other European cities such as Paris, Rome, Vienna, and Berlin, with coffeehouses playing a major role in Madrid's social life throughout the nineteenth century. Coffeehouses were indeed a favorite spot for groups of people to gather and discuss everything from gossip to politics, especially after the initial prohibition of women entering such establishments was lifted. Establishments like Fontana de Oro, Café del Príncipe, Café Suizo, Café de Fornos, Café Nuevo, Café de Santa Catalina, and Café Comercial (open since 1887 and still in operation today) were the gathering place of numerous writers, painters, and other intellectuals, as well as powerful financiers, politicians, and other influential figures. Some of these establishments witnessed political discussions that would have direct consequences for the country and played host to numerous authors and artists who would produce their art and write there.

Café Gijón

Perhaps the best-known historic café still in operation in Madrid is the Café Gijón, an establishment that has been popular since its beginning with writers, journalists, painters, and other intellectuals. The café was opened in 1888 by Gumersindo García, a native from the Asturian town of Gijón, who had migrated to Cuba and eventually returned to Spain, settling in Madrid. He invested his American earnings by opening what he called Gran Café Gijón after his native city. For decades, it would play host to numerous famous *tertulias* (a Spanish word meaning a specific type of discussion, mostly focused on literature or politics or the social, cultural, and political scene in general) and would be frequented by luminaries from the scientific and literary world, as well as artists such as scientist and Nobel laureate Santiago Ramón y Cajal, considered by many the father of modern neuroscience; painter Julio Romero de Torres; and writers Benito Pérez Galdós and Ramón del Valle-Inclán, among others. In 1914, the café's founder sold it to Benigno López, who was at the time a barber, under the conditions that the Gijón would continue to be a coffeehouse and that it would never change its name. The deal was signed, and the Café Gijón survived. During the twentieth century, it became a regular meeting spot for the poets of the group known as Generation of 27, which included Federico García Lorca, Luis Cernuda, and Rafael Alberti, among others, and the American writers Ernest Hemingway and Truman Capote met there with Spanish writers when they visited the city during the 1950s. The establishment retains its elegance today, with black marble-top tables, red-velvet chairs and curtains, numerous original paintings donated by artists who were its patrons, and golden-frame mirrors, which give it an aristocratic air of nineteenth-century elegance. The café has a privileged location on Paseo del Prado, near the Museo del Prado, and it remains popular today with a bohemian crowd, often frequented by filmmakers, actors, and writers.

Café Gijón, a historic Madrid establishment operating since 1888. *Photo by the author.*

The Embassy

The very first tea salon to open in Madrid is also the most famous and has an incredible story worthy of a spy novel, surprisingly discovered only a few years ago.[20] The Embassy was owned by Margaret Kearney Taylor, an Irish woman who arrived in Madrid in the late 1920s after having lived in Paris, where she had borne an illegitimate daughter by the Spanish diplomat José María Linares Rivas, a close counsel to Miguel Primo de Rivera (an aristocrat and military officer who, on September 1923, led a military coup and became prime minister of Spain until 1930). Taylor won a paternity case against Linares Rivas, who was forced to give his daughter his last name, and she then moved to Madrid, where in 1931 she opened an English tea salon she called Embassy on the Paseo de la Castellana, one of Madrid's principal streets.[21] When the Spanish Civil War broke out in 1936, Taylor left the country and fled to England but returned to Spain when the conflict ended in 1939, finding a country devastated by war and a city in ruins. She reopened her tearoom and slowly prospered, turning the establishment into one of the most elegant social centers in Madrid at the time, providing a pleasant place for the aristocratic and well-to-do socialites to meet for tea and pastries.

When the Second World War broke out, even though Spain remained neutral, the country became a hotbed of espionage, and the Embassy tearoom served as a meeting place for many agents of the British intelligence services. Margarita, as she was known to her friends and relations in Madrid, mingled with remarkable ease among the diplomats, members of the military, and high-ranking politicians who frequented the Embassy. An oasis in bustling Madrid, the Embassy attracted the city's high society, many of them American and British expats, as well as Spanish and European aristocrats, including Frederika, the queen mother of Greece (and mother of Sofía, who would become queen of Spain in 1975 by marriage to King Juan Carlos I), and General Francisco Franco's brother-in-law and minister of foreign affairs during the war, Ramón Serrano Suñer, a prominent Nazi sympathizer.

Franco's close alliance with Adolf Hitler had made Madrid a welcoming place for German agents, and the city was swarming with spies and Nazi soldiers. The Germany embassy, which served as the headquarters for the close to a thousand German spies operating in Madrid at the time, was just a few doors down from Taylor's tearoom.

Amazingly, for years Margaret Taylor hid Allied servicemen and Jewish refugees who were fleeing Nazi-occupied Europe and trying to reach Portugal, Galicia, or Gibraltar in order to sail to the United States or return to Great Britain. Her apartment was right above the tearoom and could be accessed through a series of doors and a hidden passage from the Embassy's bathroom, located at the back of the tearoom. Escapees would hide in the Embassy's upstairs apartment while waiting for forged documents that would allow them to continue their travels and leave Nazi Europe. As Richard Fitzpatrick writes,

> Taylor operated a safe house for escapees in her apartment above the tea salon—right under the German's noses, playing a part in helping to save 30,000 evacuees smuggled through neutral Spain during the war. . . . In a plan masterminded by MI6, which had the imprimatur of British Prime Minister Winston Churchill, Margarita helped to spirit them to Portugal and freedom.[22]

Margaret Taylor died in 1982, never having revealed her secret activities or the heroic role she played in saving the lives of so many, risking her own life to do so. She took her secret to the grave, but researchers recently discovered her story and made it public. Patricia Martínez Vicente, daughter of Eduardo Martínez Alonso, a physician and secret British agent who was one of the collaborators helping the refugees, uncovered a series of documents revealing her father's secret activities, and in 2003 she published a book revealing the story of her father and Miss Taylor's tearoom. The Embassy tearoom remained open for another thirty-five years after its founder's death, providing a quiet space for tea or coffee and delicate English pastries served in an elegant environment. It was frequented by Madrileños, as well as Hollywood stars such as the James Bond actor Pierce Brosnan, for whom the Embassy seemed like a fitting choice. Sadly, this historic establishment closed its doors for good in March 2017.

7

Madrid's Traditional Dishes

TAPAS: SMALL BITES, BIG FLAVORS

Madrid's culture of eating out and the role of food as a way of socializing with others is best represented by the ubiquity of tapas, the small plates of snack food that are served alongside drinks at every bar in the city. Enjoying tapas is very much a social affair that truly embodies the power of food to create and strengthen social bonds and personal relationships. Perhaps the most distinctive quality of tapas, besides the size of the serving, is the fact that they are meant to be shared. Everyone eats from the same plate, which is something that can be done only when there is a degree of familiarity and trust between the dining companions. This may seem like an odd practice for Americans, but it is not uncommon in many cultures throughout the world. In fact, the Spanish saying *"comer del mismo plato"* ("to eat from the same dish") is used to denote familiarity between two people.[1]

Tapas are one of the best ways to experience Madrid's food and the lively atmosphere of the city's many eateries. They are enjoyed all over Spain, with each region of the country boasting their favorite specialties, and Madrid is no exception. These small but tasty dishes are usually enjoyed very casually, standing up by the counter and accompanied by a glass of wine or vermouth, or a *caña* (draft beer served in a glass, containing roughly less than a half pint). In Madrid, a tapa is always included for free with the ordering of a drink. Tapas can be very simple or sophisticated, and organized contests among different eateries throughout the city for the award for the best tapa of the year are quite popular, with each place working hard at being creative and outdoing the others by offering a unique, especially delicious tapa.

Any time is pretty much "tapas time" in Madrid. These dishes provide an excuse for people to gather and socialize while eating and drinking and can be enjoyed as a prelude to the *comida* (main meal of the day), especially on weekends, but they are also often substitutes for *cena* (dinner, usually eaten around 10 p.m.) or part of after-work socializing on weekdays. This Spanish version of "fast food" provides a wonderful opportunity to enjoy food in a relaxed and informal atmosphere, surrounded by friends, and the chance to taste a variety of wide-ranging flavors and dishes without feeling too full. The list of tapas that can be enjoyed in Madrid is long and amazingly varied, from a slice of bread with pieces of cheese or *jamón* (Spanish cured ham) to a potato omelet; cod or ham *croquetas* (fried croquettes); *calamares a la romana* (fried calamari rings); the very popular *patatas bravas* (fried potatoes with a spicy sauce); *soldaditos de Pavía* (pieces of cod dipped in batter and fried); *callos* (tripe); *gallinejas* (chitterlings); *mollejas de cordero* (lamb sweetbreads); octopus; grilled vegetables, such as asparagus, eggplant, and tomatoes; *lacón* (ham); *jamón serrano* (cured ham); *morcilla* (blood sausage); *torreznos* (fried pork skins); *gambas al ajillo* (garlic shrimp); or *mejillones al vapor* (steamed mussels). There is also a seemingly infinite array of *tostas*, slices of toasted bread coated with a bit of olive oil and often grated fresh tomato, topped with different goodies, from pork products such as chorizo or *chistorra* to fish (sardines, cod), foie, or various cheeses combined with sweet quince paste. Ultimately, the sky is the limit in terms of creativity, and there are no rules about what can go on a *tosta*, as long as it tastes good.

Gambas al ajillo (Garlic Shrimp) from La Casa del Abuelo[2]

One of the city's most famous tapas, and the signature dish of La Casa del Abuelo, in Madrid garlic shrimp are served in a clay dish, still cooking when they arrive at the table or counter. Clay dishes and pots are cooking utensils commonly used throughout Spain, evidence of the country's Arabic culinary heritage. Clay cooking pots and dishes can withstand the fire and the heat of the oven and are wonderful at maintaining the heat, and their contents get cooked evenly and efficiently.

INGREDIENTS: White shrimp from the Mediterranean, olive oil ("Arbequina" variety if available), garlic, fresh parsley, cayenne peppers, salt

PREPARATION: Peel the shrimp and set aside. Peel the garlic cloves and chop finely. Chop also the parsley and combine with the garlic, about half and half of each. Pour the olive oil into a clay dish and set on the stove, and then add the ingredients in the following order: first, the sliced cayenne peppers (2 or 3

Gambas al ajillo. Photo by the author.

pieces, to taste), followed by the garlic and parsley mix. When the oil starts to boil, add the shrimp. Avoid overcooking and serve the dish almost immediately in the same dish where it was cooked, since the shrimp will continue to cook in the hot oil when served to the customer. Salt to taste. Serve with plenty of bread to dip in the oil.

Tortilla de patatas (Potato Omelet) from Bodega de la Ardosa[3]

Satisfying, golden *tortilla de patatas* is served in every single bar in Madrid and eaten at any hour of the day—or night. Some people love them as breakfast or as a midmorning snack with a slice of bread, but they can also be made into a sandwich, eaten for lunch or dinner, and—most often—enjoyed as a tapa accompanying a cold *caña* (draft beer) or a glass of wine. In Madrid, it is customary to serve this dish a bit underdone, with the egg inside still a bit runny, as Madrileños prefer their tortillas moist rather than dry. Bodega de la Ardosa, one of the oldest eateries in Madrid, is famed for its potato omelets, cooking dozens of them every day, which consistently sell out. This is its recipe:

Chapter 7

INGREDIENTS FOR 4 SERVINGS: 5 medium size "monalisa" potatoes (a yellow-skinned variety), 5 eggs, ½ large onion, extra virgin olive oil, salt

PREPARATION: Peel and wash the potatoes. Slice with a knife into slices of about 1½ inches and ¹⁄₁₆–¹⁄₈ inch thick. Collect the potato slices in a bowl with the onion cut into thin strips. Salt the vegetables. Heat abundant oil in a frying pan until it is hot but not smoking. Add potatoes and onion and fry for about 15 minutes, stirring the potatoes every 3 minutes or so. Remove potatoes and onion from oil and drain. Beat the eggs in a bowl and add the hot fried potatoes and onion. Prepare the potato omelet from this mixture immediately. Heat a small, heavy frying pan with high sides. Put a small amount of olive oil in the pan and extend well over the entire surface. When the pan is hot, but not smoking, add the omelet mixture. Cook for about half a minute, stirring the omelet mixture constantly. Flip the omelet over with the help of a plate and fry the other side for about half a minute. Flip onto a plate and serve.

A tapa with *tortilla de patatas* and *padrón* peppers on bread. *Photo by the author.*

Patatas a la brava (Fried Potatoes in Hot Sauce)

This extremely popular and addictive tapa, known also as *"patatas bravas,"* or simply as *"bravas,"* is present in many bars in Madrid. Although oftentimes the spicy sauce that covers the fried potatoes is made with a tomato base, some experts are adamant that the authentic *brava* ("fiery") sauce should not contain any tomato and should instead get its flavor and characteristic red color from the paprika in it. Some recipes call for a mixture of hot paprika and sweet paprika, while others use only the hot kind; still others use garlic and onion, while some omit those ingredients entirely. What all versions of the sauce have in common, however, is that it must be spicy.

Some Madrid establishments famous for their *patatas bravas*, such as Docamar and Las Bravas, keep their recipes a secret. The recipe included here for the *bravas* sauce is inspired by the one elaborated at La Máquina, a renowned restaurant chain that has several locations throughout Madrid.[4]

To prepare *patatas bravas*, start by making the sauce.

INGREDIENTS: 3 finely chopped garlic cloves; 2 large onions, finely chopped; 3 tbsp. hot paprika; 2 tbsp. flour; 2 tbsp. olive oil; homemade chicken broth

PREPARATION: In a pan with the oil, stir in the garlic together with the onion, add the flour, and let cook for several minutes. Add the paprika, stir and cook. Finally, add the chicken broth slowly until the sauce thickens. Set aside. Peel and dice several potatoes into small cubes or thin slices (depending on your preference), and fry them in abundant olive oil. Once golden, take out of the pan, drain excess oil, and dress with the *brava* sauce.

Soldaditos de Pavía ("Soldiers of Pavía," Cod Fritters with Roasted Peppers)

In his 1905 cookbook, *La cocina práctica*, famous gastronomer Manuel M. Puga y Parga, also known by his pseudonym Picadillo, mentions this cod dish as a Madrid classic that is especially sought after during Easter. The origin of the dish's name is unclear, with different theories to explain it but without clear agreement to this day. One of the theories points out that the colors of the dish resemble the red and yellow squares of the uniforms worn by the hussars of the Spanish army that fought in the Battle of Pavía in 1525, where the Spanish troops of Carlos I defeated the French soldiers of Francis I. According to this explanation, the red pepper slices that decorate these fritters would be reminiscent of the sashes worn by the soldiers as part of their uniform.[5]

Picadillo's description of this classic delicacy is below. *Note:* Picadillo's recipe uses salted and dried cod, hence the instructions to soak it in water. That step does not apply if using fresh cod.

Soldaditos de Pavía require, for their preparation, good quality cod. Cut it in square pieces of the same size and soak them in water for twenty-four hours, changing the water frequently. Drain, pat dry with a cloth, and dip in beaten egg, frying them in very hot oil. When they turn golden, drain the excess oil and let cool. Once cooled, wrap each one in a slice of red bell pepper, freshly roasted or from a jar, depending on the season.[6]

Caracoles a la madrileña (Escargots in Tomato Sauce) from Las Cuevas de Luis Candelas[7]

Snails have been eaten in the Iberian Peninsula since prehistoric times, with evidence of them being farmed at a large scale for human consumption by the Romans, and according to Pliny, the first such farms were established near Pompeii by Fulvius Harpinius. Instructions for properly eating snails appear in *Arte Cisoria*, by Enrique of Aragón (Marquis of Villena), published in 1423. Other cookery books, such as Diego Granado's *Libro del arte de cozina* (1599), Francisco Martínez Montiño's *Arte de cocina* (1611), and Juan de Altamiras's *Nuevo arte de cocina* (1758), also give recipes and instructions on how to best prepare this mollusk for consumption.[8]

Today, snails are enjoyed widely throughout Spain, either by themselves or as an addition to paella or other dishes. The recipe below shows the traditional way of preparing them in Madrid, provided by Las Cuevas de Luis Candelas (Luis Candelas's Caves), a restaurant housed in caves excavated inside of Cuchilleros's Arch, located by one of the entrances to the Plaza Mayor. The atmosphere, the decoration, and even the waiters' attire at this unique restaurant pay homage to Luis Candelas, one of the most infamous Spanish bandits of the nineteenth century. *Caracoles* are one of its most celebrated specialties, and according to the establishment's owner, Félix Colomo, they are still prepared following an authentic nineteenth-century recipe.

INGREDIENTS: 2 lb. snails, 1 onion (chopped), 1 garlic clove, 1 ham bone, 1 bay leave, 1 *guindilla* (chili) pepper, ground black pepper, *serrano* ham (cut into small pieces), tomato sauce, white Madrid wine (or another type of white wine), cognac (for flambéing), extra virgin olive oil, 1 tbsp. flour, salt

PREPARATION: Before cooking the snails, they must first be left unfed for several days, washing them repeatedly under abundant running water. When they are clean and ready, boil in water for several minutes, drain, and rinse with cold water. In a separate pan, sauté the chopped onion, garlic, and ham pieces along with the bay leaf, *guindilla* pepper, black pepper, and ham bone. Add the snails and flambé the dish with a touch of cognac. Next, add a bit of white wine, the flour, tomato sauce, and water. Let everything cook for 1½ hours, add salt if needed, and serve.

MAIN COURSES: HEARTY CASTILIAN DISHES[9]

Besides the many contributions of regional cuisines, Madrid boasts a number of dishes that are considered genuinely *madrileño*. These are generally hearty dishes, with a strong preference for meats over fish, and include delicacies such as the ubiquitous *cocido* (meat-and-chickpea stew), *callos* (tripe), roasted suckling pig, roasted lamb, ox tails, hen *pepitoria* style, and Madrid-style garlic soup.[10] Other very popular specialties include sea bream, cod prepared in a variety of ways, and kidney beans "*a lo Tío Lucas.*" The San Isidro salad, combining lettuce, olives, hardboiled egg, onion, and tuna in oil, is offered at most restaurants, either under that name or simply as "house salad."

Rabo de toro (Ox Tails in Red Wine) from Casa Alberto[11]

This rich dish was originally made using bull's meat, but it can also be made—and often is—with beef. The longer it cooks, the richer the sauce and the more tender the meat becomes; ideally, it should fall off the bone when poked with a fork. The recipe below, from the restaurant Casa Alberto, calls for just two hours of cooking, but cooking it longer at a low temperature (using an electric slow cooker, for example) will add even more tenderness to the meat and more flavor to the sauce.

INGREDIENTS FOR 4 PEOPLE: 4 lb. ox tail, 2 onions (each of them stuck with 5 cloves), 2 leeks, 3 carrots, 1 head of garlic, 2 bay leaves, 8 cups red wine, 1 teaspoon nutmeg, salt to taste, ground pepper to taste, thyme

PREPARATION: Place the ox tail, leeks, onions, carrots, garlic head, bay leaves, nutmeg, pepper and thyme in a cooking dish. Cover with the wine; if it doesn't cover all the ingredients, fill the rest with water. Boil for 2 hours; then separate the vegetables from the ox tail. Strain the vegetables with a conical strainer and mix the ox tail with the sauce. Cook for 10 minutes more. Flip onto a plate and serve hot accompanied by French fries and sprinkled with chopped parsley.

Gallina en pepitoria (Chicken in Wine and Almond Sauce) from Casa Ciríaco[12]

Early versions of this dish, consisting of hen or chicken cooked in a sauce made from ground almonds and sprinkled with cooked egg yolk, are found in thirteenth-century Al-Andalus cookbooks, as well as later medieval texts, with a similar recipe appearing in Diego Granado's 1599 cookbook, *Libro del arte de cocina*. In the works of both Martínez Montiño (1611) and Juan de Altamiras (1745), however, this dish is prepared without egg, expressly noting that no egg should be used in it and that the dish's yellow color should instead come from saffron. Even Miguel de Cervantes mentions *gallina en pepitoria* in his famous work *Don Quixote de la Mancha*, which is a testament to the popularity of this dish during the seventeenth century.[13] Fortunately, this ancient dish has never fallen out of favor and is alive and well today in many different regions throughout Spain, from Andalusia to Aragón, La Rioja, Galicia, and Asturias, although it seems to have an especially strong presence in Castile. In Madrid, *gallina en pepitoria* is considered one of the most traditional and iconic specialties. The recipe provided below is from Casa Ciríaco, a century-old restaurant in the center of Madrid that prides itself on preserving the city's culinary traditions.

INGREDIENTS FOR 4 PEOPLE: 1 chicken (or hen), water, 1 laurel leaf, 1 medium-size onion, 2 garlic cloves, fresh parsley, a few threads of saffron, 20 chopped almonds, 1 cup of white wine, 2 tbsp. of flour

PREPARATION: Clean, wash, cut up, and braise the chicken. Add water to a separate pot and cook with laurel leaf, finely diced or crushed garlic, chopped parsley, saffron, chopped almonds, and white wine. Add the braised chicken to the sauce and stew slowly for 2½ to 3 hours. In the oil left from braising the chicken, brown the diced onion and then add flour. Add the mix to the stewed chicken, cook for 10 minutes, and serve.

Cocido (Meat-and-Chickpea Stew) from La Bola[14]

As numerous scholars have noted, *cocido* probably evolved from several different stews, including *olla podrida*, or "rotten pot," a stew made with meats, legumes, and root vegetables. Some scholars also point to the Sephardic *adafina* as an antecedent of the *cocido*. Lorenzo Díaz, for example, points to the *olla podrida* as the unifying dish for all social classes in Madrid during the sixteenth and seventeenth centuries, and it eventually evolved into what is the most iconic Madrid dish, the *cocido*. Diego Granado's 1599 *Arte de cocina* includes a lengthy and extremely rich recipe for *olla podrida*, which would be impossible to prepare today given the types of meats required, since it calls for not only pork and wild boar but also beef, capon, hen, pigeon, hare, pheasant, duck, thrush, and Cornish hen, as well as sausages, chickpeas, and large amounts of various root vegetables, garlic, onions, chestnuts, and sweet spices.[15]

Despite containing less ingredients than the *olla podrida*, bacon or pork fat was—and still is—an essential ingredient of *cocido*, an addition likely due to the need to prove one's status as a "true Christian" given that, during the sixteenth century, accusations of false conversion for Jews and Muslims were a serious charge that could have dire consequences (fines, prison, and even death). The recipe below is courtesy of Restaurante La Bola, one of the restaurants best known in the city for its long history of preparing this dish. At La Bola, they follow Madrid's custom of serving *cocido* in a three-step process known as *los tres vuelcos* ("the three tippings of the pot"), with the broth and *fideos* (short, thin noodles) served first as a soup; followed by the chickpeas, potatoes, cabbage, and carrots; and, finally, the meats.

INGREDIENTS: Potatoes, chickpeas, chorizo, bacon, veal knuckle, hen, ham bones, cabbage, and *fideos* (pasta noodles)

PREPARATION: Soak the chickpeas the night before. In a clay pot, place the ham bone, veal knuckle, part of the chorizo, bacon, and chicken, and add the chickpeas. Add water and cook at a slow coal fire (preferably oak coals) for 6 hours. One hour before finishing the cooking, add the potatoes and salt. In a pan, cook the cabbage by sautéing it with olive oil and garlic. Cook the noodles separately with the remaining chorizo. *Cocido* is customarily served with an accompanying small plate of pickled hot peppers (*guindillas*) and pickled onions, as well as tomato sauce and cumin for seasoning.

Judías secas a lo Tío Lucas (Dry Beans, Uncle Lucas's Style)

Among the several legendary establishments of nineteenth-century Madrid, one of them gained prominence for the way it prepared kidney beans. La Taberna del Tío Lucas was a humble tavern located between the Plaza de Santa Ana and the beginning of Calle de Alcalá, close to several of the city's theaters. Its strategic location and the fact that it served food until late hours made this establishment popular with theater-goers, who would make a stop after the shows to have a drink and a generous bowl of the tavern's beans. This dish became very famous all over Madrid, and although the tavern is now long gone, the recipe fortunately has been preserved thanks to the writer and gastronomer Ángel Muro, who included it in his extensive 1894 cookbook, *El practicón*. Here it is, abbreviated and adapted:

Wash the beans thoroughly and leave in lightly salted water for two or three hours. Cook them in plenty of boiling water until the peel begins to wrinkle. Remove from the pot and drain.

In a separate pot, throw the beans with chopped onion, equal in volume to the beans, a spoonful of fried and refried oil and an ounce of well-trimmed bacon. Season to taste and add a head of garlic, whole, a couple of bay leaves and a dash of paprika. Let everything cook over an exaggeratedly slow fire, and when the beans fall apart when rubbed between the tips of the fingers, the onion has disappeared and the broth has a viscous appearance, add a spoonful of strong vinegar. Give it a last boil and take out of the fire, letting it rest in the pot, well covered, until it is time to serve.[16]

Sopa de ajo a la madrileña (Madrid-Style Garlic Soup)[17]

Hot soups are a common comfort food in Madrid, where winters can get pretty cold at times. This classic soup, made with the most humble and traditional of Spanish ingredients, works beautifully to warm up the body and is often served as a prelude to a hearty meal.

INGREDIENTS FOR 6 SERVINGS: day-old bread (about ½ baguette, or 9 oz.), 4 garlic cloves, 4 tbsp. olive oil, 1 tsp. paprika, 6 cups water, salt

PREPARATION: Cut the loaf of bread into thin slices and set aside. In a frying pan, cook the garlic cloves in the oil, frying them until completely golden. Add the bread and let fry well. Stir a bit and add the paprika, stirring constantly and being careful not to let it burn, since paprika burns quickly. Add the water and salt to taste, and let cook at a low boil for about 10 minutes from the moment it starts to boil. Remove the garlic cloves and serve in a tureen.

Potaje de garbanzos y espinacas (Chickpea-and-Spinach Hotpot)[18]

Potajes (hotpots) have been part of the traditional Spanish diet for centuries, especially during Lent, with recipes for different combinations of vegetables and beans appearing in cookbooks since at least the sixteenth century, such as in Rupert de Nola's *Libro de guisados* (1520), Diego Granado's *Libro del arte de cocina* (1599), Francisco Martínez Montiño's *Arte de cocina, pastelería, bizcochería y conservería* (1611), and Juan de Altamira's *Nuevo arte de cocina* (1745). This hotpot, made with chickpeas, fresh spinach, and potatoes, is a very popular hearty winter dish in Madrid:

INGREDIENTS FOR 4 SERVINGS: 1 lb. chickpeas, soaked overnight; 2 lb. fresh spinach (English spinach), washed and chopped; 1 lb. potatoes, peeled and cut into chunks; salt; 2 eggs, hardboiled; ¾ cup olive oil; 1 thick slice French bread; 2 cloves garlic, peeled; 1 onion, finely chopped; 1 teaspoon paprika

PREPARATION: Heat plenty of water in a large pot. When it comes to a boil, add the chickpeas; cover and simmer over low heat. Add the spinach, potatoes and a little salt and cook slowly for a further 30 minutes. Chop up the whites of the hardboiled eggs. Reserve the yolks. Heat the oil in a skillet. Fry the slice of bread, then remove from the pan and set aside. Fry the garlic in the same oil, remove and set aside. Slowly sauté the onion until it starts to brown. Add the paprika, stir, then quickly pour this mixture over the chickpeas. Crush the fried garlic and bread with the egg yolks in a mortar, then add to the chickpeas along with the chopped egg white. Check the seasoning. Cook gently for another 15 minutes. Taste to check that the chickpeas are cooked, then serve.

Callos a la madrileña (Tripe, Madrid-Style)[19]

Another dish with a long history in central Spain, *callos* are prepared in every traditional establishment in Madrid. They are tender, flavorful, and very filling. The way of preparing this dish may vary slightly from place to place, but everyone uses roughly the same ingredients. This is the recipe used at Madrid's historic Café Gijón:

INGREDIENTS: 1½ lb. veal tripe, ½ lb. veal snout, 1 veal knuckle, 5 oz. air-cured ham, 5 oz. *chorizo* sausage, 5 oz. *morcilla* (Spanish blood sausage), 2 medium-size onions, 1 bay leaf, 1 carrot, 2 heads of garlic, 1 cayenne pepper, 8 black peppercorns, salt, vinegar, water, 1 tbsp. flour, 1 tbsp. mild paprika

PREPARATION: Scrape the tripe with a knife and cut into pieces. Place in water with the veal knuckle. Soak, rub together, and change the water. Repeat 2 or 3 times. Place the tripe and the veal knuckle in water with a little vinegar. Bring to a boil, remove tripe from water and wash well. Place tripe, snout, and veal knuckle, all cut into pieces, in a pressure cooker with a head of garlic, one onion, a carrot, bay leaf, peppercorns, and salt. Cover with water. Close the pressure cooker. Once the pressure cooker reaches pressure, cook for 45 minutes. Allow the pressure cooker to cool without opening. Add 4 or 5 generous spoonfuls of olive oil to a kettle and fry 2 garlic gloves and diced onion until transparent. Add cayenne pepper, dried ham, and *chorizo* and *morcilla* sausages, all cut into pieces. Toss the sausages with the onion until hot and coated with oil. Then add 1 tablespoon of flour and 1 tablespoon of mild paprika. Stir while slowly adding some broth from cooking the tripe. Place the cooked tripe, veal knuckle, and veal snout in a clay cooking dish. Pour the onion and sausage mixture over the tripe, and add broth from cooking the tripe until covered. Place the clay cooking pot in the oven at medium temperature. Cook for 1 hour. Check seasoning and serve hot.

Olla gitana (Gypsy-Style Pot) from La Taberna de Antonio Sánchez[20]

Aside from their *torrijas*, this old tavern—one of the oldest in the city—is also known for this particular dish, a very filling stew made with very humble ingredients that together create a surprising harmony of flavors.

INGREDIENTS FOR 4 PEOPLE: 1½ lb. haricot beans 1½ lb. chickpeas, 9 oz. pig's ear, 9 oz. pigtail, 9 oz. chorizo sausage, 9 oz. chard, 1 head of garlic, 1 onion, 1 oz. paprika, 1 tbsp. flour, 1 cup olive oil, salt

PREPARATION: Cook the following ingredients in separate pots: (1) the pig's ear, the pig's tail, and the chickpeas; (2) the chard; (3) the haricot beans, the onion, the garlic, the spicy sausage, and the black pudding. Once everything is ready, stir-fry the flour and the paprika in olive oil, cut the chorizo and the black pudding in slices, and put all the ingredients in one pot. Cook for a short time to allow flavors to blend. Let stand for a little bit, and it's ready to be eaten.

Huevos estrellados (Fried Broken Eggs), a Specialty from Casa Lucio[21]

This dish, simple but satisfying, is the specialty of Casa Lucio. The key is to use fresh eggs and excellent potatoes and to fry both skillfully to avoid ending up with a dish that's too oily. When it comes to this dish, using fresh olive oil is essential for optimal results. This dish is Casa Lucio's claim to fame and the reason why locals, celebrities, and pretty much everyone continue to flock to the restaurant on a daily basis.

INGREDIENTS FOR 6 PEOPLE: 4 lb. potatoes, 6 eggs, olive oil, salt

PREPARATION: Peel and cut the potatoes, and add salt. Pour oil in a frying pan, and when it is hot, fry them, taking them out when they are done and placing them in a serving tray. In a different pan, fry the eggs, making sure the oil is very hot. When done, place the eggs over the potatoes. Break them slightly and let the yolk mix with the potatoes. Serve immediately.

Besugo al horno con patatas (Roasted Sea Bream with Potatoes)

Traditionally prepared in Madrid during Christmas, this simple and beautiful dish is also eaten in other parts of Spain. This recipe is adapted from Claudia Roden's amazing cookbook *The Food of Spain*.[22]

INGREDIENTS FOR 4 PEOPLE: 1 large sea bream or sea bass (about 4½ pounds), gutted and scaled, salt, 1 onion (sliced), 6 tbs. olive oil, 8–12 waxy potatoes, a pinch of saffron, 1 cup of white wine, 1 lemon cut into thin slices, 2 garlic cloves, 2 tbs. fine bread crumbs, 2 tbs. chopped flat-leaf parsley

PREPARATION: Rinse the fish and season inside out with salt. Line a baking dish large enough to hold the fish with foil. Sauté the onion in 1 tbs. of oil in a skillet over medium heat until soft and golden. Spread in the baking dish. Peel and cool the potatoes in boiling water for 10 minutes; drain and cut into slices. Add the potatoes to the onions, sprinkle with 3 tbs. of oil, add the saffron and a little salt, and mix gently. Pour in the wine. Rub the top of the fish with 1 tbs. of oil and place in the baking dish with the potatoes around it. Slash it in two places at the thickest part. Cut 1 slice of lemon in half and insert one half in each cut. Put 1 lemon slice inside the fish and the rest on top of the potatoes. Mix the remaining tbs. of oil with the garlic (crushed or finely chopped), bread crumbs, and a bit of the parsley, and sprinkle this mixture over the fish. Roast the fish in a preheated 475°F oven for 30–35 minutes, or until cooked. Serve sprinkled with the remaining parsley.

Paella

Strictly speaking, paella is not a dish typical of Madrid. Being a rice dish aromatized with saffron, it bears the unmistakable mark of its Arabic heritage, having originated in the southeast Mediterranean region of Spain in what is now Valencia, Alicante, and Castellón. Rice has been grown in that part of the country for centuries. However, paella is arguably Spain's most famous dish, and since every regional cuisine is well represented in Madrid, it is regularly offered in many restaurants; there are even a number of establishments that specialize in this dish, preparing excellent authentic paellas as good as the ones that can be enjoyed in Valencia. The many restaurants in the city center that feature colorful photos of paellas outside their doors should be avoided, however, since these are often precooked and previously frozen and would disappoint anybody with a working palate. A better option are restaurants like Carlos Arroces in the centrally located Calle de Ferraz or Que Si Quieres Arroz Catalina, Entre Naranjos, El Garbí, or Casa de Valencia in the Chamberí district (open since 1975), and, for a more upscale experience, L'Albufera Moraleja. These are establishments that take their *arroces* (rice dishes) very seriously and prepare lip-smacking, award-winning renditions of this Valencian dish.

Paella is eaten as a one-dish meal for *comida*—the day's main meal, which in Spain is eaten at 2 p.m.—but never for dinner, since it is considered too heavy a meal for *cena*, which usually takes place much later in the evening, around 10 p.m. A good paella is a dish to be shared, and because it has to be made fresh upon request and takes at least twenty-five minutes to cook, it is usually preceded in a meal by a salad and some appetizers. Once it is ready, it is customary to bring the paella to the table still in the pan and then serve it onto plates. The aroma and color of the saffron and the flavor of the rice should come through and be the dominant notes of the dish. The rice should form a thin layer and be cooked uniformly, with some of it even slightly burnt and stuck to the bottom of the pan. This does not mean that the cook accidentally burned it; in fact, for some people, that slightly burnt rice is the most desirable part of the paella. A garlic sauce called *alioli* (literally meaning "garlic" and "oil") is often served as an accompaniment. It is also traditional to season the rice after it is served by sprinkling lemon over it.

There are many variations for the recipe of the paella, and people in different towns often feel very strongly about the "proper" way to cook a paella, from ingredients to cooking methods, consistency of the rice, and so on, and people can even be a bit dogmatic about what they believe is "the right way" to prepare it. Some paellas include meat, while others do not; others are made with only fish and seafood, and some include both meat (chicken and rabbit being the most common) and seafood. In Valencia, the broth is left to boil for a few minutes before adding the rice, while in Alicante the rice is added prior to the broth. Here's a recipe from my home region, Alicante, for this popular dish:[23]

INGREDIENTS FOR 6 PEOPLE: 2.5 lb. chicken, ½ lb. monkfish, ½ lb. shrimp, 1 sweet red bell pepper, 1 tomato, 1 cup olive oil, 1½ lb. rice ("Valencian" style, medium grain), 1 *ñora* pepper (a nonspicy dried pepper also known as "pimiento choricero"), saffron, 1 head of garlic, 2½ liters water, salt

PREPARATION: Grate the tomato and set aside. Grind the *ñora* pepper in a mortar with a little salt and set aside. Pour the oil in the paella pan, and when it is hot, sauté the ground *ñora* pepper. Add also the sweet bell pepper cut into 6 pieces and the shrimp, and set everything aside once it is cooked. Next, brown the chicken, with the monkfish, garlic, and tomato, and once cooked, add the rice and stir, mixing it with all the ingredients that were already in the pan. Add the chicken broth and the saffron, season with salt, place the peppers and prawns over the rice, and let cook uncovered, without stirring at all, at medium-high for 20 minutes. After that time, cover loosely with a kitchen cloth and let rest for 5 minutes before serving.

DESSERTS

Madrid has a long tradition of enjoying scrumptious sweets, many of them associated with different religious celebrations throughout the year. Many of these sweets, such as *turrones* (nougats) or Toledo's marzipans, date back to the eight centuries of Arabic rule in the Iberian Peninsula, with recipes found in several classic cookbooks. Some of these are quite elaborate, and Madrileños prefer to purchase them at one of the many pastry shops found in the city rather than make them at home. However, some of them, like *torrijas* or *arroz con leche*, are truly simple to make and, since they use everyday ingredients, really capture the flavors of Spain.

Torrijas[24]

A very affordable sweet treat that is easy to make, *torrijas* are popular throughout all of Spain but are especially loved by Madrileños, who include them in the list of typical desserts eaten during Easter. The exact origin of the recipe is unknown, although some historians point to *torrijas* first being made by nuns in Andalusian convents during the fifteenth century.[25] Others believe they have their origin in the fried sweets of the Sephardic and Moorish traditions.[26] Recipes for *torrijas* appear in several Spanish cookery books from the seventeenth century, such as Domingo Hernández de Maceras's *Libro del arte de cocina*, published in 1607, and Francisco Martínez Montiño's *Arte de cozina, pastelería, vizcochería y conservería* from 1611.

A modest recipe initially destined to take advantage of hardened bread, it soon became a highly appreciated treat for those with a sweet tooth, especially in Madrid, where the dessert even made it into the literary works of several nineteenth-century authors. Back then, the sweets were eaten mostly at *tabernas*, with one of the places that gained fame for the quality of their *torrijas* being La Taberna de Antonio Sánchez—and they were even praised by King Alfonso XIII. Nowadays, Madrileños buy their *torrijas* mostly at bakeries, and there is fierce competition for the claim to the best ones in the city. During Easter, *torrijas* are sold everywhere around the city, even at supermarkets such as El Corte Inglés, but pastry shops like La Mallorquina, Confitería El Riojano, Moulin Chocolat, Pomme Sucre, Formentor, Antigua Pastelería del Pozo, and Viena Capellanes are among the locals' favorite places to find this sweet dessert.

Given their simplicity and the fact that they are made using just a handful of common ingredients, such as bread, milk, egg, and sugar, their popularity is not surprising. Described by many as "the Spanish version of French toast," it is a crowd-pleasing food, consisting of a slice of bread soaked in milk and sugar or wine, dipped in egg, and fried. In the past, the treat was usually eaten with a glass of sweet wine, but today's tastes have changed, and they are instead accompanied by a cup of coffee or hot chocolate. Here's a standard recipe:

INGREDIENTS: 1 day-old baguette, sliced approximately ½ inch thick, 5 cups milk, ⅔ cup powdered sugar, 3 eggs, 1 cup oil, cinnamon

PREPARATION: Mix sugar and milk. Beat the eggs. Dip the bread slices first into the milk, then into the egg, and fry them in the oil until golden. Remove from the pan, sprinkle with sugar and cinnamon, and serve.

A popular variation to the classic recipe is *torrijas madrileñas al vino* (Madrid-style "French toast" with wine), done by simply substituting milk with wine.

Flan a la madrileña (Madrid-Style Flan)

Arguably the most classic Spanish dessert, flan's beauty lies in its simplicity and the amazingly delicious results of combining just three humble ingredients: egg yolks, milk, and sugar. There are many variations of flan, adding extra ingredients for slightly different flavor or texture, but the standard Madrid style is this basic recipe.[27]

INGREDIENTS: ⅔ cup sugar, 14 egg yolks, 2 cups milk

PREPARATION: Mix in a saucepan the egg yolks and the sugar, beating with a whisk, add the milk, previously boiled and hot. Mix everything thoroughly and pour it into a mold through a sieve. The bottom of the mold needs to be previously covered with a layer of caramelized sugar, which is made by placing a layer of dry sugar in it and cooking it at medium temperature, letting it caramelize while stirring constantly. Once the mix has been poured into the mold with the caramel, boil it in a double boiler at low for 30 minutes. Check for doneness after that time by inserting a knife and making sure it does not come out wet. Take out of the double boiler, let cool, pass a knife around the edges of the mold, and turn out onto a serving plate. Refrigerate and serve.

Arroz con leche al estilo de Madrid (Madrid-Style Rice Pudding)[28]

Rice pudding is a dessert found, with some variations, in many cultures around the world. In Spain, it is made with rice, milk, sugar, cinnamon, and lemon peel, clearly being a dish inherited from Arabic cuisine. In fact, an almost identical form of this dessert is found in Middle Eastern cuisines such as that of Lebanon, although the Lebanese version also adds rose water and pistachio. Recipes for rice with milk can be found in several canonical Spanish cookbooks, as in Domingo Hernández de Maceras's *Libro del arte de cocina*, published in 1607. In his recipe, Hernández de Maceras also gives the option of making the dish with almond milk instead of cow's milk.[29]

The recipe below is from *La cocina típica de Madrid* by Simone Ortega and Manuel Martínez Llopis, a twentieth-century cookbook. However, it is identical to the one used by Maceras three hundred years earlier.

INGREDIENTS: 1¼ cup rice, 4 cups milk, ⅔ cup sugar, 1 cinnamon stick, powdered cinnamon to taste, 1 piece lemon rind

PREPARATION: Boil the rice in water in a saucepan and add a stick of cinnamon and the piece of lemon rind, letting it boil for about 20 minutes until the water is consumed. Then add the milk and the sugar, allowing it to boil until the milk is consumed and the rice is soft. When it has reached its precise point, place it in a large serving dish or several individual bowls and sprinkle with ground cinnamon. Allow to cool (or refrigerate) and serve.

Leche merengada (Merengue Milk)

Leche merengada is a typical summer drink in Spain. It is technically a milkshake since it is made by adding egg white to milk, which is usually sweetened with sugar and flavored with cinnamon and lemon peel. It is served very cold so that part of the drink is partially frozen and with a texture very similar to snow. The drink can be found in ice-cream parlors and cafés throughout Madrid and other Spanish cities. *Leche merengada* has a long history, and it is documented as one of the most popular drinks in the cafés of Madrid in the late eighteenth and early nineteenth centuries; it is even mentioned in the novel *Fortunata and Jacinta*, by Benito Pérez Galdós. This recipe is adapted from Simone Ortega's classic 1972 cookbook *1080 recetas de cocina*.[30]

INGREDIENTS: 4 cups milk, ⅔ cup sugar, the peel of 1 or 2 lemons, cinnamon (either stick or powder is fine), 2 egg whites

PREPARATION: In a saucepan, mix the milk with the sugar and the lemon peel. Adding cinnamon at this point is optional. When it starts to boil, lower the heat and let it cook for 5 minutes, stirring occasionally, then let it cool. Strain the milk and transfer it to a covered container (metallic, if possible). Place it in the freezer and leave for 1 hour. Remove from freezer and break the crystals that have formed during the freezing. Whip the egg whites with a pinch of salt and mix with the milk, then put the mix back in the freezer until it has the desired texture without being completely frozen. Serve in long glasses sprinkled with cinnamon.

Leche frita (Fried Milk)[31]

A very old-fashioned dessert, "fried milk" is a rare treat that can still be found on the menu of some Madrid restaurants.

INGREDIENTS: 3 cups whole milk, 5 tbsp. corn starch, 5 tbsp. sugar, peel of 1 lemon, 2 tbsp. butter, 2–3 eggs (beaten), powdered sugar, cinnamon, oil (for frying)

PREPARATION: Dilute the corn flour in ⅓ cup of cold milk and set aside. Grease the bottom of a mold with butter. Put the remaining milk, sugar, butter, and lemon peel in a saucepan over medium heat. When it starts to boil, add the previous mixture of milk and corn flour. Keep stirring until thick, always over medium heat, for about 5–7 minutes. Remove from the heat and pour the mixture into the mold. Cover it with film and let cool, first to room temperature, then chill for 2 more hours in the refrigerator. Once it is cold and firm, cut into squares and take them out of the mold. Flour all the pieces on both sides, and dip into the egg. Fry each piece in the oil, turning them once, until they are golden. Take out of the pan and set over paper towels to absorb excess oil. Sprinkle with powdered sugar and cinnamon and refrigerate, or eat them while they are still hot.

Buñuelos de viento (Fritters)

Buñuelos, along with *churros*, are the quintessential *verbena* (street fair) food. Deliciously delicate and fluffy, these bites of fried dough sprinkled with sugar are present in almost any street fair celebration in Spain. It is habitual to see the smoking food trucks with their big pots of frying oil, and there is something mesmerizing about watching the *buñoleros* submerge their dough in the oil and seeing how it quickly and magically puffs up.

Madrid has been celebrating *verbenas* since the sixteenth century, always as part of the year's calendar of religious festivities. Certain elements such as music, food, and often a religious component are integral parts of these celebrations. These *verbenas*, also referred to by locals simply as *fiestas* (celebrations) or *ferias* (fairs), take place primarily during the spring and summer, and each is associated with a specific saint and often a certain neighborhood in the city. The good weather and the love for traditions attract large crowds to the celebrations in honor of San Isidro (May 15), San Antonio de la Florida (night of June 12–13), San Cayetano (August 7), San Lorenzo (August 10), and the Virgen de la Paloma (August 15). San Isidro's fair is the largest and most important, since it honors the patron saint of Madrid.

Buñuelos can always be enjoyed at these events, with different variations on the classic recipe, from *buñuelos de viento* (hollow) to *de crema* or *de chocolate* (filled with custard cream or chocolate). Most people prefer to buy them at the fair as a special treat, but they are not difficult to make at home. Below is the basic recipe, adapted from *La cocina típica de Madrid.*[32]

INGREDIENTS: 2 cups water, 4 cups wheat flour, 1 tsp. yeast, salt, powdered sugar, abundant oil for frying

PREPARATION: Mix the water with the flour, a little salt, the yeast, kneading everything well until obtaining a compact and leathery-looking dough. Cover and let it ferment at rest until it grows to double its original volume. Then wet your fingers in cold water to prevent the dough from sticking to your hands and start making make balls with the dough, taking a portion that is proportionate to the size that the *buñuelo* will have and rounding it slightly—it does not have to be a perfectly round ball. Once formed, make a hole in the center with your finger and fry each ball in very hot oil. You can use a stick to prevent the holes from closing during the frying. When the *buñuelos* have puffed up and have a golden color, take them out of the oil one by one, let them cool off slightly—but not too long—sprinkle with powdered sugar, and enjoy.

Notes

INTRODUCTION

1. Susana and Fabio, "Susana & Fabio," *Eat & Love Madrid* (blog), http://eatandlovemadrid.es/susana-fabio/; my translation. Unless otherwise noted, all translations in the book are my own.

CHAPTER 1

1. "Atapuerca Mountains," *Wikipedia*, accessed February 8, 2017, https://en.wikipedia.org/wiki/Atapuerca_Mountains.

2. Xavier Medina, *Food Culture in Spain* (Westport, CT: Greenwood Press, 2005), 13.

3. Ana Ruiz, *Medina Mayrit: The Origins of Madrid* (New York: Algora, 2012).

4. Pedro Montoliú Camps, *Enciclopedia de Madrid* (Barcelona: Planeta, 2002).

5. "The Celts in Spain," Spain: Then and Now, www.spainthenandnow.com/spanish-history/the-celts-in-spain/default_35.aspx.

6. "The Celts in Spain."

7. Rafael Chabrán, "Medieval Spain," in *Regional Cuisines of Medieval Europe. A Book of Essays*, ed. Melitta Weiss Adamson (New York: Routledge, 2002), 125–52.

8. *Guía básica de cocina celtibérica: Keltiberoi, segunda semana celtibérica* (Soria, Spain: Ayuntamiento, 2004), 6.

9. Gabriel Sopeña Genzor, "El mundo funerario celtibérico como expresión de un ethos agonístico," *Historiae* 1 (2004): 56–107, www.academia.edu/1411053/.

10. Ruiz, *Medina Mayrit*, 13, 194.

11. "La villa romana de Villaverde," Parque Lineal del Manzanares, www.par quelineal.es/villa-romana-villaverde/.

12. Chabrán, "Medieval Spain," 129.

13. Pliny, *Natural History*, trans. H. Rackman, W.H. S Jones, and D. E. Eicholz, Loeb Classical Library ed. (London: William Heinemann, 1942–1963), 8:31, 43, 435.

14. Felipe Fernández-Armesto, *Near a Thousand Tables: A History of Food* (New York: The Free Press, 2002), 56. See also Andrew Dalby, *Food in the Ancient World from A to Z* (London and New York: Routledge, 2003), 305.

15. Alicia Ríos and Lourdes March, *The Heritage of Spanish Cooking* (New York: Random House, 1992), 12.

16. Medina, *Food Culture in Spain*, 23–24.

17. Claudia Roden, *The Food of Spain* (New York: HarperCollins, 2011), 12.

18. Matilde Fernández Montes, "El agua en los orígenes de Madrid," in *El agua: Mitos y realidades*, ed. José A. González and Antonio Malpica Cuello (Barcelona: Anthropos, 2003), 123–53. See also https://es.wikipedia.org/wiki/Madrid.

19. Ruiz, *Medina Mayrit*, 47.

20. Abd al-Mun'im al-Himyari, *The Book of the Fragrant Garden*, quoted in Ruiz, *Medina Mayrit*, 39.

21. "Jews in Spain to 13th Century," Spain: Then and Now, www.spainthenand now.com/spanish-history/jews-in-spain-to-13th-century/default_187.aspx.

22. Roden, *Food of Spain*, 19.

23. Medina, *Food Culture in Spain*, 25–28.

24. Miguel Ángel Almodóvar, *La cocina del Cid: Historia de los yantares y banquetes de los caballeros medievales* (Madrid: Nowtilus, 2007), 170–71.

25. Quoted in Ismael Díaz Yubero, *Gastronomía de Madrid: Cocina, historia y tradición* (Madrid: Estrellas Gastronomía, 2014), 21.

26. Díaz Yubero, *Gastronomía de Madrid*, 22.

27. Jules Stewart, *Madrid: The History* (London and New York: I. B. Tauris, 2012), 6.

28. David M. Gitlitz and Linda Kay Davidson, *A Drizzle of Honey: The Lives and Recipes of Spain's Secret Jews* (New York: St. Martin's Press, 1999), 222–23.

29. Gitlitz and Davidson, *Drizzle of Honey*, 4.

30. Roden, *Food of Spain*, 21.

31. Ríos and March, *Heritage of Spanish Cooking*, 14.

32. Ana M. Gómez-Bravo, "Adafina: The Story Behind the Recipe," in *The Converso Cookbook* (Seattle: Stroum Center for Jewish Studies, University of Washington, 2014), http://jewishstudies.washington.edu/converso-cookbook/adafina-story-behind-recipe/.

33. Roden, *Food of Spain*, 95.

34. Gitlitz and Davidson, *Drizzle of Honey*, 104.

35. Ríos and March, *Heritage of Spanish Cooking*, 14.

36. Ken Albala, *Food in Early Modern Europe* (Westport, CT: Greenwood Press, 2003), 141.

CHAPTER 2

1. Madrid has been the capital of Spain since 1561, albeit with a few intervals when the capital was relocated briefly to other cities: Between the years 1601–1606, the capital moved to Valladolid; during the War of Independence (1808–1814), to Seville in 1808 and to Cádiz in 1810; during the Spanish Civil War (1936–1939), the Republican government was moved first to Valencia and later to Barcelona; Francisco Franco's Nationalist side had its government in Burgos, but Franco moved the headquarters of the central government back to Madrid at the end of the war (1939), where it has remained since.

2. José María Escudero Ramos, *Cocinando la historia: Curiosidades gastronómicas de Madrid / Cooking History: Gastronomic Curiosities of Madrid* (Madrid: Ediciones la Librería, 2011), 62.

3. Pedro Montoliú Camps, *Enciclopedia de Madrid* (Barcelona: Planeta, 2002), 211.

4. Montoliú Camps, *Enciclopedia de Madrid*, 215.

5. Andrew Dalby, *Dangerous Tastes: The Story of Spices* (London: British Museum Press, 2000), 146.

6. Pilar Bueno and Raimundo Ortega, "Comer en Madrid: Un repaso a la crítica gastronómica," *Revista de libros* 38 (2000): 1–9, www.revistadelibros.com/articulo_imprimible.php?art=3715&t=articulos.

7. Teófilo Ruiz, *Spanish Society, 1400–1600* (Harlow, UK, and New York: Longman, 2001).

8. Ismael Díaz Yubero, *Gastronomía de Madrid: Cocina, historia y tradición* (Madrid: Estrellas Gastronomía, 2014), 27.

9. Anne Harrison Fanshawe, *Memoirs of Lady Fanshawe, Wife of Sir Richard Fanshawe, Bt., Ambassador from Charles II. to the Courts of Portugal & Madrid, Written by Herself Containing Extracts from the Correspondence of Sir Richard Fanshawe*, ed. Beatrice Marshall (1905; Project Gutenberg, 2004), p. 191, https://archive.org/details/memoirsofladyfan06064gut; italics added.

10. Fanshawe, *Memoirs of Lady Fanshawe*, 195.

11. María del Carmen Simón Palmer, "El estatuto del cocinero: Su evolución en el tiempo," *Food and History*, 4, no. 1 (2006): 255–76.

12. María del Carmen Simón Palmer, *La cocina de Palacio, 1561–1931* (Madrid: Editorial Castalia, 1997), 71. This work is the most comprehensive source of historical information about food and cooking in the Spanish court during this period, and it is highly recommended to those interested in knowing more on the subject.

13. Simón Palmer, *La cocina de Palacio*, 129.

14. Francisco Martínez Montiño, *Arte de cocina, pastelería, vizcochería y conservería* (Barcelona: Imprenta de Sierra y Martí, 1823), 13–14; italics added.

15. John A. Crow, *Spain, the Root and the Flower: An Interpretation of Spain and the Spanish People* (Berkeley: University of California Press, 1985), 177.

16. Alicia Ríos and Lourdes March, *The Heritage of Spanish Cooking* (New York: Random House, 1992), 17–18.

17. Vicente Palacio Abad, *La alimentación de Madrid en el siglo XVIII y otros estudios madrileños* (Madrid: Real Academia de la Historia, 1998), 20, 35.

18. Palacio Abad, *La alimentación*, 25.

19. David R. Ringrose, *Madrid and the Spanish Economy, 1560–1850* (Berkeley: University of California Press, 1983), 81.

20. Ringrose, *Madrid and the Spanish Economy*, 82.

21. Eva Celada, *La cocina de la casa real: Los mejores menús privados, de bodas y banquetes de los Borbones desde el siglo XVIII* (Barcelona: Belacqva, 2004), 16–47.

22. Simón Palmer, *La cocina de Palacio*, 139.

23. Celada, *La cocina de la casa real*, 33.

24. Celada, *La cocina de la casa real*, 39.

25. Recipe translated from Celada, *La cocina de la casa real*, 94.

26. Andrew Dalby, *Dangerous Tastes: The Story of Spices* (Berkeley: University of California Press, 2000), 146.

27. Juan de Altamiras, *Nuevo arte de cocina, sacado de la escuela de la experiencia económica* (Barcelona: Imprenta Don Juan de Bézares, 1758), 152.

28. Isabel del Campo, *Introducción de plantas americanas en España* (Paracuellos del Jarama, Spain: Ministerio de Agricultura, Pesca y Alimentación, 1993), 312.

29. William H. McNeill, "What If Pizarro Had Not Found Potatoes in Peru?" *What If? Eminent Historians Imagine What Might Have Been*, vol. 2, ed. Robert Cowley (New York: Berkeley Books, 2001), 413–29.

30. Del Campo, *Introducción de plantas americanas*, 313.

31. William W. Dunmire, *Gardens of New Spain: How Mediterranean Plants and Foods Changed America* (Austin: University of Texas Press, 2004), 42.

32. Altamiras, *Nuevo arte de cocina*, 44.

33. Altamiras, *Nuevo arte de cocina*, 87.

34. Dunmire, *Gardens of New Spain*, 91.

35. Carolyn A. Nadeau, *Food Matters: Alonso Quijano's Diet and the Discourse of Food in Early Modern Spain* (New York: University of Toronto Press, 2016), 97.

36. Jeffrey M. Pilcher, *Planet Taco: A Global History of Mexican Food* (New York: Oxford University Press, 2012), 39.

37. Sophie D. Coe, *America's First Cuisines* (Austin: University of Texas Press, 1994), 43.

38. Simón Palmer, *La cocina de Palacio*, 139.

39. José de Acosta, *Historia natural y moral de las Indias*, ed. Edmundo O'Gorman (Mexico City: Fondo de Cultura Económica, 1962), 180.

40. Bernal Díaz del Castillo, *Historia verdadera de la conquista de Nueva España*, ed. Miguel León-Portilla (Madrid: Historia 16, 1984), 324.

41. María Paz Moreno, "A Bittersweet Love Affair: Spain and the History of Chocolate," *Connections: European Studies Annual Review* 7 (2011): 50.

42. María Mestayer de Echagüe, *Historia de la gastronomía* (Madrid: Espasa-Calpe, 1943), 111.

43. "Chocolate: From Mesoamerica to Modern Master Chocolatiers," Food & Wines from Spain, www.foodswinesfromspain.com/spanishfoodwine/index.html.

44. Ken Albala, *Food in Early Modern Europe* (Westport, CT: Greenwood Press, 2003), 146.

CHAPTER 3

1. Pablo Jesús Aguilera, "Un episodio de la Guerra de Independencia (1811–1812)," *La Gatera de la Villa* 1 (December 2009): 12–14.

2. Pilar Bueno and Raimundo Ortega, "De la fonda nueva a la nueva cocina: La evolución del gusto culinario en España durante los siglos XIX y XX," *Revista de libros*, nos. 19–20 (1998), 42–49.

3. Maria Jesús Burgueño, "El Museo del Romanticismo enseña a comer al modo del siglo XIX," *Revista de arte—Logopress*, January 18, 2011, accessed August 10, 2016, www.revistadearte.com/2011/01/19/el-museo-del-romanticismo-ensena-a-comer-al-modo-del-siglo-xix/.

4. María del Carmen Simón Palmer, "El estatuto del cocinero: Su evolución en el tiempo," *Food & History* 4, no. 1 (2006): 255–76. Even though women cooks

were not the norm at the royal court, Simón Palmer has been able to document the presence of quite a few women cooks during the Habsburgs' rule. Beginning with Felipe II and until 1900, Simón Palmer states that there were more than thirty women who served the royal family with their cooking, even though their presence was often resented by their male colleagues.

5. Richard Ford, *A Handbook for Travellers in Spain* (London: John Murray, 1845), 664.

6. Joan Sella Montserrat, *Comer como un rey: Las mesas de Amadeo I de Saboya y Alfonso XII de Borbón* (Gijón, Spain: Ed. Trea, 2009), 15.

7. "La ilustración española y americana," *Wikipedia*, accessed October 6, 2016, https://en.wikipedia.org/w/index.php?title=La_Ilustraci%C3%B3n_Espa%C3%B1ola_y_Americana&oldid=741289297.

8. Dolores Vedia de Uhagon, *La mesa española: Arte de cocina al alcance de una fortuna media* (San Sebastián, Spain: Ed. La Libertad, 1892), 1. The original quote reads, "Una buena ama de casa debe entender el arte del cocinero, para no estar a la merced de los criados que van y vienen, para inspeccionar la limpieza, el esmero de los alimentos y proporcionar a su esposo y familia el bienestar, el confortable que les haga preferir la sencilla comida de su casa a los mayores festines fuera de ella."

9. José María Escudero Ramos, *Cocinando la historia: Curiosidades gastronómicas de Madrid / Cooking History: Gastronomic Curiosities of Madrid* (Madrid: Ediciones La Librería, 2011).

10. Quoted in *Menús de guerra* (Barcelona: Generalitat de Catalunya, Consellería de Proveïments, Departament de Premsa i Propaganda, [1937?]), prologue, n.p.

11. Miguel Ángel Almodóvar, *El hambre en España: Una historia de la alimentación* (Madrid: Oberon, 2003).

12. Paul Richardson, *A Late Dinner: Discovering the Food of Spain* (New York: Scribner, 2007), 222.

13. Quoted in Richardson, *A Late Dinner*, 222–23.

14. Ignasi Doménech, *Cocina de recursos: Deseo mi comida* (Barcelona: Quintilla, Cardona y Ca. Editores, 1941), 62.

15. Doménech, *Cocina de recursos*, 222.

16. Doménech, *Cocina de recursos*, 153.

17. José Guardiola y Ortiz, *Platos de guerra: 60 recetas prácticas, acomodadas a las circunstancias, para la conservación y el condimento de la sardina* (Alicante, Spain: Ed. del autor, 1938).

18. Miguel Ángel Del Arco Blanco, "Hunger and the Consolidation of the Francoist Regime (1939–1951)," *European History Quarterly* 40 (2010): 465.

19. Paul Richardson, *A Late Dinner*, 221.

20. Lara Anderson, *Cooking Up the Nation: Spanish Culinary Texts and Culinary Nationalization in the Late Nineteenth and Early Twentieth Century* (Woodbridge, UK: Tamesis, 2013), 3.

21. Anderson, *Cooking Up the Nation*, 150.

22. Anderson, *Cooking Up the Nation*, 150.

23. Marta Valdivieso, "Así creó Franco el menú del día," *El español*, January 2, 2016, accessed September 1, 2016, www.elespanol.com/reportajes/20160101/91240883_0.html.

24. Valdivieso, "Así creó Franco."

25. Arthur Lubow, "A Laboratory of Taste," *New York Times*, August 10, 2003, accessed September 10, 2016, www.nytimes.com/2003/08/10/magazine/a-laboratory-of-taste.html.

26. Lubow, "Laboratory of Taste."

27. Lubow, "Laboratory of Taste."

28. Quoted in Richardson, *A Late Dinner*, 227.

29. Paul Bocuse, *La cocina del mercado* (Barcelona: Argos Vergara, 1979). Bocuse's book was first published in 1974 in France, where it was highly influential. The English edition appeared in 1976 as *The Cuisine of the Market*.

30. Pilar Bueno and Raimundo Ortega, "Un cuarto de siglo en la cocina española," *Revista de libros*, nos. 55–56 (2001): 25–30.

31. Richardson, *A Late Dinner*, 227.

32. As of 2017, there are nine three-star Michelin-rated restaurants in Spain: one of them in Madrid, four in the Basque Country, three in Catalonia, and one in Comunidad Valenciana. The complete list of restaurants and their chefs includes El Celler de Can Roca, Chef Joan Roca (Girona, Catalonia); Sant Pau, Chef Carme Ruscalleda (Sant Pol de Mar, Catalonia); Lasarte, Chef Paolo Casagrande (Barcelona); Quique Dacosta, Chef Quique Dacosta (Denia, Comunidad Valenciana); Diverxo, Chef David Muñoz (Madrid); Akelarre, Chef Pedro Subijana (San Sebastián, Basque Country); Arzak, Chef Juan Mari Arzak (San Sebastián, Basque Country); Azurmendi, Chef Eneko Atxa (Larrabetzu, Basque Country); and Martín Berasátegui, Chef Martín Berasátegui (Lasarte-Oria, Basque Country).

CHAPTER 4

1. Pedro Montoliú Camps, *Enciclopedia de Madrid* (Barcelona: Planeta, 2002), 219.

2. José A. Nieto Sánchez, *Historia del Rastro: Los orígenes del mercado popular de Madrid, 1740–1905* (Madrid: Visión, 2004), 28.

3. David R. Ringrose, *Madrid and the Spanish Economy, 1560–1850* (Berkeley: University of California Press, 1983), 144.

4. Ismael Díaz Yubero, *Gastronomía de Madrid: Cocina, historia y tradición* (Madrid: Estrellas Gastronomía, 2014), 32.

5. Díaz Yubero, *Gastronomía de Madrid*, 34.

6. Virgilio Pinto Crespo and Santos Madrazo, *Madrid: Atlas histórico de la ciudad de Madrid, siglos IX–XIX* (Barcelona and Madrid: Fundación Caja de Madrid y Lundwerg Editores, 1995), 238.

7. Nieto Sánchez, *Historia del Rastro*, 50.

8. Ringrose, *Madrid and the Spanish Economy*, 82.

9. Nieto Sánchez, *Historia del Rastro*, 98.

10. Pinto Crespo and Madrazo, *Madrid: Atlas Histórico*, 220.

11. "Historia de Madrid: Mercado de San Miguel," Madridhistórico.com, accessed October 10, 2016, www.madridhistorico.com/seccion5_historia/nivel2_informacion.php?idmapa=14&idinformacion=678&pag=5.

12. Nieto Sánchez, *Historia del Rastro*, 117.

13. N. Lorena Bahamon Tabarquino, "La Plaza de la Cebada: Historia de un Madrid inédito," E-Innova: Revista electrónica de educación, no. 38 (Universidad Complutense Madrid, February 2015), n.p., accessed October 27, 2016, http://biblioteca.ucm.es/revcul/e-learning-innova/124/art1800.pdf.

14. "Mercado de los Mostenses," *Wikipedia*, accessed November 14, 2016, https://es.wikipedia.org/w/index.php?title=Mercado_de_los_Mostenses&oldid=91161963.

15. Díaz Yubero, *Gastronomía de Madrid*, 40.

16. Nieto Sánchez, *Historia del Rastro*, 50.

17. Nieto Sánchez, *Historia del Rastro,* 50, 108.

18. "Barceló: De mercado municipal a Centro Polivalente," Madrid Actual, December 18, 2014, accessed November 15, 2016, www.madridactual.es/20141218665406/images/documentos/plano-metro-madrid.pdf.

19. "Welcome to the Largest Gastro Leisure Space in Europe," Platea website, accessed November 15, 2016, http://plateamadrid.com/en/que-es/.

20. Raquel Villaécija, "El 'boom' del super en España: Ahora hay 2.500 más que antes de la crisis," *El Mundo*, September 17, 2016, accessed November 15, 2016, www.elmundo.es/economia/2016/09/17/57dbf65d268e3eb2228b4615.html.

21. "España tiene la mitad de tiendas de alimentación que hace tres décadas pero ha multiplicado por diez los supermercados," Nielsen España, September 25, 2015, accessed November 16, 2016, www.nielsen.com/es/es/press-room/2015/Espania-tiene-la-mitad-de-tiendas-de-alimentacion-que-hace-tres-decadas-pero-ha-multiplicado-por-diez-los-supermercados.html.

22. J. J. Aunión, "Emblemáticos y ahogados," *El País*, March 20, 2014, accessed November 16, 2016, http://ccaa.elpais.com/ccaa/2014/03/20/madrid/1395346828_905030.html.

23. Díaz Yubero, *Gastronomía de Madrid*, 112.

24. "Oriol Balaguer," La Duquesita website, accessed November 15, 2016, www.laduquesita.es/oriol-balaguer/.

25. "Oriol Balaguer," *So Good* magazine website, accessed November 15, 2016, www.sogoodmagazine.com/pastry-chefs/oriol-balaguer/.

26. "La Violeta," Madrid, Villa y Corte website, accessed November 1, 2016, www.madridvillaycorte.es/comerciolavioleta.php.

CHAPTER 5

1. Rafael Chabrán, "Medieval Spain," in *Regional Cuisines of Medieval Europe*, ed. Melitta Weiss Anderson (New York: Routledge, 2002), 138.

2. Carolyn A. Nadeau, "Contributions of Medieval Food Manuals to Spain's Culinary Heritage," in "Writing about Food: Culinary Literature in the Hispanic World," ed. Maria Paz Moreno, special issue, *Cincinnati Romance Review* 33 (2012): 67.

3. Translation from *Book of Sent Soví: Medieval Recipes from Catalonia*, ed. Joan Santanach i Suñol, trans. Robin Vogelzang (Woodbridge, UK, and Barcelona: Barcino Tamesis, 2008), 77.

4. Translations from Chabrán, "Medieval Spain," 139.

5. Nadeau, "Contributions of Medieval Food Manuals," 66.

6. Isabel Moyano Andrés, "La cocina escrita," in *La cocina en su tinta* (Madrid: Biblioteca Nacional de España), accessed January 20, 2017, www.bne.es/es/Micrositios/Exposiciones/Cocina/Estudios/seccion1/.

7. Chabrán, "Medieval Spain," 141.

8. Chabrán, "Medieval Spain," 142.

9. Néstor Luján, *Veinte siglos de cocina en Barcelona: De las ostras de Barcino a los restaurantes de hoy* (Barcelona: Folio, 1993), 55.

10. Chabrán, "Medieval Spain," 139.

11. Quoted in Chabrán, "Medieval Spain," 139.

12. The translation for this recipe is taken from Chabrán, "Medieval Spain," 140.

13. Translation from Alicia Ríos and Lourdes March, *The Heritage of Spanish Cooking* (New York: Random House, 1992), 199.

14. Quoted in María de los Ángeles Pérez Samper, "Recetarios manuscritos de la España moderna," *Cincinnati Romance Review* 33 (Winter 2012): 33.

15. Eddy Stols, "The Expansion of the Sugar Market in Western Europe," in *Tropical Babylons: Sugar and the Making of the Atlantic World, 1450–1680*, ed. Stuart Schwartz (Chapel Hill: University of North Carolina Press, 2004), 244.

16. Juan Cruz Cruz, "El libro de cocina de Ruperto de Nola," *Regusto: Gastronomía y cultura alimentaria* (blog), February 17, 2015, accessed January 20, 2017, http://regusto.es/2015/02/17/el-libro-de-cocina-de-ruperto-de-nola/.

17. Carolyn Nadeau, "Early Modern Spanish Cookbooks: The Curious Case of Diego Granado," *Food and Language: Proceedings from the 2009 Oxford Symposium on Food and Cookery*, ed. Richard Hosking (Totnes, UK: Prospect Books, 2010), 241.

18. Quote and translation from Nadeau, "Early Modern Spanish Cookbooks," 243.

19. Ken Albala, *Food in Early Modern Europe* (Westport, CT: Greenwood Press, 2003), 148.

20. Lorenzo Díaz, *Madrid: Bodegones, mesones, fondas y restaurantes: Cocina y sociedad, 1412–1990* (Madrid: Espasa Calpe, 1990), 34.

21. Albala, *Food in Early Modern Europe*, 149.

22. Francisco Martínez Montiño, *Arte de cocina, pastelería, vizcochería y conservería* (Madrid: Luis Sánchez, 1611), prologue, n.p.

23. Martínez Montiño, *Arte de cocina*, 163.

24. Juan de Altamiras, *Nuevo arte de cocina, sacado de la escuela de la experiencia económica* (Barcelona: Imprenta Don Juan de Bezáres, 1758), prologue, n.p.

25. María de los Ángeles Pérez Samper, *La alimentación en la España del Siglo de Oro* (Huesca, Spain: La Val de Onsera, 1998), 59.

26. Altamiras, *Nuevo arte de cocina*, prologue, n.p.

27. Altamiras, *Nuevo arte de cocina*, 49.

28. Altamiras, *Nuevo arte de cocina*, 111.

29. Barbara Feret, *Gastronomical and Culinary Literature* (Metuchen, NJ: Scarecrow Press, 1979), 32.

30. Translation from Ríos and March, *Heritage of Spanish Cooking*, 54.

31. Ríos and March, *Heritage of Spanish Cooking*, 17.

32. Juan de la Mata, *Arte de repostería, en que se contiene todo género de hacer dulces secos, y en líquido: Con una breve instrucción para conocer las frutas, y servirlas crudas, y diez mesas, con su explicación* (Madrid: Impr. y Librería de Joseph García Lanza, 1755). Translation taken from Ríos and March, *Heritage of Spanish Cooking*, 210.

33. De la Mata, *Arte de Repostería*, 165.

34. María del Carmen Simón Palmer, "La dulcería en la Biblioteca Nacional de España," in *La cocina en su tinta* (Madrid: Biblioteca Nacional de España), 81, ac-

cessed January 15, 2017, http://www.bne.es/es/Micrositios/Exposiciones/Cocina/documentos/cocina_estudios_2.pdf.

35. Quote and translation from Ríos and March, *Heritage of Spanish Cooking*, 215.

36. *La cocina moderna* (Madrid: Libr. de Anllo y Rodríguez, 1875), title page.

37. *La cocina moderna*, 153–54.

38. Ángel Muro, *El practicón*, 2nd ed. (Barcelona: Tusquets, 1997), 14.

39. Muro, *El practicón*, 735.

40. Muro, *El practicón*, 329.

41. Emilia Pardo Bazán, *La cocina española antigua* (Madrid: Sociedad Anónima Renacimiento, 1913), iii.

42. Pardo Bazán, *La cocina española antigua*, 116.

43. Pardo Bazán, *La cocina española antigua*, 209.

44. Pardo Bazán, *La cocina española antigua*, 250.

45. Ignasi Doménech, *La nueva cocina elegante española; el tratado más práctico y completo de cocina, pastelería, repostería y refrescos*, 2nd ed. (Madrid: Imprenta Helénica, 1920), 6.

46. Doménech, *La nueva cocina elegante española*, 35.

47. Ignasi Doménech, *La nueva cocina elegante española; el tratado más práctico y completo de cocina, pastelería, repostería y refrescos*, 2nd ed. (Madrid: Imprenta Helénica, 1920), 36; italics added.

48. Dionisio Pérez, *Guía del buen comer español: Inventario y loa de la cocina clásica de España y sus regiones* (Madrid: Sucesores de Rivadeneyra, 1929), 277.

49. Manuel Martínez Llopis, *Historia de la gastronomía española* (Madrid: Editora Nacional, 1981), 401.

50. María Mestayer de Echagüe, *La cocina completa* (Madrid: Espasa-Calpe, 1940), 380.

51. Mestayer de Echagüe, *La cocina completa*, 7.

52. Mestayer de Echagüe, *La cocina completa*, 15.

53. Joaquín de Entrambasaguas, *Gastronomía madrileña* (Madrid: Instituto de Estudios Madrileños, 1954), 11.

54. Entrambasaguas, *Gastronomía madrileña*, 95.

CHAPTER 6

1. RCM: Restaurantes y tabernas centenaries de Madrid website, accessed November 29, 2016, www.restaurantescentenarios.es. Information about these establishments included in this chapter is based on that provided in this website, as well as each of the restaurants' own websites.

2. Benito Pérez Galdós, *La fontana de oro* (Madrid: Perlado, Páez y Compañía, 1906), 9.

3. Mariano José de Larra, "La fonda nueva," in *Obras Completas de Fígaro (Don Mariano José de Larra)* (Paris: Baudry, Librería Europea, 1857), 376.

4. "Lhardy," *Wikipedia*, accessed December 20, 2016, https://es.wikipedia.org/wiki/Lhardy.

5. José Altabella, *Lhardy, Panorama histórico de un restaurante romántico: 1839–1978* (Madrid: Ideal, 1978), 187–88.

6. "Lhardy se ha esmerado en su confección. El pavo en gelatina está sabroso; el pastel de perdiz, en su punto; el 'rosbeef' sanguinolento, al par de blanco, y gustoso el jamón. El vino de Riscal y el champaña Munn remojan bien las viandas. Y mientras caen, lentas, a tierra la cáscaras de las naranjas y revolotea en torno del globo el papel de estaño del chocolate Marquise, Pignatelli ha elevado su copa para pronunciar su acostumbrado brindis 'porque la nación española recobre pronto el prestigio y la preponderancia que, según dicen, tuvo en otros tiempos.'" Altabella, *Lhardy*, 188.

7. Nigel Townson, *The Crisis of Democracy in Spain: Centrist Politics under the Second Republic, 1931–1936* (Brighton, UK: Sussex Academic Press, 2000), 90.

8. Teresa Sánchez Vicente, "El restaurante más antiguo del mundo está en Madrid," ABC.es website, October 21, 2011, accessed December 20, 2016, www.abc.es/20111021/local-madrid/abci-restaurante-antiguo-mundo-201110191600.html.

9. Ernest Hemingway, *Death in the Afternoon* (New York: Simon and Schuster, 1999), 48.

10. Ernest Hemingway, *The Sun Also Rises* (New York: Scribner, 2016), 197; italics in original.

11. Lorenzo Díaz, *Madrid: Bodegones, mesones, fondas y restaurants: Cocina y sociedad, 1412–1990* (Madrid: Espasa-Calpe, 1990), 287.

12. Eladia Martorell, *Carmencita o la buena cocinera: Manual práctico de cocina española, americana, francesa, con multitud de recetas especiales que no se hallan en los tratados publicados hasta el día* (Barcelona: Eugenio Subirana, 1899).

13. Martorell, *Carmencita o la buena cocinera*, n.p.

14. Julio Camba, "La cocina española está llena de ajo y de preocupaciones religiosas," in *La casa de Lúculo* (Madrid: Temas de Hoy, 1999), 33.

15. "Casa Ciriaco," RCM: Restaurantes y tabernas centenaries de Madrid website, accessed November 10, 2016, www.restaurantescentenarios.es/establecimientos/casa-ciriaco.

16. "History," La Taberna de Capitán Alatriste website, accessed December 5, 2016, www.tabernadelcapitanalatriste.com/pages_en.html.

17. Juan de la Mata, "El café disipa y destruye los vapores del vino, ayuda a la digestión, conforta los espíritus, e impide dormir con exceso," quoted in Manuel Martínez Llopis and Simone Ortega, *La cocina típica de Madrid* (Madrid: Alianza Editorial, 1987), 33.

18. Charles E. Kany, *Life and Manners in Madrid, 1750–1800* (Berkeley: University of California Press, 1932), 148.

19. Kany, *Life and Manners in Madrid*, 149.

20. Richard Fitzpatrick, "*Documentary on One* Preview: Tearoom, Taylor, Saviour, Spy," RTÉ website, updated July 8, 2016, accessed December 28, 2016, www.rte.ie/lifestyle/living/2016/0629/798935-tearoom-taylor-saviour-spy/.

21. Fitzpatrick, "*Documentary on One* Preview."

22. Richard Fitzpatrick, "The Irish Woman Who Led a Double Life Smuggling Jewish Refugees," *Irish Times*, July 8, 2016, accessed December 28, 2016, www.irishtimes.com/life-and-style/people/the-irish-woman-who-led-a-double -life-smuggling-jewish-refugees-1.2714946.

CHAPTER 7

1. More commonly, the question "*¿Cuándo hemos comido del mismo plato?*" ("When have you and I eaten from the same plate?") is used as a warning to call out somebody who may be treating the speaker with excessive or inappropriate familiarity.

2. Recipe translated from Ismael Díaz Yubero, *Gastronomía de Madrid: Cocina, historia y tradición* (Madrid: Estrellas Gastronomía, 2014), 176.

3. Recipe courtesy of Bodega de la Ardosa, see RCM: Restaurantes y tabernas centenarios de Madrid, *Recetas centenarias de la gastronomía madrileña / Ancient Recipes from the Cuisine of Madrid* (Madrid: RCM, n.d.), 7, accessed December 17, 2016, www.restaurantescentenarios.es/images/pdfs/Recetario_RCM_2.pdf.

4. José Carlos Capel, "¿Unas bravas hojaldradas?" *Gastronotas De-Capel* (blog), January 21, 2016, accessed January 11, 2017, http://elpais.com/elpais/2016/ 01/21/gastronotas_de_capel/1453411692_145341.html.

5. Teresa Barrenechea, *The Cuisines of Spain: Exploring Regional Home Cooking* (Berkeley: Ten Speed Press, 2005), 114.

6. Manuel María Puga y Parga, *La cocina práctica* (Santiago de Compostela, Spain: Ed. Galí, 1981), 125.

7. Recipe translated from Díaz Yubero, *Gastronomía de Madrid*, 206.

8. Manuel Martínez Llopis and Simone Ortega, *La cocina típica de Madrid* (Madrid: Alianza, 1987), 267.

9. Recipes in this section come from RCM: Restaurantes y tabernas centenarios de Madrid, *Recetas centenarias de la gastronomía madrileña / Ancient Recipes from the Cuisine of Madrid* (Madrid: RCM, n.d.), accessed June 15, 2016, www .restaurantescentenarios.es/images/pdfs/Recetario_RCM_2.pdf. See the individual notes for additional information.

10. Lorenzo Díaz, *Madrid: Bodegones, mesones, fondas y restaurants: Cocina y sociedad, 1412–1990* (Madrid: Espasa-Calpe, 1990), 288.

11. Recipe courtesy of Casa Alberto, RCM, *Restaurantes centenarios de Madrid*, 13.

12. Recipe courtesy of Casa Ciríaco, RCM, *Restaurantes centenarios de Madrid*, 15.

13. Martínez Llopis and Ortega, *La cocina típica de Madrid*, 285–86.

14. Recipe courtesy of Restaurante La Bola, *La Bola Taberna: La tentación de un Rey*, printed brochure.

15. Díaz, *Madrid*, 116.

16. Ángel Muro, *El practicón*, 2nd ed. (Barcelona: Tusquets, 1997), 552.

17. Recipe translated from Martínez Llopis and Ortega, *La cocina típica de Madrid*, 143–44.

18. Recipe from Alicia Ríos and Lourdes March, *The Heritage of Spanish Cooking* (New York: Random House, 1992), 61.

19. Recipe courtesy of Café Gijón, RCM, *Restaurantes centenarios de Madrid*, 10.

20. Recipe courtesy of La Taberna de Antonio Sánchez, RCM, *Restaurantes centenarios de Madrid*, 29.

21. Recipe translated from Díaz Yubero, *Gastronomía de Madrid*, 214.

22. Claudia Roden, *The Food of Spain* (New York: HarperCollins, 2001), 323.

23. Recipe translated from Antonio González Pomata, *Cocina alicantina* (León, Spain: Ed. Everest, 1998), 45.

24. Recipe translated from Martínez Llopis and Ortega, *La cocina típica de Madrid*, 380.

25. Antxon Urrosolo, *La cocina del monasterio: Recetas para el cuerpo y el alma* (Barcelona: Plaza y Janés, 2009), 296.

26. José Carlos Capel, "Las 12 mejores torrijas de Madrid (y dos sorpresas)," *El País, El Viajero*, March 8, 2016, accessed January 10, 2017, http://elviajero.elpais.com/elviajero/2016/03/07/actualidad/1457348428_371286.html.

27. Recipe translated from Martínez Llopis and Ortega, *La cocina típica de Madrid*, 369.

28. Recipe translated from Martínez Llopis and Ortega, *La cocina típica de Madrid*, 370.

29. Ken Albala, *Food in Early Modern Europe* (Westport, CT: Greenwood Press, 2003), 146–47.

30. Recipe translated from Simone Ortega, *1080 recetas de cocina* (Madrid: Alianza Editorial, 1996), 708.

31. Recipe adapted from Simone Ortega, *1080 recetas de cocina* (Madrid: Alianza Editorial, 1996), 680.

32. Recipe translated from Martínez Llopis and Ortega, *La cocina típica de Madrid*, 372.

Bibliography

Acosta, José de. *Historia natural y moral de las Indias*. Edited by Edmundo O'Gorman. México: Fondo de Cultura Económica, 1962.

Aguilera, Pablo Jesús. "Un episodio de la Guerra de Independencia (1811–1812)." *La Gatera de la Villa* 1 (December 2009): 12–14.

Albala, Ken. *Food in Early Modern Europe*. Westport, CT: Greenwood Press, 2003.

Almodóvar, Miguel Ángel. *El hambre en España: Una historia de la alimentación*. Madrid: Oberon, 2003.

————. *La cocina del Cid: Historia de los yantares y banquetes de los caballeros medievales*. Madrid: Ediciones Nowtilus, 2007.

Altabella, José. *Lhardy, panorama histórico de un restaurante romántico: 1839–1978*. Madrid: Impr. Ideal, 1978.

Altamiras, Juan. *Nuevo arte de cocina, sacado de la escuela de la experiencia económica*. Barcelona: Imprenta Don Juan de Bezáres, 1758. Originally published 1756 by Impr. y Libreria J. García Lanza (Madrid).

Anderson, Lara. *Cooking Up the Nation: Spanish Culinary Texts and Culinary Nationalization in the Late Nineteenth and Early Twentieth Century*. Woodbridge, UK: Tamesis, 2013.

Anonymous. *The Book of Sent Soví: Medieval Recipes from Catalonia*. Edited by Joan Santanach i Suñol. Translated by Robin Vogelzang. Woodbridge, UK, and Barcelona: Barcino Tamesis, 2008.

Baeza, Miguel. *Los quatro libros del arte de la confitería, compuestos por Miguel de Baeza.* Alcalá de Henares, Spain: J. Gracián, 1592.

Bahamon Tabarquino, N. Lorena. "La Plaza de la Cebada: Historia de un Madrid inédito." E-Innova: Revista electrónica de educación, no. 38 (Universidad Complutense Madrid, February 2015). Accessed October 27, 2016. http://biblioteca .ucm.es/revcul/e-learning-innova/124/art1800.pdf.

Barrenechea, Teresa. *The Cuisines of Spain: Exploring Regional Home Cooking.* Berkeley, CA: Ten Speed Press, 2005.

Biblioteca Nacional de España. "La copla en la Biblioteca Nacional de España." In *La cocina en su tinta*, 62–81. Madrid: Biblioteca Nacional de España, 2009. www.bne.es/es/Micrositios/Exposiciones/Cocina/documentos/cocina_ estudios_2.pdf.

Bocuse, Paul. *La cocina del mercado.* Barcelona: Argos Vergara, 1979.

Bueno, Pilar, and Raimundo Ortega. "Comer en Madrid: Un repaso a la crítica gastronómica." *Revista de libros*, no. 38 (2000): 35–38. www.revistadelibros .com/articulo_imprimible.php?art=3715&t=articulos.

———. "De la fonda nueva a la nueva cocina: La evolución del gusto culinario en España durante los siglos XIX y XX." *Revista de libros*, nos. 19–20 (1998): 42–49.

———. "Un cuarto de siglo en la cocina española." *Revista de libros* 55–56 (2001): 25–30.

Burgueño, Maria Jesús. "El Museo del Romanticismo enseña a comer al modo del siglo XIX." *Revista de arte—Logopress*, January 18, 2011. Accessed August 10, 2016. www.revistadearte.com/2011/01/19/el-museo-del-romanticismo-ensena -a-comer-al-modo-del-siglo-xix/.

Camba, Julio. *La casa de Lúculo.* Madrid: Temas de Hoy, 1999.

Celada, Eva. *La cocina de la Casa Real: Los mejores menús privados, de bodas y banquetes de los Borbones desde el siglo XVIII.* Barcelona: Belacqva, 2004.

Chabrán, Rafael. "Medieval Spain." In *Regional Cuisines of Medieval Europe*, edited by Melitta Weiss Anderson, 125–52. New York: Routledge, 2002.

Coe, Sophie D. *America's First Cuisines.* Austin: University of Texas Press, 1994.

Corral, José del. *Ayer y hoy de la gastronomía madrileña.* Madrid: Avapies, 1987.

Crow, John A. *Spain, the Root and the Flower: An Interpretation of Spain and the Spanish People.* Berkeley: University of California Press, 1985.

Dalby, Andrew. *Dangerous Tastes: The Story of Spices.* London: British Museum Press, 2000.

———. *Food in the Ancient World from A to Z.* London and New York: Routledge, 2003.

Del Arco Blanco, Miguel Ángel. "Hunger and the Consolidation of the Francoist Regime (1939–1951)." *European History Quarterly* 40 (2010): 458–83.

Del Campo, Isabel. *Introducción de plantas americanas en España*. Paracuellos del Jarama, Spain: Ministerio de Agricultura, Pesca y Alimentación, 1993.

Díaz, Lorenzo. *Madrid: Bodegones, mesones, fondas y restaurants: Cocina y sociedad, 1412–1990*. Madrid: Espasa-Calpe, 1990.

Díaz, Lorenzo, and José Luis Cabañas. *Ilustrados y Románticos: Cocina y sociedad en España (Siglos XVIII y XIX)*. Madrid: Alianza Editorial, 2005.

Díaz del Castillo, Bernal. *Historia verdadera de la conquista de Nueva España*, Edited by Miguel León-Portilla. Madrid: Historia 16, 1984.

Díaz Yubero, Ismael. "El hambre y la gastronomía: De la guerra civil a la cartilla de racionamento." *Estudios sobre consumo* 17, no. 66 (2003): 9–22.

———. *Gastronomía de Madrid: Cocina, historia y tradición*. Madrid: Estrellas Gastronomía, 2014.

Doménech, Ignasi. *Cocina de recursos: Deseo mi comida*. Barcelona: Quintilla, Cardona y Ca. Editores, 1941.

———. *La nueva cocina elegante española; el tratado más práctico y completo de cocina, pastelería, repostería y refrescos*. 2nd ed. Madrid: Imprenta Helénica, 1920.

Dunmire, William W. *Gardens of New Spain: How Mediterranean Plants and Foods Changed America*. Austin: University of Texas Press, 2004.

Entrambasaguas, Joaquín. *Gastronomía madrileña*. Madrid: Instituto de Estudios Madrileños, 1954.

Escudero Ramos, José María. *Cocinando la historia: Curiosidades gastronómicas de Madrid / Cooking History: Gastronomic Curiosities of Madrid*. Madrid: Ediciones la Librería, 2011.

Fanshawe, Anne Harrison. *Memoirs of Lady Fanshawe, Wife of Sir Richard Fanshawe, Bt., Ambassador from Charles II. to the Courts of Portugal & Madrid, Written by Herself Containing Extracts from the Correspondence of Sir Richard Fanshawe*. Edited by Beatrice Marshall. Reprint of the 1905 London and New York edition, Project Gutenberg, 2004. https://archive.org/details/memoirsofladyfan06064gut.

Feret, Barbara. *Gastronomical and Culinary Literature*. Metuchen, NJ: Scarecrow Press, 1979.

Fernández-Armesto, Felipe. *Near a Thousand Tables: A History of Food*. New York: The Free Press, 2002.

Fernández Montes, Matilde. "El agua en los orígenes de Madrid." In *El agua: Mitos y realidades*, edited by José A. González and Antonio Malpica Cuello, 123–53. Barcelona: Anthropos, 2003.

Flandrin, Jean-Louis, and Massimo Montanari, eds. *Food: A Culinary History from Antiquity to the Present*. New York: Columbia University Press, 1999.

Ford, Richard. *A Handbook for Travellers in Spain*. London: John Murray, 1845.

García del Real, Matilde. *La cocina de la madre de familia*. Madrid: Sucesores de Hernando, 1908.

Gitlitz, David M., and Linda Kay Davidson. *A Drizzle of Honey: The Lives and Recipes of Spain's Secret Jews*. New York: St. Martin's Press, 1999.

Gómez-Bravo, Ana M. "Adafina: The Story Behind the Recipe." In *The Converso Cookbook* Seattle: Stroum Center for Jewish Studies, University of Washington, 2014. http://jewishstudies.washington.edu/converso-cookbook/adafina-story-behind-recipe/.

González Pomata, Antonio. *Cocina alicantina*. León: Ed. Everest, 1998.

Granado Maldonado, Diego. *Libro del arte de Cozina: en el qval se contiene el modo de guisar y de comer en cualquier tiempo, así de carne, como de pescados, para sanos, enfermos, y convalecientes, así de pasteles, tortas, y salsas, como de conservas al uso español, italiano, y tudesce de nuestros tiempos*. Madrid, Luis Sánchez, 1599.

Guardiola y Ortiz, José. *Platos de guerra: 60 recetas prácticas, acomodadas a las circunstancias, para la conservación y el condimento de la sardina*. Alicante, Spain: Ed. del autor, 1938.

Guía básica de cocina celtibérica: Keltiberoi, segunda semana celtibérica. Soria, Spain: Ayuntamiento de Soria, 2004.

Hemingway, Ernest. *Death in the Afternoon*. New York: Simon and Schuster, 1999.

———. *The Sun Also Rises*. New York: Scribner, 2016.

Hernández de Maceras, Domingo. *Libro del arte de cocina*. Salamanca, Spain: Ediciones Universidad de Salamanca, 1999.

Hernández de Maceras, Domingo. *Libro del arte de cozina: En el qual se contiene el modo de guisar de comer en qualquier tiempo, ansi de carne, como de pescado, ansi de pasteles, tortas, y salsas, como de co[n]seruas, y de*. Salamanca, Spain: En casa de Antonia Ramírez, 1607.

Herrera, Ana María. *Manual de cocina. Recetario*. Madrid: Sección Femenina de F.E.T. y de las J.O.N.S., 1962.

Kany, Charles. *Life and Manners in Madrid, 1750–1800*. Berkeley: University of California Press, 1932.

La cocina moderna. Madrid: Libr. de Anllo y Rodríguez, 1875.

Larra, Mariano José de. "La fonda nueva." In *Obras Completas de Fígaro (Don Mariano José de Larra)*. Paris: Baudry, Librería Europea, 1857.

Luján, Néstor. *Veinte siglos de cocina en Barcelona: De las ostras de Barcino a los restaurantes de hoy*. Barcelona: Folio, 1993.

Martínez Llopis, Manuel. *Historia de la gastronomía española*. Madrid: Editora Nacional, 1981.

Martínez Llopis, Manuel, and Simone Ortega. *La cocina típica de Madrid*. Madrid: Alianza, 1987.

Martínez Montiño, Francisco. *Arte de cocina, pastelería, vizcochería y conservería*. Bareclona: Imprenta de Sierra y Martí, 1823. Originally published 1611 by Luis Sánchez (Madrid).

Martorell, Eladia. *Carmencita o la buena cocinera: Manual práctico de cocina española, americana, francesa, con multitud de recetas especiales que no se hallan en los tratados publicados hasta el día*. Barcelona: Eugenio Subirana, 1899.

Mata, Juan de la. *Arte de Repostería, en que se contiene todo género de hacer dulces secos, y en líquido: Con una breve instrucción para conocer las frutas, y servirlas crudas, y diez mesas, con su explicación*. Madrid: Impr. y Librería de Joseph García Lanza, 1755.

McNeill, William H. "What If Pizarro Had Not Found Potatoes in Peru?" *What If? Eminent Historians Imagine What Might Have Been*, vol. 2, edited by Robert Cowley, 413–29. New York: Berkeley Books, 2001.

Medina, F. Xavier. *Food Culture in Spain*. Westport, CT: Greenwood Press, 2005.

Menús de guerra. Barcelona: Generalitat de Catalunya, Consellería de Proveïments, Departament de Premsa i Propaganda, [1937?].

Mestayer de Echagüe, María. *Historia de la gastronomía (Esbozos)*. Madrid: Espasa-Calpe, 1943.

———. *La cocina completa*. Madrid: Espasa-Calpe, 1940.

Montoliú Camps, Pedro. *Enciclopedia de Madrid*. Barcelona: Planeta, 2002.

Moreno, María Paz. "A Bittersweet Love Affair: Spain and the History of Chocolate." *Connections: European Studies Annual Review* 7 (2011): 50.

———. *De la página al plato: El libro de cocina en España*. Gijón, Spain: Ediciones Trea, 2012.

Moyano, Guillermo. *El cocinero español y la perfecta cocinera*. Málaga, Spain: Librería de Francisco de Moya, 1867.

Moyano Andrés, Isabel. "La cocina escrita." In *La cocina en su tinta*. Madrid: Biblioteca Nacional de España. Accessed January 20, 2017. www.bne.es/es/Micrositios/Exposiciones/Cocina/Estudios/seccion1/.

Muro Goiri, Ángel. *El Practicón*. 2nd ed. Barcelona: Tusquets, 1997.

Nadeau, Carolyn A. "Contributions of Medieval Food Manuals to Spain's Culinary Heritage." In "Writing about Food: Culinary Literature in the Hispanic World," edited by Maria Paz Moreno, special issue, *Cincinnati Romance Review* 33 (2012): 59–77.

———. *Food Matters: Alonso Quijano's Diet and the Discourse of Food in Early Modern Spain*. North York: University of Toronto Press, 2016.

———. "Early Modern Spanish Cookbooks: The Curious Case of Diego Granado." In *Food and Language: Proceedings from the 2009 Oxford Symposium on Food and Cookery*, edited by Richard Hosking, 237–46. Totnes, UK: Prospect Books, 2010.

Nieto Sánchez, José A. *Historia del Rastro: Los orígenes del mercado popular de Madrid, 1740–1905*. Madrid: Visión, 2004.

Nola, Ruperto de. *Libro de Guisados ma[n]jares y potages, intitulado Libro de Cozina: En el qual esta el regimiento de las casas de los reyes y grandes señores, y los officiales de las casas dellos cada uno como tiene*. Medina del Campo, Spain: Pedro d' Castro impressor d' libros; A costa d' Fra[n]cisco gallego librero, 1549.

Norman Makanowitzky, Barbara. *Tales of the Table; a History of Western Cuisine*. Englewood Cliffs, NJ: Prentice-Hall, 1972.

Ortega, Simone. *1080 Recetas de cocina*. Madrid: Alianza Editorial, 1996.

Palacio Abad, Vicente. *La alimentación de Madrid en el siglo XVIII y otros estudios madrileños: Clave historial*. Madrid: Real Academia de la Historia, 1998.

Pardo Bazán, Emilia. *La cocina española antigua*. Madrid: Sociedad Anónima Renacimiento, 1913.

———. *La cocina española moderna*. Madrid: Sociedad Anónima Renacimiento, 1917.

Pérez, Dionisio. *Guía del buen comer español: Inventario y loa de la cocina clásica de España y sus regiones*. Madrid: Sucesores de Rivadeneyra, 1929.

Pérez Galdós, Benito. *La fontana de oro*. Madrid: Perlado, Páez y Compañía, 1906.

Pérez Samper, María de los Ángeles. *La alimentación en la España del Siglo de Oro*. Huesca, Spain: La Val de Onsera, 1998.

———. "Recetarios manuscritos de la España moderna." *Cincinnati Romance Review* 33 (Winter 2012): 27–58.

Perry, D., and T. Leonard. "La mesa española en el Madrid de Larra." *Mester* 10.1–2 (1981): 58–65.

Pilcher, Jeffrey M. *Planet Taco: A Global History of Mexican Food*. New York: Oxford University Press, 2012.

Pinto Crespo, Virgilio, and Santos Madrazo. *Madrid: Atlas histórico de la ciudad de Madrid, siglos IX–XIX*. Barcelona and Madrid: Fundación Caja de Madrid and Lunwerg Editores, 1995.

Pliny. *Natural History*. Translated by H. Rackman, W. H. S. Jones, and D. E. Eicholz. Loeb Classical Library ed. London: William Heinemann, 1942–1963.

Puga y Parga, Manuel María. *La cocina práctica*. Santiago de Compostela, Spain: Librería-Editorial Galí, 1972.

Rementería y Fica, Mariano. *Manual del cocinero, cocinera, repostero, pastelero, confitero y botillero: Con el método para trinchar y servir toda clase de viandas, y la cortesanía y urbanidad que se debe usar en la mesa*. Madrid: Impr. de Norberto Llorenci, 1851.

Richardson, Paul. *A Late Dinner: Discovering the Food of Spain*. New York: Scribner, 2007.

Ringrose, David R. *Madrid and the Spanish Economy, 1560–1850.* Berkeley: University of California Press, 1983.

Ríos, Alicia, and Lourdes March. *The Heritage of Spanish Cooking.* New York: Random House, 1992.

Roden, Claudia. *The Food of Spain.* New York: HarperCollins, 2011.

Ruiz, Ana. *Medina Mayrit: The Origins of Madrid.* New York: Algora, 2012.

Ruiz, Teofilo F. *Spanish Society, 1400–1600.* Harlow, UK, and New York: Longman, 2001.

Schwartz, Stuart B. *Tropical Babylons: Sugar and the Making of the Atlantic World, 1450–1680.* Chapel Hill: University of North Carolina Press, 2004.

Sella Montserrat, Joan. *Comer como un rey: Las mesas de Amadeo I de Saboya y Alfonso XII de Borbón.* Gijón, Spain: Ed. Trea, 2009.

Simón Palmer, María del Carmen. "El estatuto del cocinero: Su evolución en el tiempo." *Food and History* 4, no. 1 (2006): 255–76.

———. *La cocina de Palacio, 1561–1931.* Madrid: Editorial Castalia, 1997.

———. "La dulcería en la Biblioteca Nacional de España." In *La cocina en su tinta,* 63–81. Madrid: Biblioteca Nacional de España. Accessed January 15, 2017. www.bne.es/es/Micrositios/Exposiciones/Cocina/documentos/cocina_estudios_2.pdf.

Sopeña-Genzor, Gabriel. "El mundo funerario celtibérico como expresión de un ethos agonístico." *Historiae* 1 (2004): 56–107.

Stewart, Jules. *Madrid: The History.* London and New York: I. B. Tauris, 2012.

Stols, Eddy. "The Expansion of the Sugar Market in Western Europe." In *Tropical Babylons: Sugar and the Making of the Atlantic World, 1450–1680,* edited by Stuart Schwartz, 237–88. Chapel Hill: University of North Carolina Press, 2004.

Townson, Nigel. *The Crisis of Democracy in Spain: Centrist Politics under the Second Republic, 1931–1936.* Brighton, UK: Sussex Academic Press, 2000.

Urrosolo, Antxon. *La cocina del monasterio: Recetas para el cuerpo y el alma.* Barcelona: Plaza Janés, 2009.

Vedia de Uhagon, Dolores. *La mesa española: Arte de cocina al alcance de una fortuna media.* San Sebastián, Spain: Ed. La Libertad, 1892.

Villena, Enrique. *Arte Cisoria, o Tratado del arte del cortar del cuchillo.* Madrid: En la oficina de Antonio Marín, 1766.

Index

About the Author

Maria Paz Moreno is an essayist, poet, and literary critic. She is professor of Spanish at the University of Cincinnati, Ohio. A native of Spain, her research focuses on the literature and gastronomy of her native country. Moreno is the author of seven books of poetry and several scholarly books and critical editions, among them *El culturalismo en la poesía de Juan Gil-Albert* [Cultural References in the Poetry of Juan Gil-Albert] (2000) and *De la página al plato. El libro de cocina en España* [From the Page to the Plate: The Spanish Cookbook] (2012).